HILARY

HILARY

The brave world of Hilary Pole

by

Dorothy Clarke Wilson

MOWBRAYS
LONDON & OXFORD

© DOROTHY CLARK WILSON *1972*

First published by Hodder & Stoughton Ltd, 1972
This edition published in 1978 by
Becket Publications
Saint Thomas House, Becket Street
Oxford OX1 1SJ

ISBN 0 7289 0004 1

Printed in Great Britain by
Lowe & Brydone Printers Limited, Thetford, Norfolk

Tho' much is taken, much abides: and tho'
We are not now that strength which in old days
Moved earth and heaven; that which we are, we are;
One equal temper of heroic hearts
Made weak by time and fate, but strong in will
To strive, to seek, to find, and not to yield.

Ulysses, ALFRED, LORD TENNYSON

ILLUSTRATIONS

facing page

KEY TO ACKNOWLEDGEMENTS

[1] R. M. Jefcoate

[2] R. G. Miller

THE CAR PARK PORTER at the Queen Elizabeth Hospital in Birmingham looked stolidly adamant. "Sorry, mate, y' can't come in 'ere."

The young man in the Bedford van smiled persuasively. "But I've come from Stoke Mandeville, the Spinal Injuries Centre, to see a disabled patient here. I have an appointment."

On most occasions this approach had provided entry to the limited and privileged parking spaces available within such institutions. Not this time.

"Sorry, mate." The stolid visage remained icily unyielding. "Only ambulances and doctors' cars with permits are allowed in here. You must use the visitors' car park over there."

The young man looked dubiously towards the distant area indicated. "O.K.," he agreed, "if I must. I've come to see Miss Pole — "

Instantly the ice melted. The crusty face burst into a smile. "Oh, you mean Hilary! She's on Ward East 1A right now. Just go straight down the road," a helpful finger pointed the way, "and park where it says, 'Ambulances only'."

"But I thought — "

"No need to worry. Stay there as long as you like."

Delighted with this unexpected V.I.P. treatment, the visitor started his van in the direction indicated.

"She's in an iron lung, you know!" shouted the porter as he drove off.

Such was Roger Jefcoate's introduction to the young woman he had come to assess as a possible candidate for the remarkable electronic device known popularly as "Possum", which was bringing new life to dozens of severely disabled people. Roger was even more bewildered than delighted. What sort of person was this that the mere mention of her name to the porter of one of the best known teaching hospitals in Britain could open doors to a stranger?

He parked as instructed and found his way, after several inquiries, along the maze of corridors to Ward East 1A and Sister's office.

"I'm Roger Jefcoate from Possum," he said. "Is it possible to see Hilary Pole, please?"

"Certainly," replied Sister, smiling. "At this moment she's in the middle of a blanket bath. I'll just see how long she will be. Can you wait?"

Roger nodded. Sister Brown was soon back to say it was all right. He followed her down the corridor to a door marked "closed", and they entered a small hospital room.

"This is Hilary," said Sister, "and with her is Nurse Crowder. Hilary, this is Mr. Jefcoate from Possum. Nurse Crowder will explain Hilary's method of communication."

Roger's sharp eyes, accustomed by much experience to a swift evaluation of many types of disability, noted instantly that this case was different from any he had yet encountered. There lying on the bed, surrounded by bowls, towels, and toiletries, was a pale-skinned girl, perhaps in her late twenties, head supported with a bandage, tongue strangely protruding, eyes closed. The same sharply discerning glance revealed beautifully lacquered finger and toe nails, their rosy hue blending with the delicate pastel pink nightdress and brighter bedspread; a jade ring and bracelet flashed counterpoints of colour. Between the big toe of her right foot and the bedside locker was a length of hospital bandage, in the middle of which was suspended a small bell.

Roger was neither shocked nor discouraged by the limp and apparently lifeless figure, nor by the clicking and hissing in the background — no "iron lung", as the porter had described it, but a ventilator pumping air to the lungs through a tracheotomy tube. In fact, some years before he had worked for the makers of this very machine which had kept this girl alive for the past seven years. He knew that the figure was not lifeless, that, though she could not see, breathe, move, she could hear every word he said.

"Hello, Hilary," he began.

"Do you mind if I stay and translate for you?" asked Rachel Crowder. "You see, Hilary cannot speak, and it will save time if I act as interpreter."

Disconnecting the bandage, she sat down by the bed and placed her first finger on the Archilles tendon of the girl's right foot. Instantly her touch was rewarded by a small flick of the toe. "She's listening," said the nurse encouragingly.

Roger continued. "I'm from a group known as the P.O.S.M. Research Project. As you may know, your father talked recently with our director, Mr. Maling. The letters stand for 'Patient Operated Selector Mechanisms', but we're usually known by the word 'Possum', which is the Latin for 'I can'. It's a happy designation, because that's exactly what we're trying to do, make it possible for disabled people to do more for themselves."

Another flutter of the toe, this time a little stronger.

"We're a small organisation," went on Roger, "that started life at the National Spinal Injuries Centre, Stoke Mandeville Hospital, and last year we moved into our own premises close by. We design and develop systems intended to help severely disabled people regain at least some independence. The most popular item of our equipment is the environmental control unit, the Possum Selector Unit Type One, that is provided for suitable cases under the National Health Service." He hesitated. The girl on the bed looked so devoid of life. "I hope I'm getting some of this across."

This time the flick was noticeably sharp. "Don't worry," said Rachel, smiling as if amused. "I doubt if you could say anything that Hilli couldn't understand."

"This machine," continued Roger, feeling somehow rebuked, "is about half the size of a television set and will operate a number of electrical items around the house, such as bell, light, radio, television, and so forth, and is really intended to help disabled people in their own homes. We've also developed a range of typewriter controls to help those who, through their disability, are unable to write. You can see that this offers untold possibilities of communication, education and perhaps even employment."

Devoid of life, had he thought? Fascinated, he kept his gaze on the toe, which was indicating avid interest by occasional quick flicks. "I'm listening," he sensed it trying to say. "Go on!"

He did. The boyish eagerness in his voice made his sum-
mary seem less and less like a sales talk, for Roger was as
selflessly committed to his work as the most fervent and dedicated missionary.

"You see, Hilary, as we told your father in our telephone
conversation, this unit is a simple computer and to operate it
we need to use as a source of control whatever residual movement
remains to the user. Some operate it by mouth by puffing and
sucking through a tube. Some use the hand, some the foot.
We have one who uses a side movement of the chin. But for
those who can't manage any of these, we have to look elsewhere. The Possum environmental control requires sustained
pressure on just a single switch, but I believe you would be
especially interested in the typewriter control, which requires
two inputs to operate two switches."

Yes — yes — yes — *yes*! A steady stream of flicks revealed
mounting excitement to match his own. He could read them as
easily as if they had been words.

"Fortunately one doesn't need sight to operate them — "
he glanced at the girl's eyes, their lids swollen and tight
shut — "because the user gets feed-back from the control by
counting clicks." He hesitated again, enthusiasm suddenly
checked. Now came the crucial moments of the whole interview.
Never, in all his hundred and more assessments had he felt
more uncertain, inadequate. "I can see," he temporised, "that
you have your toe movement, but — "

Rachel broke in. "Do you want to speak, Hilli?" There was
a positive flick of the toe.

Speak! The nurse used the word as casually as in normal
conversation. First bewildered, then with fascination Roger
observed and listened.

"Beginning? l, m, n, o, p, q, r, s, t . . . Beginning? l, m,
n, o, . . . Beginning? l, m, n — Sorry, Hilli, a, b, c, d, e — Toe.
Is that what you wish to say?" An affirmative flick.

"Hilary says" reported Rachel after further interchange,
"that her toe is her best available movement." Again she turned
to the patient. "Yes, Hilli, beginning? a, b . . . Beginning?
a, b, c — sorry — l, m, n, o, p, q, r, s, t, u — Is it 'but'? Yes.
Beginning?"

Roger soon learned the code. If the desired letter was in the
first half of the alphabet, it was indicated by a movement of

Hilary's toe; if in the latter half, there was no movement. With each foot motion there was a contraction of the calf muscle, hence the finger placed on the Achilles tendon. The bell, he discovered, could also be used, but this method was a bit quicker and more efficient for those who had become experienced in using it. It was a slow and laborious method of communication but surprisingly effective. In the following exchange Hilary explained that her best movement was in her toe but she could not hold it. The disease, myasthenia gravis, which was responsible for her near immobility left her with less than one-sixteenth of an inch movement in each big toe, but the right foot — which was being used then for communication — was the stronger.

Roger was even more uncertain. He was a passionate believer in Possum and in its adaptability to the needs of every form of disability — to date, that is. Now it was facing its supreme test. For the girl who lay there on the bed was certainly the most disabled person he had yet encountered, probably the most disabled (short of complete paralysis) in the whole of Britain, perhaps in the world. It was already clear to him that any existing switches would be insufficiently sensitive to respond to the very limited force available in the big toe, but that didn't mean that one couldn't be created! Never yet had he and Possum faced a challenge they could not meet. Would this be the first time?

He explained some of the difficulties to Hilary and was astonished by her grasp of the situation. He expressed cautious confidence that he could fix her up with a Possum typewriter control, but warned that she must not raise her hopes too high.

"Don't worry," flicked Hilary as speedily as Rachel could translate. "Always take my hopes with a pinch of salt."

Roger regarded her with renewed interest, mixed with wonder. Courage? She certainly had that, even after seven years of life which would have broken an average spirit. Mental keenness? She had responded to his scientific jargon with a terse and clear comprehension. Pride? Those perfectly manicured and lacquered nails, the blending of colours with their accent of jade — yes and the delicate elusive fragrance reminding one of wild flowers. All this and a sense of humour too! It was unbelievable.

"Well, mate," the car park porter hailed him on his way out, "did you see our Hilary?"

"Yes," said Roger, "I saw her. We had a good talk together." Talk! He was using the word as naturally as Rachel.

The porter nodded with satisfaction. "Quite a girl, ain't she?"

"Yes," said Roger, "she certainly is."

PART ONE

Upway

My World

I have a world that's mine alone,
A world where no one else can roam,
Of books I've read and plays I've seen,
An opera, a ballet theme;
Of roads I've walked and hills I've climbed,
Woods and fields all stored in mind.
So if at night I cannot sleep
I do not end up counting sheep.
Instead I think of days gone by,
Of picnics 'neath a clear blue sky,
The thrill of watching unawares
A pair of boxing mad March hares.
I walk down Lapal Lane again,
I find a nest, I see a wren;
The fields are full of ripening wheat,
The banks are white with meadow sweet,
And searching closer to the ground,
Bashful violets I have found.
I squelch along the bridle path,
Thus evoking Mother's wrath;
I tear my coat, I cut my knee,
But there's a squirrel's drey to see.
The landscape blurs, light fades fast,
I smile, and fall asleep at last.

HILARY J. POLE

SHE WAS WELL NAMED.

"You must call her Joy," urged Grandfather Oates, Mona's father, "for she will bring you so much happiness."

Mona and Eric were not impressed with the name, but they loved Grandad. Why not find something else which meant "Happiness"? Hilary! A doubly satisfying discovery, for St. Hilary is the patron saint of Cornwall, where they had spent their honeymoon, and the new arrival was a honeymoon baby. A second name? It must be rhythmic and long enough to balance the short, blunt surname. Jennifer! Not only a favourite Cornish family name, but one signifying "white wave", also reminiscent of that spray-swept honeymoon at Newquay. Good! Soon after her birth on May 27th, 1938 the full name appeared on the register of Sheffield, Yorkshire: Hilary Jennifer Pole.

Even in the act of arrival she gave evidence of two dominant qualities, independence and vigour. "No birth until Monday," assured the doctor on Friday. That night Eric was dispatched post haste to fetch him, running all the way up the steep hill where he lived. No doctor, no car. But just as he was leaving in near panic, the car drove up. The doctor dashed into the house for his bag, and he and Eric rode full speed to the house at 28 Avisford Road. Arriving at the gate, they heard a baby's cry. It was a girl.

When all was quiet Eric dragged a mattress to the floor of Mona's room and spent nearly the whole night gazing at his beautiful baby. But delight in this perfect offspring did not keep him from the cricket field on Saturday.

Hilary was herself only three weeks old when she joined the cricket fans. Grandad Oates took her and Mona to see Eric play for Barnsley on June 18th and succeeding Saturdays. Washed and changed in the car, undressed and stowed in her carry cot in the back seat, already she was absorbing that milieu of magic which would quicken her blood for a lifetime.

In a family which had run mostly to boys, and many of them short-lived, the baby girl was an object of adoration especially to Grandad Oates. Every night he came to look at her, even after returning late from a distant conference, carefully removing his shoes before tip-toeing upstairs. If she cried, he would go outside unable to listen to the sound. If business called him away for an extended period, he would send her a card every day.

It was well that he enjoyed this early excess of affection, for when she was six-weeks-old, one day before his own fiftieth birthday, he suffered a fatal heart attack. The family were bereft, shattered. Now Hilary would never know the delightful, whimsical Grandad who had so adored her. And he would never share the magical unfolding of bud into flower.

For she was a beautiful baby. Strangers as well as relatives fell captive to her charms. Like the woman in Blackpool, where Mona went for a brief holiday in September to recover from the depression following her father's death. She was standing in front of a book shop looking at the display, the pram behind her, fingers firm about its handle. Someone tapped her shoulder.

"Is this your baby?"

"Yes."

"It's the most gorgeous baby I have ever seen. You are lucky parents."

Mona watched mutely as the fashionably dressed woman bent down, placed some glinting coins in the chubby fingers, stepped into a huge chauffeur-driven limousine, and was whisked away. The good fairy, she thought, bringing gifts to the princess's cradle; then remembered with a wry smile that there had been a bad fairy, too, who came late. But certainly all had been good so far, their gifts portending well-being, if not wealth : perfectly formed body, fluff of blonde hair like a halo, wide curious eyes, contagious laughter, and that incredible energy, accompanied by a streak of stubbornness and an indomitable will. Were the two latter, perhaps, gifts of the bad fairy — or of another good? Only time would tell.

The combination was sometimes baffling, even to an equally strong-minded parent like Mona, trained as a teacher and versed in infant psychology. A child who could cry every night yet refuse to be cuddled, who could climb upstairs alone at ten months yet show not the sign of a tooth until well past twelve, whose acrobatic feats after being put to bed could result in a head stuck fast between the bars or a body purple and blotchy and barely conscious from burrowing deep beneath the covers. Life for Mona was a constant struggle of wits, putting drawing pins in the soles so she could locate the pattering of feet, searching the shops for a sleeping harness, moving objects higher and higher.

Already war was casting its shadow. One day Mona went to take Hilary from her cot. She drew the window curtains. There in the field behind the house were tents massed and soldiers moving. She was terror-stricken, thinking war had started. Not yet. But rocking Hilary in her arms that morning, unable to put her down, she felt greater fear than in the actual horror of the years ahead.

It came all too soon. In September 1939 they moved to Southey Green Road, fortunately nearer to Nan Nan. They moved on a Friday. Nan Nan shook her head. "Friday flit," she quoted darkly, "short sit." Too true! All that weekend they unpacked, tacked down carpets, so that Sunday night they were fairly tidy. At teatime Monday Eric came home with the bad news. "We have to move again."

Because of the war and dispersing factories, he was being sent to Blackheath, Birmingham, where a new factory was being built. He must go immediately, returning home at weekends. He would look for a house. It was December, raw and cold, when the next move was made. The furniture had been sent, the new house in Quinton made ready. It was nearly five o'clock and already dark when they arrived by bus at Quinton terminus. The country was in blackout. Still a good mile and a half to the house in Manor Lane, through darkened streets, laden with hand luggage, and with a nineteen-months-old child! They could not carry her. It was Mona who found the long trek almost unbearably tiring. Hilary kept pace without a murmur, her small sturdy legs pumping steadily. They arrived at last, toiled up the steep drive, unlocked the massive, nail-studded door which was the house's chief claim to beauty, and entered into cold darkness. With curtains drawn and lights on, the familiar furniture still brought no hint of home. They put Hilary to bed with hot water bottles. Mona made tea and sandwiches, but neither of them could eat. Huddled by a feeble fire, they sat in dumb misery, strangers in a hostile world.

It did not remain so. The house, appropriately named "Upway", began to seem like home. Soon neighbours across the road waved. People always waved and smiled at the sight of Hilary. They quickly changed from "the Johnsons" to Auntie Norah and Uncle Arthur. The Newburys next door, George and Kath, became firm friends, and the two families shared an air raid shelter at the foot of their adjoining gardens. Mort and Edna Beck, two houses away, recommended their doctor and became the godparents of Ian, born the following July. Hilary celebrated acceptance into the community by taking first place at a garden fete in a "beautiful and bonny baby contest".

She appropriated not only the house but the whole surrounding world as her own. Just before her second birthday Mona went to look for her in the back garden where she had been settled for play with both gates securely fastened — yes, and with the latches placed higher than she was able to reach. No Hilary. The side gate was open and a pile of seed boxes beside it. Panic stricken, though seven months pregnant, Mona ran down the drive. No child in sight.

"Looking for a little girl?" asked a passer-by.

"Yes — oh, yes!"

"In a white-spotted blue dress?"

Just then they both saw her crossing the main road at the S-bend two hundred yards away, cars speeding by in both directions. "There she goes!" Mona stood transfixed, unable to move or shout, even to breathe, until the tiny figure had safely gained their side of the road. Then she started after her, down the road, into a farm drive beside a brook. There she was, sitting on a bank under a willow, ball in hand, watching the ducks, dangling her feet over the water. At sight of Mona's outraged face she announced with instant forethought, "My ball wanted a walk."

Her zeal for experimenting was unflagging. Nothing within reach of her curious fingers was sacred. She cleaned Mona's dressing table with metal polish, mixed her nail varnishes and face powder in a crystal powder bowl, sucked clear gums to wafer thinness, then wedged them between the piano keys. Even baby Ian was not safe from her well-intentioned but misguided experiments.

"A doll!" she exclaimed delightedly after his appearance on July 20th. And, though her preference in toys was for balls and things that moved on wheels, she found this new plaything irresistibly intriguing. Not long after his arrival Mona had just got him undressed for his bath when the telephone rang. She hastily deposited him on the dining room couch well back among the cushions — he could not possibly roll off, and Hilary was safely in the garden — and ran to answer it. Terrified screams brought her rushing back, to find the baby on the floor and a baffled Hilary close by. "That doll's too heavy!" she complained, suddenly deciding it was time to run.

"Could have accounted for a lot of things since," Ian was to chuckle many years later.

But he survived in spite of such sisterly solicitude, and, thanks to Mona, life at Upway went on according to plan. Only two things could disturb the routine — Hilary's strong will and war.

2

Hilary moved blithely through the years of blackouts and bombings. She could not remember lighted windows, and sirens were almost as normal interruptions as train whistles. She thrived on the half pint of milk allotted to children under five, later on the quarter pint, relished dried milk and egg powder, especially the sweets Eric concocted every Saturday night out of dried milk, margarine, and a few drops of peppermint. The two grandmas, who did not take sugar in their tea, would hoard their four-ounce ration and send packages of home-made cakes, biscuits and toffee, Nan Nan's often arriving a mass of crumbs, so they always put it on a tray to unpack it.

Mona managed to make the grim exigencies seem like fun — living in the kitchen because fuel was rationed, using candles when the power was cut off from seven p.m. to seven a.m., cooking breakfast on an old paraffin stove. For weeks after the first sirens sounded in August 1940, Hilary went to bed on a camp bed under the stairs. Ian slept in her doll's pram, Mona sitting on a camp stool close by. They laughed over the sight of Ian enveloped in his baby gas mask, only arms and legs dangling, and christened Hilary's own small mask "Mickey Mouse", making practice at putting it on more play than grim necessity.

Hilary was a little over two the night Coventry burned, its lurid glow in the south eastern sky visible from the front doorstep. Bombs soon began to fall much nearer. Eric was on fire-watching duty at the steel factory nearly every night, leaving Mona alone with the children.

One night when the sirens shrieked the warden called. The bombing was close, and she must go to the shelter immediately. Grabbing Hilary and Ian from under the stairs, she put the sleeping baby in the pram, Hilary at its foot, and ran down the steep drive to the underground Anderson shelter. That night nobody slept on the three bunk beds along the wall. The tiny steel box was crowded : George and Kath with their two boys and dog; their next door neighbours Edie and Raymond with their little girl; Arthur and Norah from across the road; Mona with Hilary and Ian. Kath had prepared a great plate of dripping toast and jugs of cocoa, which were soon empty. George wanted to get more powdered milk for the children, but each time he reached the door the whistle of another bomb would drive him back. Some of the children cried — not Hilary. She was even more fascinated by the proximity of the dog than by occasional glimpses of the flares. Though the night passed without imminent danger, they never did get the extra milk. As soon as the siren wailed its all clear, another shrill alert would sound.

Bombs soon came closer, however. Once there was a rare daytime raid. Mona and Eric were taking the two children for a walk, Ian in his pram, when they heard a German plane, and then saw bombs fall from it and drop in the fields beyond Illey. At the sight of the huge barrage balloons rising into the air all around Birmingham, Hilary jumped up and down with delight. "Mummy, Mummy, the big balls!" For her, thanks to Mona's deliberate restraint, the shriek of the sirens held no terror. The bombs, intended either for Birmetal's, very near at Woodgate, or for Austin's at Northfield, never reached their targets. They

saw Spitfires arrive, the German plane veer off with the Spitfires chasing. Later, they heard, it was brought down near
Bristol. After this day air raid they went over to the field and
saw the bomb craters. For years afterward one could tell where
they had been, for the grass would remain a different colour,
the corn growing over them a browner hue.

Hilary was to remember other things: the notice board at
the bottom of the garden with messages for the fire wardens;
school children going by with gas masks on their shoulders; the
night the bombs came nearest of all and dropped in the fields
only a few hundred yards away.

Even though he was in an essential industry, Mona feared for
months that Eric would be called into the army. One day in
1943, just after her third child was born, a gypsy came to the
door. Ian and Hilary were out of sight in the garden. "You have
just had a new baby," said the visitor. "It's a girl. You have two
others. You are worried about your husband. Looking for the
letter calling him up. Your eldest daughter will make her name
dancing. She will achieve fame. Your son will be the charming
one, will have good fortune."

When she had gone, Nan Nan, who was visiting, was shaking
with laughter. "Posh! Saw the pram outside, probably saw the
other two in the garden. What woman isn't afraid her man
will be called up? And as for Hilary — Heaven knows she can
move fast enough, but — that little skoppydiddle a dancer!"

Dad had been reading *Peter Pan* to the children, so when
the baby came Hilary insisted that it be called Peter, even
though it was a girl. Ian of course agreed. It would be a long
time before he challenged her superior strength of mind and
body. When Mum finally convinced them that Peter was for
boys, they reluctantly settled for Wendy.

In spite of the war Hilary started kindergarten at four. She
could already read, not by being taught, but by having books
read to her and asking questions. Her curiosity and overpower-
ing energy needed more direction than Mummy was able to
give. Being trained as a teacher, Mona must have the best. State
schools would not take pupils under five, so she began looking
for a private school with a fully qualified staff. A cricketing friend
of Eric's recommended Garry House. It was a journey of more
than half an hour by bus, but they found that a pupil of eight
or nine named Elspeth Smart lived close by. They took Hilary

to the corner where she could meet Elspeth, who took her safely on the bus to school.

Hilary liked kindergarten. She liked Miss Rosher, the head-mistress. She liked drawing, especially animals, birds, and flowers. She liked modelling with plasticine, again animals, and tried to see how small she could make them, an elephant no bigger than a marble but with ears and trunk which hung down. She liked her French lessons and was soon giving new names to everything in the house : *la chaise, la table, le plancher.* She liked milk and biscuits during the morning break. She got into trouble helping herself to spoonfuls of Ovaltine from the desk of a boy who was absent — not to put in her milk, just to eat. Caught in the act, she was forced to apologise. She was terribly ashamed, and, Ovaltine being hard to acquire, had to repay her debt with Milo. She loved nature study and collecting : butter-flies, worms, grubs, tadpoles, not to kill and preserve them; to find, observe, keep for a little, and let go. It was akin to her passion for stray dogs and cats. If there was one loose in the neighbourhood and she didn't find it, it found her! "Mummy, please, can't we keep this one?" Then followed the inevitable visit to the police station. The local police must have groaned at the sight of Hilary.

She won the kindergarten prize that year at Garry House, a book called *Janet and the Fairies* — for progress in her work, not for superior conduct.

"Good," stated her school report in 1943, "but inclined to talk too much."

"Most lively and energetic," Miss Rosher recalled long after-wards. "Could be argumentative. Very hard to keep still."

Life was war, yes. It was also fierce conflict of wills with bitter and fuming frustration when you couldn't get your own way. But it was so many other interesting things that sirens and bombs, even acts of discipline, seemed relatively unimportant. It was going on holiday to Great Aunt's in Sussex and feeling the salt spray in your face. It was playing with marbles on the lounge floor with Ian and giving every one of the two hundred a name, the weirder the better, like Bloody, Scotty, Bluey, Pimply. It was collecting wooden animals from since you couldn't remember, until you had more than you could count. It was watching Dad taking a wicket and scoring a run at cricket. It was the soft fuzziness of a pet caterpillar named

Foxy. It was the taste of Grom's toffee and the lollypops Dad made from dried milk and the whole two-pound jar of strawberry jam that you and Ian snitched from the cupboard and ate every bit with a mustard spoon, because it was all you had time to find. It was purple candles on the buddleia tree at the foot of the garden and dandelions in a blue bowl on the carved monk's bench and the fringed petals of daisies.

But most of all it was MOTION — beautiful, swift rhythmic . . . running into the wind, turning somersaults, leap-frogging, climbing a tree even though you were terribly afraid of high places, squelching through mud, kicking dry leaves, throwing a ball farther than Malcolm, who was older and lived next door.

Was it irony of fate or mercy of Providence that could prelude utter dependence with such fierce independence of spirit, immobility with such incredible vitality? Perhaps a little of both.

3

Hilary was four when she first left home, an act of rebellion following a battle of wills. She tried to persuade Ian to go with her, but he resisted, not being permitted to take along his hot water bottle. Unlike his sister, he prized comfort above liberty.

When the time came for Ian to go to school, Garry House was considered too far away. He had suffered a hernia operation when nearly three — to Hilary's disgust, for it had interrupted her fifth birthday party — and was still not strong, so they both went to the local, Lapal Primary School. Hilary dutifully digested the three Rs, absorbed with greater gusto the side relishes — a book read by teacher called *Wurzle Gummidge* (almost as fascinating as the *Jemima Puddleduck* of kindergarten days) and a lesson on bees by one of the pupils' fathers, complete with nets, honeycomb, queen, drones, workers. Swarms of the fuzzy creatures mingled with the rabbits and elephants cavorting along the margins of her exercise books.

The school's real diet was less pleasing. Lunch was served at long trestle tables : grey potatoes, stewed cabbage, and other unpalatable items. A member of staff sat at the head of each table, but had different food. Hilary resented the inequality even more than the food. However, there were bonuses, such as her first boy friend, Peter, handsome, dark hair, merry black eyes, who walked with her to the golf course during lunch hour. first of a succession of Peters to encounter her life.

The next one, and far more important, was Peter Tetley, son of one of Eric's cricketing friends who had lost his wife when his two boys were twelve and ten. Lonely for home life, Peter and his brother often rode out to the Poles' from the city on their bicycles and were accepted as members of the family. This Peter was not handsome like the other. He was too thin, too gangling, a little like a bean pole. His high cheek bones made his cheeks look even more thin and hollow, and his thick dark hair emphasised their slight sallowness; but he was full of fun and laughter and liked children. Though there were seven years between them, he and Hilary were kindred spirits. Both liked to read, to take long walks, to study flowers and birds, to go browsing through fields and woods. From the time they were small children he would take Hilary and Ian for walks round Manor Lane.

During all her childhood Peter was a "big brother", someone who would take her part when others mistook her genuine wisdom for stubbornness and insubordination, to whom she could talk, who was big and strong yet willing to play with younger children, who did not tease and aggravate like Ian. They walked for miles around Lapal Lane and its environs, Hilary, Ian, and Peter, once even as far as Catshill. Ian became tired, planted himself on the grass verge, and refused to budge. It was Peter who had the bright idea of bribing him. "There's a shop around the corner, we'll buy ice cream!" He played games with them and the other children of the neighbourhood, mad games like British bulldogs, rough and tumble, leap frog, racing, all the exhilarating feats of motion which Hilary loved.

She loved going to his house in Hall Green. Uncle Tom who liked to call her "Peaches and Cream", would show them films — Charlie Chaplin, Laurel and Hardy, a fascinating one of a mongoose baiting and killing a cobra. There was always a banquet — ham, tongue, pork-pie salad, French roll with shrimps (how she loved shrimps!), jellies, fruit salad, trifle, cream, cake, biscuits. After tea the grown-ups would go next door to watch television, while the children, including Peter, played Monopoly, Pontoon, Canasta, Newmarket, and ate up

all the leftovers. Oh, she hated to think what childhood would
have been without Peter! He was a bonus supreme.

Another bonus during her early years was that she was
allowed to keep a cat. During the war she had had a tabby
kitten which she had called Toozelum (after the story of the
calico cat), Toozie for short. Unfortunately he was killed while
very young, but that was a long time ago. A friend's pet had
kittens. Hilary asked for one. "No." "Oh, please," she pleaded.
"NO." The next day she came home heart-broken because they
were going to be drowned that evening. Mum relented. Joyfully
Hilary ran down the road to Sarah Martin's house and brought
back a small, fluffy, black kitten which also must be named
Toozelum. "But you called the other one that," protested Mum.
Purpose was undeflected. "Yes, but this is Toozelum Two."
He grew into a beautiful tom with thick long black hair,
fluffy tail, amber eyes, a half Persian. She kept him for eight
years.

She made a pact with Malcolm Newbury, who played with
the young Poles in the dingle a few yards down the road. When
they grew up they would be married. Malcolm would be a
farmer, and she would be the farm vet. There was no romance
involved. It was to be solely a marriage of convenience. Oddly
enough, Malcolm would turn to farming, after studying law.
Hilary, who seldom swerved from her purpose once her mind
was made up, cherished her ambition for many years.

Because of the wartime dearth of teachers, Mona went back
to teaching, agreeing to substitute for a sick neighbour for two
weeks, a stint which was to last a quarter of a century and
more. When she took a permanent post at Olive Hill School,
she transferred the children there. Hilary liked Olive Hill much
better, especially the meals. There were only nine at each table,
and the staff ate with them having the same food. It was
served cafeteria style by four women: meat, potato, greens,
gravy. You could choose what you wanted. But you always
chose pudding, especially if it was FRESH CHERRIES AND
CREAM MADE WITH POWDERED MILK. Years later she
would remember and write the words in capitals. Also she
would recall, "Got slapped for chatting!" She took Australia
for her project at Olive Hill and acquired an Australian pen
friend.

Here she revealed an innate aptitude for drama, dancing,

art. The dancing was but a slight co-ordination of the muscles which had always dictated perpetual motion. As one of her teachers commented, "I don't think she could have walked sedately all the way home, *ever*!" She came to art naturally enough. Father was an excellent painter, with oils, pen and ink sketching and figure drawing. He especially favoured landscapes, and when the family went on a picnic he would take a sketch pad, sit and draw. He was a very active member of the Halesowen Art Society. The children often helped at the exhibitions. Hilary had started sketching with him at an early age. Her holiday greetings were as pictorially illustrated with small animals as her exercise books. In this as in other areas her teachers found her uniquely unconventional.

"I remember one painting she did of her idea of the jungle," recalled her art teacher at Olive Hill, "many brightly coloured patterned snakes, rearing up among brilliant trees and tall, yellow grasses. Most of her classmates had painted animals on four legs."

As for drama, each Christmas the family was given evidence of her theatrical instincts, as author, producer, director, costumier, prompter, manager, and principal actor. Admission was charged, a three-penny bit. During rationing the play was performed in a cold room, where there was a deep bay window with curtains going straight across, like a proscenium arch. Aunts and uncles, grandmas, neighbours, friends, all were herded together for an audience.

"She would always have about five roles for herself," Wendy remembered long afterwards with a chuckle, "and would give Ian and me one thing to do. He might have to be a snowman, so he'd be undressed, or a fairy, with little on. Then Hilary would be the little boy with mufflers and three big coats."

Christmases were always gala occasions at the Poles'. Even in wartime, when there were few toys, they somehow emerged : doll clothes, a steam roller hammered out of tin cans by Dad in the garage, a "gollywog" made for Hilary out of an old black stocking. The three pillowcases hung over the banister on Christmas Eve would be full on Christmas morning.

The Christmas cake was the annual pièce de résistance. It was different each year, its form kept secret from the children until Christmas morning. It might be in the shape of a church or a train or a house with a roof of chocolate drops and windows with red shiny paper and lights. It was cut on Christmas day at tea, when dozens of friends came to join the relatives who had been there for dinner.

Guy Fawkes days were almost as exciting as Christmases. The mats on the red tiled kitchen floor were taken up and the door closed into the rest of the house. The children could wallow in mud, get plastered from head to toe, as long as they did not go beyond the kitchen. A huge bonfire was built on the stone terrace. There would be potatoes roasted in their jackets, chestnuts, cheese, gallons of cocoa, treacle toffee, black, delicious to suck. Dad would set off fireworks.

"Why do you put so much time and effort," a fellow teacher asked Mona, "into a Bonfire Night party for the children?"

"Because," replied Mona, "I look back with such pleasure to all those things I had as a child. I want to fill my children's minds with such things to remember when they grow up." How thankful she would be later that she did!

It was Mona's sister Betty who filled a void in Hilary's tempestuous childhood with which Mona herself, equally independent and strong-minded, was never quite able to cope. When Hilary was six, Ian four, and Wendy a small baby, Betty had a serious illness, confining her to hospital for nine months. When she was discharged, the doctors insisted that she should go to a more rural area than Sheffield. Where better than the house in Manor Lane, near to open fields and lanes, an old bridge and canal, with wood-crowned Clent Hill in the distance? A divan bed was cut down and fitted into the bay window of the dining room. For nine months she lay there, companion for games and stories, confidante for childhood grievances, both foil and butt of bickering, fights, and pranks.

Betty was more than aunt to Hilary, more like an older and understanding sister. Often she would liaise between mother and daughter, Mona and Hilary were so alike! What annoyed one would annoy the other, and being a person who always knew exactly what she wanted and was determined to get it, but the smaller and weaker of the two, Hilary would often end the day in a storm of rebellion.

"Please," she would beg Aunt Betty again and again, "come upstairs with me."

There would follow a recounting of all the day's frustrations, whereupon Betty would use reason and persuasion. Even to her their relationship was at times bewildering. She loved the other two, but Hilary was somehow different, special in some way she could not define. Even knowing she was flagrantly at fault, Betty felt she had to defend her. She would have fought for her like a tigress protecting her young. It had been so from Hilary's babyhood. She was such a bundle of joy, so strong, so ramrod straight, so determined, such a "four square to the wind" child! Yet — why that strange feeling that maturity would bring her ill luck or unhappiness? Not failure certainly, she would accomplish what she set out to do — perhaps an unfortunate love affair?

Betty's own romance was already in the offing. She had been corresponding with a service man, friend of a neighbour in Sheffield. Before leaving for an overseas commission, he wanted to meet her. Arriving late at night, he was put to bed downstairs on the studio couch. At five thirty in the morning he was roused by a descending avalanche of three squealing, yelping children, shouting lusty greetings, dancing about him, ruffling his hair.

"Our new uncle! Our new uncle!"

As all male family friends became "uncles" automatically, no assumption of future marital status was intended, but Uncle Doug was quite willing to follow up the suggestion. His courtship proceeded by post from Malaya.

For the big celebration of Aunty Betty's twenty-first Hilary made her some plasticine brooches and bought her a silver cardboard key — with Aunty Betty's money! She had been sent to a local shop on an errand and bought the key out of the change. It wasn't the first time she had practised such questionable ethics. Mona had once sent her to the shop for a small purchase, giving her a pound note, and she had come back with a huge box, containing a beautiful doll for Wendy. "But, Mummy, it was only change!" Fortunately Mona was friendly with the shopkeepers.

It was at New Year that Betty's courtship reached its culmination. The children were not allowed to stay up for the late night celebration, but later Aunty Betty came into Hilary's room and showed her a sparkling engagement ring. "Look! See what Uncle Doug has given me!"

The wedding took place in July 1947. Hilary and Wendy were bridesmaids, Ian a page boy. The two girls looked and felt

very grown up in long pale blue dresses, roses and larkspur in
their blonde hair, which was plaited and fastened high on their
heads, a posy wrapped in a silver doyley in their hands. Eric,
scheduled to give the bride away, had flu, so "Arber" (Wendy's
version of Arthur appropriated by the whole family) took his
place. The reception held at Raybould's was an anticlimax,
because the couple sneaked out and cheated the party of throwing confetti. Hilary was indignant.

She loved visiting them at their rooms in Norton. There
were animals. The landlady had a beautiful bull mastiff,
Zanny, whose playmates were John Pool, a spaniel with one
blue and one brown eye, and a Scotch terrier called Whisky.
Uncle Doug took her to watch outdoor greyhound racing, such
glorious rapturous motion! At a farm near Dodford, their next
home, she was allowed to stroke a two-day-old calf. She loved
the village of tiny pink cottages, the plums, raspberries, and
strawberries. She helped make bramble jelly. Even the lack of
a proper "loo" seemed more novelty than deprivation. Most
of all she loved the freedom of escape. It was always to Aunty
Betty's that she planned to go on the many occasions when she
ran away.

4

Strange, how you could be so passionately loyal to home and
family yet long to run away from them! How you could say
again and again to Mum, "I hate you, I hate you, I hate you!",
then drop a note over the bannister saying, "Dear Mummy,
sorry I was naughty. I love you very much!" How you could
"bounce" Wendy up and down, up and down, on your knee,
making her squeal with delight, then pull the stair carpet from
under her so that she got a big bruise on her back, afterwards
enjoining her, under pain of dire punishment, not to tell! How
you could raid cupboards and the pantry and share generously
with Ian at midnight feasts, then, when setting the table, fling
at him a whole bundle of knives and forks! Fortunately doing
less damage to him than to the black-tiled floor!

In fact, of all perplexing things in life, you yourself were the
hardest to understand. You could climb trees like a cat, clamber

over rocks, shin up the drain pipe and wriggle head first through a tiny window into the "loo" when you got yourself locked out, yet turn giddy on the edge of a sheer slope, a swing bridge, or a fire escape. You could chatter like a magpie to people in bus queues and trains, to street cleaners, school janitors, and shop keepers, yet shake like a leaf when you had to stand up and read the lesson. When Aunty Betty was ill at home, you could spend hours sitting beside her, yet balk at a single visit when Dad was in hospital. You could want to do well in school and please your teachers, yet torture them mercilessly with mischievous pranks.

Though Oliver Hill was a junior school, normally keeping a child until the age of eleven, at this time it was overcrowded and all nine- and ten-year-olds were transferred to a local secondary school. Mona disapproved of this, so Hilary was sent again to Garry House. Her irrepressible energy was soon seeking outlet in unacademic pursuits.

"Conduct can be a trifle too exuberant," was the mild comment on her first report.

The remedy was unorthodox. "You're inclined to be mischievous, my dear," said the wise headmistress. "You're also a born leader, and you can have great influence for good. Perhaps you will be able to curb yourself in helping to curb others. We are making you school captain."

Hilary gasped. "Set a thief to catch a thief," she thought. She was thrilled. At first the idea was not too successful. She participated in some pranks she should have stopped. A stern censure was forthcoming : if she did not show more responsibility, she would be relieved of her captaincy. Hilary was both humiliated and chastened. Though perfection was never attained, she did apply herself to her task of leadership more seriously.

"Slight lapses of responsibility," her teachers commented. "Keen and interested. Full of enthusiasm for things she likes, impatient over things she does not like. Popular with most, but shows an occasional intolerance of those of less ability than herself."

And a faculty for coping with the unavoidable, the headmistress was to remember years later. For Mona as well as for the children it was a major tragedy. Measles and whooping cough, scabies during the war, had been bad enough, especially the latter. She had had to scrub them with a nail brush until they bled, then bandage them. But this! They had gone to the seaside for a holiday. Returning, she noticed a little patch of dry skin behind Wendy's ear. It grew. "A bit of seborrhoea," soothed the doctor and prescribed a medicated shampoo. Increasingly worried, Mona consulted a specialist. "Have you more children?" he asked. "Yes, two." "I want you all here in my surgery in the morning by nine thirty, husband, yourself, children, animals." Mona gasped. "What on earth — !" The doctor shook his head. "I'm very sorry if it's what I think it is."

They all went. Each was subjected to a special X-ray. The cat was cleared. Eric and Mona were cleared. Wendy was badly infected, the other two children slightly. Looking through the doctor's lens, Mona was horrified. The whole scalp seemed to be moving. It was not ringworm, but it belonged to the same family. The children had contracted it on holiday, during exceptionally dry weather, from contact with horses. The cure was execrable. Before undertaking it, Mona had to sign a paper saying that if hair never grew again, she would not sue the doctor.

She went home. She cut their lovely blonde hair to a quarter of an inch, Hilary's and Wendy's baby-fine and straight, Ian's a mass of curls. At the hospital they were given X-ray treatment. "Their hair will fall out," said the doctor. "It will die at the roots. They will be completely bald." Would they go to school? "Why not?" demanded Hilary calmly. Mona made them little caps, the girls' like sun-bonnets, Ian's small and white like a cricketer's.

"At her age most children would have been unwilling to face their schoolmates," commented the headmistress, "but Hilary took it in her stride and appeared quite unselfconscious."

Embarrassment was one thing. Pain was quite another. After a week bandages of Elastoplast were applied in strips, left on for four days, then ripped off. Their heads were scrubbed with a nail brush and permanganate of potash. By the time Mona got them in bed, she could have cried the rest of the night herself. Hilary's case was most stubborn of all. "Scrub it with washing soda," advised the doctor with apparent heartlessness. Hilary wept. She screamed. She had always found pain abhorrent, an insult perhaps to her superior health and vigour. If Ian were ill, he would be perfectly content lying in bed with his hot water bottle and a book, daydreaming. Not Hilary! Approach a scratch or a splinter with a bit of cotton wool and she would cry out, "Oh, it hurts! No, no, don't do it!"

But, like other childhood tragedies, this one passed. The day came when Mona exclaimed delightedly, "Oh, look at them in the light! I think some hair's growing." So it was, a bit of yellow fuzz. Ian's came out thick and curly, Hilary's and Wendy's as fine and unmanageable as ever.

In spite of its conflicts and frustrations childhood was a happy time. There were the cricket matches on Saturdays and Sundays. Dad had joined the Smethwick Cricket Club in the Birmingham League. On Sundays he played for the Warwickshire Acorns. The family nearly always accompanied him. Hilary loved every minute of it — the early morning, with Mum cutting sandwiches, preparing a picnic, packing Dad's bag, not forgetting her score book, rolling sleepily into bed after an exciting day. As she grew older, interest became more serious. They went to watch county matches, and the Test match was THE big event. The whole family sat glued to the radio, holding its composite breath. If anyone had to leave, one was left on score duty. One evening Hilary came plodding home from school, satchel clutched in one hand, portable radio squawking in the other.

There were the quiet evenings when Dad read from the classics — *Black Beauty, Robinson Crusoe*, and, most memorable of all, *Masterman Ready*, which ended in tragedy. When Dad finished the book with the hero's death, all went to bed in tears, Ian's grief giving vent to loud moans of "Poor — po-oor old Masterman Ready" until he cried himself to sleep. But such shared experience was sobering, not unhappy.

In fact, it was often the sobering things that made life most fascinating, like a neighbour's old Granny who, though blind, could read books with her fingers. Hilary stood at her feet and watched her for hours, wondering, admiring. Like Robert, a spastic pupil at Olive Hill, who could not speak well or control his movements, yet was so very lovable that you wanted terribly to help but didn't know how.

There were the visits to Nan Nan in Sheffield where you

stored up memories to last a lifetime : meat and potato with Yorkshire pudding, home-made cakes, dough rising on the hearth; the huge kitchen with its mangle, tub, posher, copper boiler, and drying rack; feeding a little goat-kid from a bottle, playing with Jenny, the fat white bulldog that lived next door; ginger biscuits and dark sticky parkins that made your mouth water.

Visits to Grom's, Dad's mother, were fun too, with the toy cupboard filled with all sorts of surprises — bits of cloth, sweets, dolls' clothes. "Where's the key? Where's the key?" you would demand as soon as "Hellos" were over. Then you three would rush to empty it, each one claiming what he had found, and since you were the oldest and strongest, you always got the lion's share.

Grom was pretty and tiny. At ten you gleefully discovered you were the same height; at fifteen you could hold out your arm straight, and she could fit under it. She was generous to a fault. If you went into her house and said of something, "Isn't that lovely!" she would say, "Oh, you can have it." Generous, yes, but cantankerous. If you were hot, Grom felt a draught. If the government said yes, Grom said no. You named one of your wood carvings, a little Indian figure with hat and blanket drawn closely about head and shoulders, "Grom in a Draught". Memories stored up at Grom's were more pungent, adventurous, lively — home-made pickled cabbage, onions; a coal cellar with dark narrow steep stairs; noise of a factory; a sports field at the bottom of the garden; outside loo and a chamber in your bedroom.

But most precious of all memories would be those of your small world round Upway, of three children romping, running, shouting, eyes open wide to all the wonders of unfolding life; of roaming the countryside searching for wild flowers, nuts, conkers, mushrooms, coming home with hands full of strange plants, never resting until you had learned their names, Latin as well as English; bird watching, knowing where each kind made its nest and how its song sounded; fishing the streams for tiddlers with a bent pin; tracking small animals; climbing Clent; tobogganing in winter, cricket in summer; often getting into trouble because of your torn clothes and muddy shoes. Long afterwards, when your limbs were motionless, your voice stilled, your eyes unseeing, you would take them out of hiding and relive them.

Out of our gate, down the road, past a herd of Friesians (I call them Nestlés' milk cows), past an orchard and a field of sheep with lambs, across the road, down a steep incline to the towpath of an old disused canal. As we walk, coots and moorhens dart off to hide in the reeds, scolding as they go, but George and Henrietta, the pair of resident swans, sail majestically to the water's edge, heads slightly askew on long graceful necks, eyeing us speculatively as we fish in our pockets for bread. A vivid flash of russet and blue, as the kingfisher streaks by.

We turn off the towpath, down the bank, wriggling under a barbed wire fence into the grounds of Manor Abbey farm. High up in the Abbey ruins a pair of kestrels build each year and in the old barns swallows nest among the beams. Through the farmyard to a stream, crossed by an ancient stone bridge, moss-covered with hart's tongue and maidenhair fern clinging to the crevices. The banks of the stream are steep, clothed in hazel, alder and grotesquely shaped pollarded willows, where we used to build tree-houses. Once, wandering along the path, I come face to face with a fox. I'm not sure which of us is more surprised. He freezes, head raised, tongue lolling, staring at me, crafty insolent eyes agleam with curiosity. Then in one bound he leaps the stream and disappears, leaving only his strong pungent odour behind.

We follow the stream as it meanders through the barrows and come to a stile guarding a field of mowing grass, dotted with harebells, yellow rattle and moon-pennies. Clambering over, we cross the field, keeping strictly to the path, through the gate into a lane. Here and there in the tall hedges are tangles of dog-rose, woody nightshade and bryony. The air is heavy with the scent of meadowsweet.

A little way up the lane, turning left, we tiptoe up the dark, mysterious fairy footpath. Making sure the bull is not with the cows, we cross another field, climb another stile and pause awhile, to watch a dragonfly hovering over a stagnant pool, before making our way into a cornfield. There is a sunny bank on one side of the path where we sit and eat our picnic. Butterflies and bees flit from flower to flower, and grasshoppers play leapfrog among the stalks. If the sun gets too hot, we can share the shade cast by the old oak with the last foxglove. Then, the hamper empty, we stroll home-ward, listening to the larks as we go.

5

She was thirteen when she went to her first symphony con-cert. Peter took her. Rudolph Schwarz conducted the City of Birmingham Symphony Orchestra at the Birmingham Town Hall, and Dennis Matthews played Beethoven's Fifth Piano Concerto, the *Emperor*. She listened, spellbound, nerves tight-strung and vibrating to the exquisite harmonies. After that she was often in the audience, occasionally in the main body of the hall but more often in the two-shilling benches behind the orchestra.

There had been music in her life before. Dad played the violin, not as expertly as he painted, but passably. She had taken lessons from an early age, but hated her first teacher. Examination reports commented, "Good pace but scales un-tidy" . . . "Sight reading, rhythm very poor. Why not count?" . . . "Pace variable." Yet by June 1950, she had passed the Academy Grade V examinations in Theory and Practical.

There had been evenings of music with their neighbours, Ernest and Hattie Jones, coffee and much hilarity punctuating the harmonies — or discords — of piano, violins, and cello. She played the hymns for junior church held at St. Peter's, which met in a hall at Lapal Halesowen . . . badly. No matter how perfectly she could sight-read them at home, in public she always made mistakes galore.

This sudden new awareness of SOUND was different. It was as elemental, as exhilarating as Motion. It flung open doors of joyous experience which she hadn't known existed : choir festivals at Gloucester, Hereford, Worcester; opera, symphonies, promenade concerts. Often she scribbled terse, discerning com-ments on her programmes.

"Very, very, very good," she wrote of Berlioz' *Royal Hunt*

and Storm, played by the Symphony Orchestra; but of another feature of the programme, "The soloist is a bit too showy off."

"Rather monotonous," she described a performance of Strauss's *Don Juan*. Another number, "Powerful beginning and finish, middle inconspicuous and uninteresting."

Her tastes in music proved as wide as her interest in sports :, country and western as well as classical; folk and Irish rebel songs along with opera; Glenn Miller, Jimmy Shand and Bach — but always Beethoven's *Emperor* would be her favourite.

When she was twelve years old, after a year at King Edward's Grammar School in Handsworth, she was accepted for six years' studying at King Edward's High School for Girls. This was an imposing brick and stone building with bewildering long corridors polished to such glassy smoothness that you were tempted to get a running start and slide the whole length — and sometimes did. Hilary loved everything about it, the green, black, and white uniform (the grammar school one had been disappointing, with no tie); her A Form of twenty-six girls, which happened to contain the "sporty" crowd, her new friends; the tuck shop, which sold sweets, chocolates, biscuits, Horlicks, cream buns. She could resist everything but the chocolate. The first year her best friend was Caroline, a professor's daughter, with hair as dark as Hilary's was blonde, and mischievous green eyes. They were a diabolical combination.

"Such charming conversationalists, both of them," Dr. Smith, the principal, said to Mona. "I love to sit at Hilary's table because I know I'm going to enjoy myself. But what freak of chemistry brought those two girls to the same school and the same form in the same year I shall never know !"

They were equally exuberant, equally inventive. Miss M., their history teacher, was a prime target. Caroline brought a small bow and arrow to class and shot a dart through the open window. Hilary, sitting close to the window, climbed out to get it. Miss M. continued her lecture, quite unaware. They turned the desks around so that when she came into the room she saw rows and rows of backs. This time she was equal to the challenge. She taught the class from the other end of the room. Their tormenting was not due to dislike. She was just easily teased and upset. In spite of the torture she became a firm friend of Hilary, even presenting her with her wedding bouquet.

"Has good intentions," Hilary's report noted at the end of the year, "but her conduct has been unreliable and sometimes very foolish. Needs more effort."

At least she was not nondescript. Even members of staff who did not teach her were conscious of her presence. One, Elsa Freeman, remembered her from the entrance examination she had taken in March 1949, one of some seven to eight hundred girls trying for seventy-five places. Why should she have noticed her, even remembered her name, when she had forgotten the names and faces of the other twenty-four girls in the room where she invigilated? Because she was different, her blonde hair cropped short at a time when most girls did not favour that style? Perhaps — but mostly because of her liveliness, the sheer energy which exuded from her lithe, compact body. She looked as if she were bursting to be out and running about the playing field. Could she really sit still long enough to pass the examination? If so, how would she adjust to life in a highly academic school?

Hilary had passed the examination and been put on the waiting list. Now here she was, a year later, as exuberant as ever, hair still cut short, streaking through the dark corridors like a bright flash of quicksilver. But she had had to be warned by the headmistress, it seemed, that she must be more disciplined in work and conduct. Miss Freeman felt oddly relieved when at the beginning of each new term the blonde head reappeared.

The second year showed improvement, and she tackled her studies with zest. A new friend, Molly, was a steadying influence, but still there were lapses of decorum; worse, acts of madness, as when Hilary climbed the partitions of the lavatories, one after the other, locking the door of each in turn. She loved to visit Molly, her petite merry mother, her studious but fun-loving father, a cage of hamsters, and Leo, the spaniel. So great was her craving for a dog of her own that once she had bought a leash, fastened it to her neck, and persuaded a playmate to lead her round! She and Molly went riding together every week, patronising a small stable belonging to a boys' prep school. Hilary's horse was usually Jimmy, a skewbald gelding, who proved allergic to trains. As the field was next to a railway line, she was thrown unceremoniously, until she adjusted to his charging up the field the minute he heard a train and stopping dead in his tracks as it passed!

School mornings were pandemonium at Upway. When Wendy started Grammar School, the three young Poles were scheduled to catch the eight-twenty bus which went from Webbs Green up Manor Lane to Birmingham. Missing it would have meant a twenty minute walk and being late for school. However much Mum insisted that satchels be packed, shoes cleaned, clothes prepared the night before, something was always forgotten. The one who finished breakfast and tooth cleaning first would grab belongings, dash out of the front door, leaving it open, and stand at the bottom of the drive. The bus sighted, he or she would yell, and the other two would drop everything, grab coat, hat, scarf, satchel, and sort them out as they ran. Meanwhile Isobel, who lived up the road, would be running for the bus too, often dashing across the road trying to flag it down.

Going home, if Hilary and Isobel got to Bearwood too early for the bus, they would visit a small milk bar, "The Ship", for chocolate biscuits and a milk shake. On "high days" the snack might be supplemented with a quarter of a pound of Brunner's home-made rum truffles. If they caught one of the buses which did not go down Manor Lane, they had either to walk a mile or wait for a local bus. Here, when they had time to spare, they patronised the small fish and chip shop near the bus stop known as "The Stag", after the local pub close by. One stood sentry to warn when the single-decker turned the library corner at the bottom of Long Lane, and they dashed out for the hundred-yard sprint. They never missed it.

At this stage Hilary was becoming fiercely appearance-conscious. In spite of the ministrations of the Dunns ("Uncle Leslie" and "Aunty Joan"), good family friends as well as hairdressers in Halesowen, her baby-fine hair was the bane of her life. Bubble cuts and perms either wilted or frizzled. She complained bitterly about a persistent case of acne.

"Doctor says I must drink more water, eat fruit, and cut out carbohydrates," she said to her friend Pat Thompson, then proceeded every break to stock up on sweets at the tuck shop.

Pat, usually called "Baby Elephant", was also a bus companion and a partner in an adolescent discovery of the other sex. At thirteen they each nourished a *grand passion* — several, in fact. For some weeks Hilary's swain, Marsh, met the 2B bus and rode with her to the Ivy Bush, before the romance died a natural death. She and Pat often manoeuvred buses to join that of their particular heart throb of the moment, quite oblivious to the obviousness of two giggling school-girls planting themselves again and again in his vicinity. Pat's embarrassment was to come years later when, starting as a dental student, she was to find the object of their attentions in the fourth year of the same faculty!

However, these were minor concerns for Hilary. She was plunging with genuine ardour into her studies — botany, French, trigonometry, calculus, art, especially English literature, where they read Shakespeare and she studied poetry, which she loved to read while hating its mechanics. Still, her reports revealed much room for improvement.

"1953. English, erratic, varies in quality. Latin, does not make sufficient effort. Fusses rather than works. Careless mistakes. Energy often misplaced."

"1954. Latin superficial. Art erratic. Work not good enough, and a great deal of thorough learning is needed to make any improvement."

Yet that same year one of her paintings, illustrating wheels and gears, won honourable mention in an open competition conducted by the *Daily Telegraph*, and her scraperboard design was chosen to decorate the cover for the Benjamin Britten Ceremony of Carols at the Festival of Christmas. It revealed not only artistic skill but refreshing imagination: the holy family at one side, a star shining on a burst of angels' wings and streaming hair, trumpet-shaped, sheep-folds and sheep, and at the bottom the faint suggestion of an audience.

Erratic, yes, for little elephants, rabbits, and pigs continued to frolic up and down the margins of her Rough Book and on bus tickets, all dressed differently and doing a variety of things — skiing, running, eating, sleeping. In art, hair style, or whatever, she would never be a conformist. Who else in school would have dared challenge the school's rigid uniformity by going down to lunch with a red ribbon in her hair — and got away with it? Even in subjects where she excelled her rating suffered.

"Gymnastics," stated her school report for 1955, "Does excellent free movement, but her apparatus is not so good." (*Rebel*, scrawled Hilary after this notation)

But on the playing field she was in her element. MOVEMENT.

She had known its language from birth. Now she could speak it with all the fluency of a strong, lithe, perfectly co-ordinated body. Cricket, hockey, squash, rounders, badminton, netball — she played them all with a fierce will to win, expending every ounce of energy. She played right half at hockey, Molly right back, each seeming to know by instinct what the other would do, an unbeatable combination.

It was in these years also that she discovered the joys of swimming. The family developed a habit of going to the local baths at Bearwood, five miles away, early on Sunday mornings. After their swim there would be a picnic breakfast of cold bacon sandwiches, and coffee. Their friends the Dunns often went with them. "The perfect pupil," the swimming instructor described Hilary, "highly intelligent and quick to grasp instructions."

Even this did not compare with dancing. Here, in the interpretive dance, was true freedom of fulfilment. It was mathematics, poetry, drama, music, art, all the choicest values of life for which she had never been able to find expression. Yes — even religion. For surely the leap of a fawn, the soaring of a lark, are akin to worship. It was the form she liked best in gymnastics at school. She and Wendy had had ballet lessons with a Mrs. Dayus, whose brother, John Knight, also taught dancing. One year they both performed at Lapal Fair. Wendy took part in a Welsh dance and Hilary a Norwegian. And at the time of the Festival of Britain to her great surprise and delight Hilary was asked to demonstrate the Coronation Waltz with John Knight.

The Coronation! She almost saw it. She and her mother and father were invited to the May Day celebrations at Whitelands Training College, where Miss Frederick (Freddie), who had been Mum's biology lecturer at college, was assistant principal. They came back through London on the eve of the Coronation, saw the splendid decorations in the Mall, the banners on the lamp-posts, the Pakistani guards in their kilts and resplendent turbans, white spats over their plaid stockings. Far more thrilling to Hilary, however, was a trip to the Zoo. Since Freddie was a fellow, she was allowed inside some of the cages — the chimpanzees', the Bush babies', and through the feeding fences to the polar bears' and rhinos'. She entered without the slightest fear.

Three years later Hilary saw Queen Elizabeth when, with the Duke of Edinburgh, she visited the High School in November 1955. Of course it had to be raining. Mr. Lunt, the headmaster, conducted the Queen into the building under an umbrella. An impressive array of guests joined the royal couple on the dais, including the Lord Mayor of Birmingham, the Lady Mayoress, and the Lord Lieutenant of Warwickshire.

Holidays on the coast, at Bournemouth, at Great Aunt's in Sussex, at Llangennith on the Gower in Wales, could be even more exciting than one in London, for they involved physical activity. For three consecutive years four families went together for a fortnight at Llangennith. The place was made for cricket, great expanses of flat firm sand with high rocks at the back, acting not only as wickets but wicket keeper and shelter for the ladies' supporters club. Hilary was chief organiser for cricket and rounders. They would trek to the beach with all their paraphernalia, five Poles, Uncle Doug and Aunty Betty, the Dunns with their son Robin, Uncle Norman and Aunty Marjorie with their daughter Joyce, and perhaps others. The main object in cricket was to play high and far. Hilary and Ian were usually deep sea fielders, and it was a marvel that they never lost a ball. Afterwards they would trek home over the dunes, all in single file, each carrying his share of goods and chattels, looking like an overloaded camel train.

It was on one of these holidays, the usual trip to Bournemouth over Easter for the spring hockey festival, that family tensions, for Hilary at least, rose to boiling point. In addition to her independence, she jealously guarded what she considered her privileges as the eldest. After years of being served supper on a tray in the bedroom, she was looking forward to joining the grown-ups for the evening meal. To her horror, despite her frantic pleadings, Ian and Wendy were allowed to stay up too! There were other similar episodes. When she was twelve or thirteen, a family they had made friends with invited her to attend a village hop. No, she was too young. Two years later she was allowed to go, but, to her outrage, so were Ian and Wendy. There were tempests of rebellion when Wendy was permitted to wear make-up, nylons, high heels and other accessories of womanhood at an earlier age than she. The very closeness of the family made occasional friction all the more abrasive.

"We know each others' raw nerve ends," admitted Hilary long afterwards, "and just where to rub the salt in."

Even Dad, patient, honest, jocular, always the keen sportsman, sometimes yielded to temper. Once, after much provocation, when Hilary responded "I shan't" to a simple request, it was the last straw. He exploded, picked up the kitchen stool and started after her. She was out of the kitchen, through the hall, upstairs and under her bed in half a minute flat.

However, it was Mona, so like herself, with whose equally dominant will Hilary's was more often in collision. After Wendy's birth Mona endured years of mental and physical tension with an ulcer, often culminating in periods of intense pain. Hilary's assertion of will, it seemed, rose in direct ratio to her pain level. Once, when Hilary had been so perversely stubborn that she was ready to drop, she reached a peak of frustration.

"Young lady," she said, "when you are older, if you are ever ill, I hope people will have as little sympathy with you as you've got with me."

She was aghast the moment she had said it, and for years afterwards it was to haunt her with an obsessive sense of guilt.

Hilary had many faults, most of them byproducts of virtues, but neither vindictiveness nor injustice was one of them. If Wendy, the less aggressive, had committed some misdemeanour, Hilary would invariably take the blame. If she herself had been at fault, she would usually confess and take the consequences.

Her thirst for independence was somewhat assuaged when in 1954 she took her first trip to France. Miss Freeman arranged an exchange visit for her with a family named de la Genardière, who lived in a charming old chateau a few miles outside Autun. There were eight children, Alix, near her own age, then Jacques, Simone, Xavier, Dominique, Alain, Philippe, and two-year-old Claude.

She loved it all; the ancient chateau with its big farm and tiny chapel, its huge stone-floored kitchen with massive wooden table, big chest for food, antique stove, and sink literally hewn out of rock. The high point of the trip was the journey with Alix and her Guide Company to Corsica. Sailing on the Sanpiero Corse, she slept that night with a pair of feet for her pillow. They belonged to a scout who had another pair for his pillow. No one slept on hers since she was near the rail. She and the scout discussed Chopin, Haydn, and piano techniques far into the night, and she was thrilled to discover that he did not know she was English until morning, her colloquial French had been so good. Of course she had started learning it in kindergarten.

Corsica held memorable adventures, pleasant and unpleasant but all thrilling. The journey up Cap Corse from Bastia in a rickety charabanc, clinging dizzily to her seat, shutting her eyes to the sheer drops and trying to pretend she couldn't hear the corner stones plop into oblivion as they charged around hairpin bends. Sleeping on the wooden floor of a half-ruined house in a tiny mountain village, bats hanging from the rafters. Palm, quince, and olive trees, and cacti growing wild in the hedges. A beautiful snake wriggling out of the grass, green with two red stripes down its sides, a brief gorgeous flash of colour. Camping in a sun trap and taking your turn cooking over a roaring open fire in a shade temperature of eighty to ninety degrees. Long walks through the sweet chestnut forest, tracking and stalking game. Learning French songs and teaching your "beaver patrol" to sing "There's a Hole in My Bucket" and "Down among the Deadmen". Climbing to the top of San Piedro and lighting a fire at ten p.m. to let the villagers of Croce know you had reached the top. A greetings telegram from home.

"Congratulations. Seven passes. Mummy."

Returning with Alix to the chateau, she so captured the hearts of the big French family that they became lifelong friends. Indeed, it became a real family exchange, for they invited Ian to visit them the following year. And later Hilary herself was able to make a second trip to France.

Later she had an Italian pen friend too, a boy named Francesco, whose life, though she had never seen him, became almost as vividly real as that of the de la Genardières'. And for a while, during these high school years, there were letters from Peter in Hong Kong and Canada.

Peter was still her "big brother". During her early teens he took her to many concerts and was her escort to the Three Choirs Festival. He continued to be a frequent visitor at Upway. Hilary often baked on Sundays — scones, coconut pyramids, cakes of all kinds, shortbread, meat and fruit pies, crumbles. Peter was often there at weekends. If he came during a busy time, he would help, peel potatoes, shell peas, set the table.

Hilary always made him dry the dishes. She didn't mind washing, but loathed drying. They always made evening coffee together. Usually they would argue, about books, plays, cricket, anything but politics, in which Hilary was not interested. When he debated such subjects with Mum and Dad, often with mounting heat, for all had determined views, she would get very much upset and leave the room. Strange, because she found arguing with him fun!

Then Peter spent two years in National Service, some of them in Hong Kong. His letters were regular and interesting — if you could read his dreadful writing! She pored over them, fascinated by his descriptions of army life and the mysterious Orient. He was in Hong Kong for his twenty-first. She tried to think of a way to send him a cake but couldn't, so he had to celebrate on eggs and chips! She was fifteen when he returned, bringing her a delicate moonstone bracelet and a pair of blue silk pyjamas — men's! — a beautiful Chinese pattern embroidered in darker blue. Later she made them into shorties.

It was the following year, when she was sixteen, that their relationship, on her side at least, begun to change. He was feeling unsettled at home and work and decided to go to Canada.

"I'll come back for your twenty-first," he promised lightly.

Suddenly she knew that he meant more to her than just a brother and that she was going to miss him very much. She looked eagerly for his letters. A small powder compact with pictures of H.M.S. *Saxonia* on the lid became a most treasured possession. When, after ten months, his letters revealed a dangerous depression, she became intensely worried if none came. She was very much relieved when he decided to come home to study at night school for his A levels, leading to university entrance. Though his attitude towards her remained apparently unchanged, she knew that she was in love with him. Foolish! She tried to pretend that she was not, and was determined that no one should guess her secret. If he so much as suspected how she felt, it would most certainly spoil their friendship.

Meanwhile, during these last years in high school Hilary was forming a new, far more congenial relationship with her own "little sister". Until now her feelings towards Wendy had been protective, usually tolerant but sometimes antagonistic, and just a bit contemptuous. The antagonism had sprung from a conviction, shared by both, that the other was her parents' favourite. The tinge of contempt was the outgrowth of physical superiority. For Wendy, it seemed, was never quite equal to the challenge of a boisterously active older brother and sister. She was always falling behind on walks, getting tired, complaining of pains in her legs, though doctors could find nothing wrong with them. An excuse, Hilary had thought, for getting out of long walks and vigorous games. Then something happened to turn the last vestige of contempt into contrition. One day when Wendy was getting into the car with Mum, she caught her knee on the door handle, turned ashen and drawn, and was obviously in great pain. Mum took her to a doctor, who sent her to a consultant. He diagnosed osteochondritis, a very painful disease, which demanded treatment and might — later did — require surgery.

Hilary became not only contrite but more discerning. Emerging into adolescence, tall, blonde, attractive, popular with both sexes, Wendy was becoming a sister not to tolerate, to share midnight feasts and play childish games with, but to be proud of and enjoy. She was developing skills that Hilary could not only admire but envy — sew a dress that looked tailor-made, whip up a flan or soufflé that would do justice to a French chef. She was a keen gardener, loving every variety — flower, vegetable, bog, water, indoor — and could make anything grow. She talked of being a horticulturist. The two girls began borrowing each other's clothes cosmetics, jewellery. Hilary took Wendy to her first symphony concert. They sat behind the orchestra and heard Rachmaninoff's Second Piano Concerto. Love of music became a strong uniting bond. Their new relationship welded the family even more closely together.

Preparations for Hilary's own life work were all too imminent. During her fourth year in secondary school, she had to choose among a wide variety of courses. Art, gymnastics, especially dancing, were obvious choices. There were mathematics and French, and of course zoology and biology, essential for a future veterinary surgeon. Greek, German, geography? She finally chose geography, while Molly turned to Greek.

Art was fascinating. For her three practical papers, prepared for A level examinations, Hilary chose imaginative composition, flower paintings, and still life.

For her theory paper she chose the history of painting from prehistoric cave painting to the present day. Too big a subject for a lifetime, much less two years! As she was the only one studying that particular subject, she could choose her own course. She decided to make a very superficial study of western art so that she could understand the various influences, then concentrate on her favourite schools — the Italian, especially the Venetians, from Veronese, Titian, Tintoretto to El Greco; Spanish, Dutch, Flemish, and German, the French Impressionists, Renoir, Cézanne, Dégas, Manet, Van Gogh, Gauguin. As for English, she was not much interested in early English or pre-Raphaelites but loved the more contemporary style — Nash, Turner, Piper, Spencer. Greek sculpture and architecture fascinated her, so she studied that, too. She spent hours wandering around the Barber Institute, just across the road from school, and the Birmingham Museum and Art Gallery.

She laboured over her art notebooks One, for her course in the Lower Sixth, told the story of painting in England to Hogarth's time. She illustrated it with drawings from the Winchester Bible which were almost professional in their conception and technique. Her notebook for Miss Crisp on the History of Art was illustrated by dozens of drawings ranging from Egyptian tomb and temple masterpieces, through Greek and Roman sculpture and the Renaissance, up to modern times, many so realistic as to be easily recognised. She struggled for days over an elaborate diagram showing the open work of the famous twelfth-century candlestick at Gloucester Cathedral, its intertwined monsters, dragons, and tiny human figures painstakingly produced in intricate detail.

"Lively minded," Miss Crisp commented. "Good in her gay fresh way at art."

"Art promising," rated her school report in 1956. "Original and courageous, though sometimes a little too free." (REBEL, appended Hilary again.)

During the two Easter vacations in her A level years she went to the Dale Fort Field Centre on marine biology expeditions with her teacher, Gladys Wilson. Ten or twelve girls were in the party. The journey to Dale was almost as exciting as its scientific studies. The road lay through the rich red farmlands of Hereford, past the grim Black Mountains and the smiling Brecon Beacons, across Wales and out along a peninsula to the western sea. Here at Dale they became "Beachcombers for Science". Each girl took a hand lens and knife for winkling out specimens, going to the beach each morning to study zonation. Working in a group of four, they would construct a frame enclosing a square yard of beach, then count or estimate the number of different animals or algae within the frame. Winkles, cockles, barnacles, whelks or whatever, they would bring them back for study, then as the last act of the day restore them to the sea. Hilary plunged into the study with all her abundant energy and *joie de vivre*.

Plunged into more than study! The first year some of them went a little mad, deciding to dance in the moonlight, then take a midnight swim. The second year Molly was with her, and conduct was a bit more stable. Still, she managed to startle her companions by some daring combinations in dress — maroon jeans, scarlet sweater and socks, maroon smock. In 1956 it was almost a crime, certainly a *faux pas*, to put such colours together. (Again, REBEL.) "Fabulous," she rated the experience.

She loved working with Molly. Often the two could be seen dissecting in the biology laboratory during the lunch hour. In spite of her love of animals, Hilary enjoyed dissection. For one project she made a thorough study of the diet of the dogfish by examining the stomach contents of as many specimens as she could procure.

People tried to discourage her ambition to become a veterinary surgeon. It would require six years of training, and there were not many openings for women. However, advice had never deterred her, once she had made up her mind. She would go and train at Edinburgh University. Then something happened. She saw a cat run over! A car hit it, split its head open. Instead of lying still, it jumped up and flapped around, still on its side, rolling into the gutter, leaving blood in its path. She felt physically sick, as unable to go to its aid, even approach it, as to fly. Veterinary surgeon? In that moment she knew it would be unwise, if not impossible. Yet she had had no other ambition since early childhood. Here she was in her A level year of high school, facing the necessity of choice. She felt plunged into a vacuum.

Nursing? Hospital almoner? Physio- or occupation therapist? None of them set her on fire. She had almost decided to read biology at the university and decide after that when somebody

— or something — suggested teaching Physical Education. Teaching! With Mum a teacher, all three children had sworn they would never teach. Yet Mum loved it. True, Hilary excelled at games of all kinds. She enjoyed gymnastics. Then suddenly her pulses quickened. Dance! Modern educational dance! Surely as a Physical Education teacher one could specialise. Though dancing was taught in many infant and junior schools, it was rarely a subject for secondary students. Why shouldn't it be? All the better if one had to pioneer!

She began writing to various training colleges for prospectuses. Miss Jaques, one of her teachers, recommended the I. M. Marsh College of Physical Education in Liverpool. She was a close friend of Miss Crabbe, the principal. To Hilary's delight the courses offered there seemed tailor-made for her: gymnastics, dance, biology, physiology, anatomy, English, music, art, education. A three-year course with all the subjects she liked best! The college also had the best reputation for dance. She applied and kept her fingers crossed.

Her last year at King Edward's! She worked furiously on her chosen subjects, botany, zoology, art. She was Senior Library Prefect and a Fourth Form Prefect, one of twelve selected by her class to supervise the junior forms. She enjoyed not only the responsibility but her lively group of associates and the sociability of the small prefects' room, with its even tinier kitchenette where coffee could be made on a gas ring. She did not share their craze for bridge; if one had to sit down for a game, she preferred chess. At last she was turning from an exuberant and energetic adolescent into an equally energetic but responsible woman.

She was invited to come to I. M. Marsh College for an interview. The prospect both delighted and appalled. In spite of her gregarious nature, she had always hated new confrontations — like her first communion after Confirmation. She had been away the first Sunday and went alone three weeks later; had gone to the church door, stood quaking, turned around and gone home.

Ever conscious of appearance, she prepared for the interview with meticulous care, wearing a dark grey dress with white saddle stitching on the bodice, a grey flannel coat, red shoes, gloves, bag, and red square bonnet-shaped hat. Mum and Dad drove her to Liverpool, straight into a glorious sunset, pink and molten gold, silhouetting everything, including her own future, in a bright golden glow. She stayed in digs in a side street near Lime Street Station. The interview lasted an entire day, with gymnastics, games, talks with staff, and dance. To her delight much of the latter was spontaneous movement. The pianist would improvise a phrase. The qualities inherent in it would be practised, each girl choosing her own interpretation, until three or four movements were developed, first in a group, then in pairs. Best of all, solo work was required. She ended the day exhausted, hopeful, stimulated. And — she was accepted.

Independence at last, escape from all the entwining tentacles which at times had seemed so irksome! It was like tearing herself up by the roots. Family, home, things she loved best became doubly dear : the beautiful front door, the copper beech that had been planted in the back garden for Ian's birth, the apple tree for Wendy's, the great heavily carved monk's bench. She had always had a strong emotional attachment to things she loved — like the buddleia tree.

It had grown on the right side of the sloping front garden, a beautiful tree with long purple flowers like candles, perfect when small, but when it grew too tall and broad it threw the whole garden out of balance. Eric, with Ian's help, cut it down with a hatchet, but, oh, dear, when Hilary came home from school!

"It was my tree," she sobbed, tears flowing from both rage and bereavement, "my lovely gorgeous tree! You had no business — how could you!"

Mona told the caretaker at school about the incident. "Don't worry," he had comforted. "It's the best treatment you could give to a buddleia. It will grow even bigger and stronger."

Would it be so with this sense of loss she was feeling now? Was she perhaps just cutting away this first growth of family and home, not tearing it up by the roots? As time passed, might she become, like the buddleia, even more inextricably rooted in its clinging soil? Did the thought bring hope or foreboding?

PART
TWO

West Riding

Spring

Gentle warmth, coaxing the last lazy seed,
To split its coat, root and shoot without heed,
As, like earth-bound suns, the Celandines
Spread shining pools beneath the trees,
And shy white flowers dance, blushing in the
    breeze.

HILARY J. POLE

I

IT WAS A NEW WORLD. Strange, how you looked forward to being independent for nearly eighteen years, even attempted to run away from home at times, then when you finally achieved the identity you craved, you were almost as much in bondage as before! You had exchanged a family of five for one of twenty. You were as prone to conflict with your new room-mates, Bunty (Maureen) and Estelle, as with Wendy — more so, for she had been younger and less assertive. When you wanted to read, study, or listen to concerts on the radio, those two were often prone to chatter.

After being top competitor in sports at King Edward's, you were now just average among a group picked for its aptitude in Physical Education. Though you were eighteen years old you found yourself humiliatingly immature and inexperienced, ashamed to confess to a bevy of peers sharing confidences of their romances that not only had you never been kissed but had never had your hand held — at least, not since you were eight! Though you had been the life and soul of the party at socials and dances at your Youth Fellowship at St. Peter's Church, here you were so conscious of ignorance and lack of confidence that you stayed away from all such functions, though you would have loved to go. You prided yourself on your superior strength and physical stamina, yet with the first rigorous sessions in gymnastics and games you, like all the others, were in sheer agony, even having to walk downstairs backwards! Being on the third floor of Barkhill, you had two long flights to negotiate.

But slowly you adjusted. Rules were not too stringent. Though doors were locked at ten thirty p.m. on week days, eleven at weekends, you could obtain late leave from the Principal, Miss Crabbe, for almost any evening and be given a key. A friend would set the alarm at the time you were due in, and you would switch it off on arrival. If you were late, you were reported, but not for discipline, only to ensure safety. Though there was a formal uniform — grey skirt, round-necked pull-over, V-necked cardigan, blue, green, or yellow shirt, blue blazer or blue cloak — mufti was in order for most meals and lectures.

Food was plentiful, mid-morning "elevenses" and afternoon tea in addition to the three substantial meals, plus a quota of milk and biscuits to take to your room at night. Still you remained unsatisfied.

"Please send a tin of Horlicks, raisins, apples, butter too if possible," a letter home urged that Autumn of 1956. "I can't help being hungry and I'm NOT getting fatter!!!"

The same letter reported with enthusiasm on her various courses. She was learning lacrosse, enjoying art, overjoyed with the emphasis on freedom of movement. "Movement comes into everything. There are quite a few 'budding artists', but perhaps the buds will drop off." Music she described as "a lot of theory".

She made friends. Just before leaving for college she heard about a girl in Dudley who was to attend I. M. Marsh, Janet Skilbeck. They arranged to travel together. Arriving, they discovered they were to occupy rooms next door to one another. The intimate friendship with Skilly was to last throughout life. Bunty, who came from Blackpool, would make the third of the close threesome. She and Hilary had much in common, a sister named Wendy, a passion for games (Bunty was a keen Blackpool Football Club supporter), a gay liveliness which made their room in Barkhill a favourite rendezvous for late gossip and snacks. However, even Bunty could not compete with Hilary for liveliness, an excess of which was not always popular with her room-mates.

"Bubbling over," one of them described her. "She would bounce around, fling open all the windows, no matter what the weather, bounce back from breakfast before the rest of us were up. Almost drove us mad with her enthusiasm!"

Staff and second and third year students were also impressed with this enthusiasm, not always favourably. Some of the latter found her boisterous, schoolgirlish ways, her tendency to overdo helpfulness, a bit annoying. "Her zest," commented Miss Crabbe in retrospect, "was sometimes greater than her control so that on occasions she gave the impression of a young cart horse sensing his ability and eager to show his strength and power."

However, some new friends were completely uncritical, merely adoring, like Annie East who cleaned their rooms. A woman well over seventy, she "kept" the top floor of Barkhill like a new pin, and if a student failed to make her own bed or left dirty dishes about, she could become both angry and aggressive. Hilary dubbed her affectionately "The Barkhill Dragon", and, though other students aroused her temper, with Hilary she was kindness and gentleness personified.

Hilary had always been on friendly terms with cleaners, kitchen staff, porters, and other workers at school. Her sense of humour, willingness to listen, sympathetic concern with people's problems, reached out to include individuals of every age and class. "Look at that," she would chide one of her room-mates who dropped a uniform on the floor. "Who do you think's going to pick it up? You're not leaving it for poor Mrs. East, are you? Shame!" "Come on," she would tease when they were having a sing-song in the room, "sing us a tune, Mrs. East. We know you can sing." Then, when the cleaner would cheerfully oblige, she would jibe, "Good grief, Mrs. East, you're out of tune! I'll tell Miss Church, the music lecturer, about you!"

"She was so smart, and with such a wonderful figure," Annie East would recall more than a decade later. "Oh, and I did have such a good time with her!"

Others would remember Hilary's spruce appearance, her almost fanatical insistence on neatness and cleanliness, her fondness for certain combinations of dress, like her white broderie anglaise blouse worn with a scarlet dirndl skirt.

When she became homesick that first year Hilary would visit the Dransfields. She had met Ethel Dransfield on the train, returning from a brief holiday at home. "Come down for the carol service," she begged Mum and Dad, who were seeing her off. "We'd love to come," replied Mum. "When is it?" "I'm not sure. I'll ask Miss Crabbe and let you know."

"Excuse me." The other occupant of the carriage, a pleasant-faced woman, interrupted. "The college carol service is —" She told the day and time.

It was the beginning of a lifelong friendship. The home of the Dransfields, only a five minute walk from college, became a second home to Hilary. Jim, Ethel, and their three sons, Ralph, John, and Peter, helped compensate for the absence of her family. And Chakra and Chulah, their two beautiful seal-point Siamese cats, bewitched her with their exquisitely shaded coats, their musical voices and sapphire blue eyes.

One weekend when she knocked at the door of 423, it was opened by an excited John urgently bidding her to come and see. She saw — Queeen Chakra surrounded by four squirming kittens. It was the instant birth of desire. She knew that some day she must have a Siamese.

Her appetite was further whetted when one of the lecturers at college brought her Siamese cat back with her. Ming would walk along the corridors as if she owned them, ask in her deep voice to be let into a student's room, snuggle her way down the bed, and start blissfully to suck her victim's pyjamas. When the same lecturer bought Tiny, another Siamese kitten, from the Dransfields to keep Ming company, the whole college was entertained by the pair of them — Ming suddenly deciding to be terrified of Tiny's smutty face and fleeing as if a pack of devils were in pursuit, or the pair of them rushing about pretending to be cowboys and Indians.

The first year of college was one of self-discovery, of tentative venturing into the new world of independence. Hilary was more listener than participant. Many of her excursions were solitary, walking on the promenade, visiting the Museum and the Walker Art Gallery, listening to concerts and plays on radio, absorbing the sights, sounds, and smells of the great seaport city — salt tang of ocean, smart young sailors from the Merchant Navy hostel for midshipmen in Aigburth, the muted whistles of tugs at high tide, towing out the big ships when they sailed. In spite of new friends and days filled with activity, she often felt curiously alone.

The feeling of isolation during her first term in college was increased by family worries. In September Wendy went into Woodlands Orthopaedic Hospital in Northfield for a serious knee operation. One knee cap had to be removed and a wedge of bone cut from inside the knee on each leg, in the hope that, with the outer knee continuing its growth, the legs would be straightened. Another operation was performed in November for the removal of cartilage. Fortunately all the surgery was completely successful. In fact, Wendy became a prime exhibit for her surgeon, who showed her off to other orthopaedic surgeons, students, nurses. She was home again in time for Christmas, and there was great family rejoicing.

However, Hilary let nothing — homesickness, worry, loneliness — interfere with her studies. She knew exactly what she wanted and, being Hilary, was determined to get it.

"I don't want to waste my time," she told her first year dance lecturer rather bluntly. "I've come here to become a lecturer in dance."

Not that she neglected other forms of sport. Hockey, netball, cricket, and tennis — in all she was both ardent participant and enthralled spectator. Though cricket would always be her first love, tennis became a close second, especially during Wimbledon fortnight.

Now, during the magic fortnight, Hilary could see as well as hear, for, though Miss Crabbe's attractive flat on the first floor of the original building was usually out of bounds to students, they were generously invited to view important sporting events — with certain stipulations. A visitor might be dumbfounded by what resembled a second-hand shoe shop outside the flat, while inside the owners sat barefoot on the beautiful pale carpet, eyes glued to the television set. Now, also, Hilary learned all about top spin, back spin, volleys, half volleys, and drop shots. She had to clamber into the umpire's chair, score and study tactics. Her respect for the Wimbledon giants increased daily. During Wimbledon fortnight she spent every available minute in front of the television screen, giving it her full attention — except when the event clashed with cricket Test Matches. Then she applied one ear to a radio.

2

Peter. Though college activities filled her days full, the thought of him was always there, like a wistful minor refrain, and she still dreamed impossible fantasies. They corresponded, as always, and he visited her at the college. As the holiday season approached, mingled with the joyful excitement of seeing Wendy again, on the way to full recovery after her operations, was another stirring of anticipation. Peter was always with the family for Christmas. Who knew? Perhaps —

But Peter was not at home for Christmas. He was away climbing mountains with a friend in Wales. In spite of all the family fun, the day was somehow spoiled. Then he telephoned. He and his friend were unable to make it for the usual celebration, but they would meet the Poles on Boxing Day at Aunty Betty's. Hope soared again. Hilary dressed for the party with even more than her usual pains, brushing her blonde hair until it shone, donning one of her favourite outfits, a very full scarlet cotton dirndl skirt with a black bodice — broad belt at the waist, long sleeves, low, very wide V-neck.

There was a big group going in spite of unfavourable weather. Ookie (the family car so named because the first symbols of its licence were OOK) led the way, with Dad, Mum, Wendy, Nan Nan, Grom, and Hilary all crowded in. Because of snow and ice they did not go the usual way through country lanes, but the main road was bad enough. Suddenly the car turned in a half circle and went into a violent skid, the soft snow on the side of the road and pavement mercifully stopping it between a brick wall and a telegraph pole, missing both by inches. It all happened in the moment it took Dad to exclaim, "Oh, God!", yet the pole and wall seemed to be rushing towards them for an eternity before they stopped. Narrow escape indeed, for the pole they just missed was the only one on that stretch of road without a steel hawser which would have cut the car in two!

However, Hilary was as much worried as relieved. Peter would be travelling on just such roads, either riding pillion or, at best, in a sidecar. She endured agonies until he arrived safely. Then relief was suddenly enhanced by delight when his eyes widened in obvious admiration and he remarked, "You are looking very, very attractive tonight!"

It was not much, but enough to brighten the whole holiday, even though his subsequent visits to the house were as impersonally casual as ever. Then came another flash of hope. After his next visit to Liverpool she went to Central Station to see him off. When the train came in, he put his arm around her shoulders and kissed her. It was so unexpected, she was struck dumb with confusion. She could only hide her face against his shoulder and mutter, "You'll miss your train," then, instead of managing a more suitable remark, repeated inanely, "You — you'll miss your train." This also was enough. She went back to college walking on air.

When she saw him again, after a few weeks, she still felt shy and confused. Their relationship was spoiled. For the first time, instead of easy companionship, there was tension between them, and neither had the sense or the understanding to break it. At last it was Peter who tried.

She was home on holiday and he was visiting. As she sat writing at the dining table, she was uneasily conscious of his tall lanky figure standing on the other side of the room, feet apart, hands thrust in his pockets. Her fingers tightened on the pen, and she stopped writing in mid-sentence. There was an electric tension in the air. She didn't know whether she was more frightened or excited.

"I want to talk to you," he said. "Now, while I have the courage to say it."

Fright won. She was plunged into trembling panic. "I — I don't think I've the courage to hear it," she blurted.

He came close to the table, leaned over, spoke in quick sharp accents. "Dammit, woman, I'm in love with you!"

Was it good luck or ill that at that moment Mum came in, saying she was going up the road to the shops? "I'll come with you," said Hilary, rising so hastily that her papers fluttered to the floor. Mum must have sensed that something was wrong, but fortunately she did not ask, because Hilary couldn't possibly have told her. Nor could she explain her inexplicable behaviour to herself. For two years she had hoped and dreamed for this very thing to happen, and here she was running away like a frightened child. She deserved what followed, for Peter did not mention the subject again. They tried to resume the old relationship, but it was hopeless. Hilary avoided being alone with him. Words which might have broken the impasse were frozen inside her. The summer gave promise of being the most unhappy ever.

The family borrowed a caravan at Towyn for their summer holiday. While there, Hilary received a woeful letter from Francesco, her Italian pen friend. His mother had died. He was heartbroken, *desolé*. Instead of the weekly letter she began writing to him every day to try to cheer him up, as he had no other family. Once he nearly caused a national disaster by addressing a letter to her, "Wales, England". Concern for Francesco was a blessing, for it took her mind off her own problems, though the family misunderstood. Ian began teasing, and Mum obviously thought she was falling in love with Francesco.

Peter and Uncle Tom came to visit them at Towyn. They spent the morning on the beach, then took the guests to Borth-y-gest for tea. Peter and Hilary hardly spoke.

Peter was at the house again when they returned from their holiday. In silent constraint they washed the dishes after coffee, Peter looking as miserable as she felt. Suddenly she summoned courage to reach for his hand and blurt out, "I'm sorry. I didn't mean to upset you," then dissolved into tears. The impasse was over. They remained in the kitchen, had a heart to heart talk, and by the time he went home that night, they both felt light-hearted and happy. At last each knew how the other felt.

The next Christmas was the happiest she had ever known. Peter and Ian went to the college ball, Peter as her partner, Ian as Skilly's. At home the holidays mounted to a perfect climax. One night Peter parked in Arber's drive, opposite Upway. She went across with him to say good night.

"One day," said Peter suddenly, "I will ask you to marry me."

This time she felt no fright, no confusion. "One day, when you do, I shall say 'Yes'."

"Unless you count that as a proposal," he said, almost as an afterthought.

"I do," she replied instantly.

She told Wendy that Peter had asked her to marry him, but the fourteen-year-old was unimpressed. Ian, the only other person she confided in, was sceptical. She was too happy even to ask why.

"Shall we get engaged on your twenty-first?" suggested Peter. "Then we can be married on my birthday in September."

Hilary gasped. Although she was only nineteen, it sounded so soon, so very final! For the moment she wanted to leave things as they were, secure in an understanding, yet not committed as to future plans. It was enough to be in love, to know that you were loved. Peter, older and wiser, understood — perhaps too well.

3

This, her second year at college, was far happier than the first. She was begnning to find her place in this new world. She and Bunty and Skilly decided to room together, again on the top floor of Barkhill. Hilary was again bursting with energy, but the childish exuberance was ripening into the steady competence and confidence of maturity. As well as having a third class "mum", she now had two college daughters, since there were more first year students than second year — Margaret Denner, whom Bunty had known at school, and Anne Tsoi-a-Sue, a Chinese girl from Trinidad. Anne was petite and charming. She had needed a lot of advice on what to bring from Trinidad and what she could safely leave to buy in England.

Hilary no longer felt tongue-tied and inexperienced when the other girls chattered about their romances. Strange what the knowledge of being loved and desired could do for your ego! Letters from Peter arrived, if not daily, with punctual regularity, and he sent her flowers. His picture was displayed proudly on her bureau. Not a handsome face with its too thin lines, but with fine understanding eyes and a smile that reminded you of hundreds of miles walked, years of jokes bandied, concerts and books, plays, and films shared.

"Go out more and meet other men," Peter urged. "You're young. You must have a good time."

"No. I love you. I don't want to go out with anyone else."

He kept urging and finally quashed her objections. She went to a dance without an escort and found to her surprise that she was not a wallflower. She accepted dates with several men from the navy school and discovered to her confusion that she was undeniably attracted to at least one of them. Or — was it the dancing, always a stimulus of gay excitement? She spent weeks in doubt and uncertainty. Was she belatedly experiencing the mercurial emotions of a fifteen-year-old, in love with love? Almost as a penance she knitted feverishly on a sweater for Peter.

Even Peter's presence in the flesh restored no sense of certainty. Did she — or didn't she? She felt more relaxed in the

company of Ian, who, now that he was seventeen and in the
Upper Sixth at school, tall, handsome, and a rugby ace, had
smoothed away all the sharp edges of a teasing little brother.

Her diary recorded everything but the indecision which was
making life a jigsaw puzzle with half the pieces missing.

"Started term well. Dance first! Good photo of Pete and
myself in the chair at home . . . Skilly cut my hair to make it
look tidier . . . Dance first. We used percussion. Great fun . . .
Bought pale blue blouse in sale. Nice. Now have no money . . .
Letter from Pete . . . P.C. from Pete. English lecture deadly
. . . Gorgeous frost. Letter from Peter . . . Theory of dance with
Miss Carr. Great fun. Letter from Peter . . . My hair's a plague.
Mum said I could have a perm . . . Phone from Peter. Gee whiz!"

But finally the diary reflected her ambivalence. "Letter from
Pete. He thinks he's going to marry me. I wrote to him. Very
difficult. I'm very unsure again." The following day she met a
naval cadet named John. A few days later she was confiding,
"Can't wait till tonight. Wrote up my lessons during the day
so I could see John. He arrived at eight. Wow! He's great."
They went to the Philharmonic to hear Dvorak's *Eighth
Symphony*. Soon after this John sailed for Java, and the entries
in her diary were more decisive.

"Went to the cinema to see *Ali Baba*. Pete was there. I do
NOT love Peter. All the time I was thinking of John. Bad! . . .
Peter came. We had a talk. I told him I wasn't in love with him,
etc. He said he'd stick around 'cos I keep on changing my
mind. He's sweet, but I do not love him, not enough to marry
him . . . Back to college. Spent all the time thinking of John.
Silly! I've only seen him three times!"

In May she met Jim. Gareth, Bunty's boy friend, asked if
he could bring a sailor friend with him for a date with her
room-mate. Hilary had the evening free, so she said, "Yes".
She was introduced to a very tall (six feet four), handsome
young man, well built, light brown wavy hair, hazel eyes,
pleasantly shy. They watched the rugby league final, then went
to the cinema.

"He's very nice indeed," she noted on that May 10th, 1958,
"but not like John!" Later she added in black firm writing,
"No! Much nicer!"

When he rang the next morning asking if she would like to
see *Bridge on the River Kwai*, she agreed. After that she saw

him every day, or they talked on the phone. A little more than a month and he would be gone to the far ends of the earth. It was a month of mounting happiness, her diary exploding with superlatives and exclamations, interspersed with more earthy prose. "Jim rang. Meeting him in town for lunch. He's smashing! . . . Started throwing the javelin. What a lark! . . . I had to stand on the gym steps so that Jim was on my level. He kissed me good night. Said I ought to wear stilts! . . . Jim coming . . . He came . . . Met Jim, saw *East of Sumatra*. Gee! ! ! Phew! That's all I can say. Just — wow! . . . Heaven knows what I'll do when he goes! . . . Met Jim . . . Rang Jim . . . We've won the test by 205 runs . . ."

It was strange, perhaps, that their rapport was so instant and complete, for they had few interests in common : cricket, crossword puzzles, ships and sea, a mad sense of humour. The latter was an ever-strengthening bond. The commonest things aroused laughter. Umbrellas were a constant source of merriment. If she held one, it poked Jim in the eye. If he held it, she got soaked. Luckily it rained little that month! Hilary often ended an evening wearing his naval cap, which almost covered her eyes as well as her ears. They went to cinemas, sat on the Promenade watching the cargo boats go down the Mersey carrying bananas, coal, timber, the tugs going up blowing their sirens; listening to the gulls and the sound of surf; carving their initials on one of the benches.

She was falling in love with Jim. Love? Long before the month was over she knew that until then she had not known the meaning of the word.

At Whitsuntide the college had a long weekend holiday. She invited Jim to visit her at home. He came on the Sunday excursion train. She drove with Ian to New Street station to meet him. Not a sign of him. She rang Mum. "Has Jim phoned?" "Yes." "Where is he?" "Waiting at the top of the steps." Still no sign of Jim. Impossible to miss that tall figure with the white uniform cap, even in a crowd! After frantic inquiries they found out that the train had arrived at Snow Hill station. Rescuing a forlorn-looking Jim, they took him home to lunch. To her great relief the family seemed to like him. After lunch they all went to see Wendy at a guide camp near Ludlow. A picnic tea had been prepared for visitors, but they had to leave early in time for Jim's train.

Back at college Hilary saw him nearly every night. It was examination time, but she could not let swotting interfere with the most important thing that had ever happened to her. Jim also was supposed to be studying, so both worked in the early evening, then they would meet about eight thirty, walk along the promenade, sit in "their" shelter, where Jim had carved their initials. During those days she learned almost as much about buoys, ships, navigation, international codes, as about anatomy, biology, theory of movement, and English.

Jim's last week in Liverpool unfortunately coincided with her examinations. Though she had no compunction about going out, she wasn't quite cheeky enough to ask for late leave. She had done much preliminary work for anatomy, there was so much detail to learn — origins and insertions, names, functions of muscles, special treatments for deformities, and so on; but she had done little work for biology. The night before this exam she met Jim as usual at Pierhead at eight thirty p.m. They had coffee and went to the News theatre, which Hilary always enjoyed, being partial to cartoons, Mickey Mouse, Donald Duck, Tom and Jerry, Kat and Canary, and others. Horrors — biology tomorrow! When she got back to college, she got ready for bed, wrapped herself in a cloak, armed herself with coffee, a tin of biscuits, a cigarette, and, to her roommates' disgust, took her notes to Mrs. East's laundry cupboard, the only place where the light wouldn't disturb anyone. She went to bed about two a.m. Then, to their further disgust, she completed her paper early — gaining distinction — and had a nap!

The day before Jim was to sail, he rang her about midday. "Put something gay on, woman. We're celebrating." He wouldn't say where. Something gay? She chose one of her favourite outfits, a white sleeveless broderie-anglaise blouse with a deep V-neck, and a very full scarlet dirndl skirt.

"Gear," was Jim's comment, his term for "smashing".

They went to the Grafton Dance Hall and had a table upstairs. She had not asked for late leave and offered to go home by herself, but to her relief Jim would not hear of it. They had agreed there would be no sorrowful farewells, so they walked up the road to a whistled accompaniment of "Swinging Shepherd Blues", which had somehow become "their" tune. In the grounds she was treated to snatches of such appropriate numbers as "Now is the Hour" and "Give Me Five Minutes More". Was Jim feeling as miserable as she under his flippancy? He was going for a "long jag", nine months. How could she bear it? When it was time for her to go in, she was marched to the door, given a last perfunctory kiss, a very smart salute, and summarily abandoned. She went in sadly, her misery somehow enhanced by his nonchalance.

His flippance was belied the next morning, when he rang at eight a.m. for a last minute goodbye. "Don't forget to write," he begged. No fear! "Just a very good friend," she assured her diary. ("!!!!" she amended later in bold black ink.) "I wish he hadn't rung me up. It makes me feel terribly, terribly lonely. Golly, it hurts!"

It hurt more as the weeks passed. She had company in misery, for her room-mates also had boy friends on the high seas, Bunty's Gareth and Skilly's Ken. She found it far easier to give them sensible advice than to apply it to herself. She missed Jim far more than she had expected. If there was a letter from him, she felt on top of the world, dejected if there was not. This was utterly illogical, since she knew perfectly well that he could post letters only when his ship was in port. He must always find a letter from her when he docked!

In spite of her preoccupation with romance, sickness, loneliness, late nights on the town, or whatever, Hilary finished her second year with an excellent record. Nothing could temper her zest for the career she had chosen. For her solo dance assessment she chose parts of Elgar's beautiful *Chanson de Matin* for the music. She would play a few phrases on the piano, remember the tune, make up the movement, cut out unsuitable bits, and practise, practise, *practise*. It was hard work, but she loved every minute of it. When the day came she felt inspired. She *was* the "song of morning", joyous, expressing from her innermost being all the wonder of newly awakened life. "It was good," she could say afterwards with satisfaction, "very good."

Yet she flung herself into every subject and activity with the same fiercely persistent energy. Her room-mates were to remember her practising handstands in her gym rompers, minutes at a time, against the wardrobe; sweating through intricate routines in her black dance tunic; never resting, meticulously careful about her appearance; forever worrying about her

hair yet loving to scrape it back from her face into a tiny knot
at the back of her head; tending to be either an up, up or a
down, down person, but almost invariably up.

She performed her rota duties with the same vigour and
thoroughness — waking people in the morning, laying tables
for breakfast and supper, feeding, cleaning, and grooming the
animals, whitening pads, painting hockey balls, flicking lights
on and off at ten twenty-five to warn students saying fond
farewells, locking doors and windows.

Art, music, drama — the college years were replete with
opportunities for widening her horizon in every direction that
challenged her eager exploration. She haunted the Walker Art
Gallery in Liverpool, managed a visit to the Tate or National
Galleries on rare trips to London. On her second trip to France
to see Alix she spent some time in Paris and visited the Louvre,
to be awed for ever by the Greek *Victory of Samothrace*, though
her favourite sculpture would always be *The Girl*, by Uli
Nymptch. (Mum and Aunt Betty maintained that Hilary could
have posed for it herself!) Her favourite picture in the Walker
Art Gallery was Salvador Dali's *Christ of St. John of the Cross*.
She liked to boast that she had helped to buy Rodin's *Le
Baiser* for the Tate. (She had contributed a small amount to
the open subscription!)

There were excellent theatres in Liverpool. She became a
member of Sam Wannamaker's New Shakespeare Theatre
where he staged such controversial works as *Tea and Sympathy,
Cat on a Hot Tin Roof, The Rose Tattoo*. She saw *Pyjama
Game* and other musicals at the Royal Court Theatre. There
were symphony concerts at the lavishly furnished Philharmonic
Hall and promenade concerts at the boxing stadium. She crossed
the Mersey to the Continental, where the best foreign films
were shown, among them *The Red Balloon* and *Crin Blanc*.

Then, of course, dance! While she studied the technique
and theory of movement, designed new routines, practised teaching, and impressed her classmates by dancing herself "like a
dervish", she was absorbing some of the world's finest choreo-
graphic magic. Many dance companies came to Liverpool en
route for London — the Russian Folk Dance Group, the Israel
National Ballet, "Imbal" and the New York Negro Ballet —
superb! She saw Anton Dolin dance to Ravel's *Bolero*. It was
unforgettable!

There were football and rugby matches, Saturday night hops at the Student Union, quiet moments in the lofty sandstone cathedral, walks in the parks and along the promenade. Once she saw the *Empress of Britain* at anchor in midstream, beautiful during the day but at night with all her lights reflected in the water, a veritable fairyland. All these pleasures, so carelessly enjoyed, would become precious memories endlessly recounted.

By no means least, there was cricket. Her next door neighbour, Gill, who became one of her special friends, was the daughter of George Emmett, then captain of the Gloucestershire County Cricket Club. Aigburth cricket ground was only a five-minute walk from the college, and as Lancashire played there now and then, she and Gill were able to pop down in their free time and after lectures. Hilary never wore her college blazer on these occasions. She, a Yorkshire lass, watching Lancashire with a dirty red rose emblazoned on her pocket? She would rather die!

During the summer holidays she went to visit Bunty in Blackpool. Pure chance, of course, that the week she chose happened to be that of the Blackpool Cricket Festival! It would have been expensive if she had gone as a visitor, so she craftily joined the Blackpool Cricket Club and had a deck chair right at the front of the members' enclosure all week! It was a wonderful holiday. After a fairly late breakfast they went into town for fresh batch cakes, then packed their bags — salad, hard boiled eggs, tomatoes, cheese, a lavishly buttered batch cake each, and fresh fruit. They assembled score cards, pencils, some knitting (to do in the lunch break), and set off. The West Indians were playing, and in between showers they saw some entertaining cricket.

Cricket was, of course, part of her college curriculum. She loved playing in the nets and practising catching at the cradle, though she did not enjoy the formal intersets or inter-college matches. The only part she took in them was as scorer or umpire. Scoring was fun but umpiring a real trial. Her knees were quaking when she was asked, "How's that?" or she had to make an important decision.

That summer was one of marking time, its high points days when letters came from Jim — from Port Said, Aden, Djakarta, Melbourne, Sydney, Singapore. Other events recorded in her diary, even moving into the new house which Dad and Mum had been building at Walsall, were valleys between the heights.

"Had navy blues yesterday . . . Mum finished at Olive Hill . . . Dad returned from Denmark bringing me a gorgeous hand-carved duck. Got distinction in biology. Wow! . . . Never felt so empty before. Another eight months to wait . . . Moved things to the house. Feel dreadfully tired, so tired I can hardly move. Almost too tired to think of Jim . . . We move. Chaotic, but should be nice when finished."

She saw Peter for the first time in many months. They had met and talked after she had written telling him her decision. It had been a painful interview. It would have been easy if she could have said frankly, "I'm sorry, I've met someone else", she was passing through a temporary phase. Now she knew that she was not. He came to the house and they took one of the old-time walks across the fields.

"Sorry, Hil," he said after a long silence, "but I must ask you. No regrets?"

"No regrets," she could now reply quite honestly.

She breathed a deep sigh of relief. They were friends and companions again.

In August she visited Molly in Wales, climbed "The Rivals" and found the view magnificent. In September there was the week of cricket with Bunty at Blackpool. "Sobers was hitting sixes and fours all over the place!" She returned to college. "Bunty going out with Gareth, lucky girl!"

That third year she and Bunty and Skilly lived in Holmfield, a large house in the grounds for about twenty-five students. A lovely old house with three storeys plus basement and attic, with rooms in all sorts of unexpected places! There was a social room with a piano, coal fire, large table, and an odd assortment of easy chairs. They had a room on the ground floor, to the right of the front door, looking out across the drive to the garden.

Hilary was on school practice this year and loving it. She knew now that she had chosen well. Even the joy of one's own creative movement could not compare with the excitement of bringing out the best in others. What better medium could there be than modern educational dance? It developed poise, grace, imagination. It combined music, painting, poetry, voice, body awareness, group awareness, and integration of all one's faculties. No pupil need feel left out. Naturally some were more skilled than others, but each one could find her own level. Gymnastics, games, swimming — all required aptitude. Not so dance. She could not wait to get really launched on her career. She would teach for perhaps three years, go to the Laban Studio in London for a year of further training, then get a lectureship, maybe at I. M. Marsh, or — who could tell? There were tempting posts abroad in New Zealand, Canada, the United States. It would depend on Jim.

She was disappointed to find herself in Miss Primrose's group for special dance instead of Miss Carr's, not because of any personal dislike but because she favoured Miss Carr's type of movement. She grew impatient with "Prim's" persistent "gather and scatter" techniques, though any type of dance was fun. The students made up a short programme of Group Dances and toured Liverpool schools, hoping to inspire in the pupils an interest in dance. They used Jamaican rumba for three dances — the card game, seduction, and the fact and fantasy of fire; part of Schumann's *Kinderscene* for two studies, ending with *Teddy Bear's Picnic*. They did a programme for a garden party, in costume — great fun! She loved dancing on the grass.

Only one activity equalled in thrill that of teaching dance. With other volunteers she took turns going to Garston baths, once in three weeks, to help polio children with swimming. It was an unforgettable experience. Some of the children could not walk, some were in huge calipers, most were painfully thin. However, once in the water, a miracle took place. They could swim, move freely, play with joyous abandon. She could not pity them. They were too happy, too triumphant in their accomplishment. It could be a chore. On a cold wet night, when she was tired and cosily settled in her room, it took all her will power to dress warmly, get out her bicycle (for the baths were not on a bus route) and make the long disagreeable journey, but it was always worth it.

She seemed to lack will power for many activities these days. For the first time in her life she did not spring out of bed each morning with a burst of exhilaration. Sometimes it was an effort to get up at all. She would start a game of netball, hockey or lacrosse, and before it was finished strength would begin to flag. Natural, of course, to be tired after severe physical exertion, but it was a strange feeling not to snap back immediately.

She found it disturbing. Surely the emptiness she felt without Jim could not be wholly responsible!

Even Jim's absence could not dull the magic of the Christmas ball. It coincided with Gill's twenty-first, which made it extra special. Gill's boy friend, Roger, was able to come. Gill's roommate, Tommy, was going with her boy friend, Tom. As Jim was chugging round the east coast of Australia, Hilary invited Ian. Her friends chaffed her for being old fashioned. "Really! Your brother for an escort!" But Hilary loved dancing with Ian. Since neither Bunty nor Skilly was going to the ball, she invited Wendy to come and share in the excitement of the preparations and see the college. They put her to bed on a mattress on the floor, highly illegal.

Hilary always loved getting ready for a dance, especially if it entailed wearing a long dress. She revelled in the smallest details — the soaking bath, the best talc, perfume (her favourite *Molyneux numero cinq*), nail varnish to match her dress, the last touches to her shining hair, then the final thrill of donning the dress. Fresh from laundering and an hour's painful bout with the iron, the delicate fabric fell about her like a soft mist. If only Jim were here to see her! Though if Jim were here, she would not be going, for he hated dancing. She could never coax him into a dress suit.

She was as thrilled as Gill when a green orchid arrived from Roger. Gill had never had a corsage before. The crowning enchantment came when Hilary looked out of the window, for it had begun to snow, large soft flakes drifting slowly and silently against a backdrop of black velvet. It was so beautiful her throat ached in sudden painful ecstasy. Time, the world, stood still. She exulted in the sheer joy of being alive. Movement, action, achievement — all the things she loved best — were for a rare perfect moment unimportant. It was enough to feel, to know, to *be*.

4

The holidays in the new home were disappointing. Hilary liked the house, very new and modern in a wide suburban road, with a garden at the back and broad grounds in front crying out to be landscaped. The new decor, suited to the modern and functional construction, was in perfect taste and satisfied her artistic senses. The location was nearer Mum's school and Dad's work than Upway had been. She approved of the name, "West Riding", a good old Yorkshire one suggesting high winds and flaming sunsets and, above all, Movement. Still, she missed Upway and all its environs, and the many friends and associations they had there.

After Christmas the holidays would have been boring indeed without the Test matches. "Woke at six forty-five to listen. England finished at 190-6. Swetman is playing very well. Letter from Jim . . . Australia 353 all out, 138 runs ahead. We batted for one over and Bailey got one run . . . England 174-3. Boy, there may be a glimmer of hope for us now! . . . Back to college."

With the New Year anticipation mounted with the lengthening days. "Hurrah, 1959! I shall see Jim this year."

The weeks crawled and rushed. She laboured over the routines for the Final assessment in dance, practised them for long sweating hours in her black dress. Skilly had her twenty-first. Hilary consulted with Miss Crabbe about possible teaching posts. Jim wrote from Sarawak. Only forty-eight days to go! She spent a whole evening writing him a long dissertation on religion and marriage. He reached Borneo, then Colombo. She found it harder and harder to get up in the morning. She finished two paintings and hung them on the wall. She went to early communion on Ash Wednesday. A letter came from Manila with a photograph. "Whew! How does he expect me to concentrate on teaching with that in my mind!" Mrs. East had a birthday, and they took her some flowers. The "Barkhill Dragon" wept for joy. "My dears, may God bless you, I can't bear to think of you leavin'." Gareth came back, and Bunty was in heaven. Jim wrote from Aden. "Gee, a week on Friday!" Bunty had her twenty-first. For some reason the end of each day brought unnatural exhaustion. Strange, she had never felt this way before! Jim wrote from Port Said, seven pages of moodiness. Had she written something to upset him? She had her final assessment. "Phew! I'm tired. My dance was fine. Lisa Ullman, Miss Carson, and Mori were there. It's all over and done with now, thank the Lord. Jim should be back tomorrow."

"JIM BACK!" Her diary fairly shouted the good news. They

had arranged that he should ring her at four forty-five p.m., when his ship docked. What a day! She was so excited she was ill. He rang dead on the agreed time. The sound of his voice tingled through all her nerves like an electric current.

Ken had secured tickets for the six of them, Jim and Hilary, Gareth and Bunty, himself and Skilly, to see *South Pacific*. Hilary was on tenter-hooks again but managed supper without dire results. She put on a pair of new shoes and was ready. When the male trio arrived, she was tongue-tied. So was Jim. But once they were on their way and he had taken her hand, she no longer felt shy. When they reached the bus stop, he gave her a small flat box.

"It's not wrapped in tissue paper," he said, "and it doesn't have 'I love you' written all over it, but it means about the same."

Inside were a beautiful brooch and earrings in Siamese silver with a white background. Lovely! She enjoyed *South Pacific*, but the cinema got very hot, and she yielded to her usual silly impulse of kicking off her shoes. Of course when it was time to go she could just squeeze them on. Walking to the bus, she suddenly realised that she was not forced to execute the usual hop, skip, and jump to keep up with Jim's long stride. She looked up inquiringly. "I'm wearing new shoes," he confessed with a rueful smile, "and they're pinching." She burst into laughter, confessed in turn, and they giggled sporadically all the way back to college.

Jim stayed in Liverpool for the weekend, then went home to Whitstable in Kent. They seemed to spend most of their time saying goodbye. During the Easter holiday he rang her up. Would she like to visit him and his family for a week? Would she! He met her at Whitstable station and took her home in time for lunch. She liked his family, especially his sister Ann, tall, dark, attractive. They did crosswords, took long walks around the harbour, visited Canterbury Cathedral. "Magnificent! But I don't like it very much, prefer small old churches." She went with Jim and his father to a pub called "Noah's Ark" and was introduced to hot cockles and oysters. "I shall probably be classed as a heretic for ever, but I can't see why people rave about them. You're supposed to swallow them without biting, like a heron swallowing eels, and I found them, dare I say it, tasteless!"

All earthly heavens must come to an end. She returned to Walsall, cooked, sewed, cleaned, had a frightful row with Ian, returned to college, swotted for the education examination, had her second assessment in dance. "Not so bad, but, cor, do I get tired!" Jim came to Liverpool for another two weeks before sailing, and she saw him every day. It was *her* brief heaven now. Bunty's Gareth was in Aden, Skilly's Ken in Singapore. Then Jim went to London, preparatory to sailing for six weeks. "Feel all empty inside. Silly!"

She had little time to mope, however. All the third year students were looking for jobs. Miss Crabbe gave them valuable advice : how to fill in or make out application forms, how to dress for an interview, what to look for in a position. They drew a map of England, and when a student was accepted she wrote her name on a small flag and stuck it on the appropriate town. All obtained posts fairly early : Bunty at Whitby, east Yorkshire, where she had gone to boarding school; Skilly at Kingswinford and Tommy at Crosby, both able to live at home; Gill at Cinderford on the edge of Wye Forest.

Not at home! thought Hilary. Now that she had tasted independence, it was the last thing she wanted, especially in an open-plan house with no privacy. She would have loved a post just outside Liverpool, with all its advantages of music, drama, art, sports. Miss Crabbe arranged for her to visit a comprehensive school close by. Its size overwhelmed her — 2,000 pupils! She did not apply. She was getting very concerned when Miss Crabbe stopped her in the corridor.

"Ah, Miss Pole, New Heyes will have a vacancy; it will be advertised in two weeks."

Hilary was thrilled — until she remembered. There were two Physical Education mistresses at this school. She plucked up courage to ask, "Which one is leaving?"

It was the wrong one. She shook her head. "I'm sorry, I could not teach with Miss S." She knew the relationship would be disastrous. Miss S. would rob her of what little self-confidence she had. In spite of Miss Crabbe's annoyance she held firm to the decision.

That week Walsall advertised two vacancies. She applied with little enthusiasm. She was called for an interview on a Saturday morning. Knowledge that she looked chic and competent in a pale brown tweed suit, pink blouse and scarf, shoes, gloves, and handbag to match the suit, and floppy angora beret, did little to allay her nervousness. However, the Director of Education was a kind, fatherly person, who put her instantly at ease. They discussed her ideas about general education, physical education, dance, eleven plus. Would she be prepared to teach other subjects. Oh, yes! Art and biology. He offered her a choice of two posts, one in a school with modern buildings, excellent equipment, good playing fields. Edward Shelley, the other school, had an old building, poor equipment, no fields. The pupils must walk to a park for games. Of course the first was by far the better post, but there Wendy would be in the Lower Sixth, an embarrassing situation for both of them. She accepted the post at Edward Shelley. She would live at home at first, perhaps later find a flat in Walsall.

She was not thrilled with the prospect but pleased and relieved to have the matter settled — until she returned to college and told Miss Crabbe. The Principal hit the roof. She asked pertinent questions about the post which Hilary was unable to answer. Stupid, gullible, apathetic! Meekly, but with inward indignation Hilary accepted the storm of rebuke, knowing she undoubtedly deserved it. Miss Crabbe only wanted the best for her students, and she felt Hilary had let her down. Hilary could understand.

The weekend had proved doubly disappointing, for Jim had promised to ring and hadn't. She found an appropriate card. On the front it said "Grrrrr", over a picture of a tiger. Inside it said, "I've a bone to pick with you." She cut out a picture of a telephone and stuck it on, then sent it without signing. It was fortunate that they possessed the same brand of humour, for Jim had been ringing the college, swearing because no one answered. "Big nit!" she wrote in her diary. "I had told him I would be at home." He was off with his ship now, and the months of waiting had begun again.

May 27th came, her twenty-first. On the actual day Mum and Dad came to the college, bringing her a beautiful make-up case. Her college "family" gave her an exquisite powder compact. There were cards galore and, as for all birthdays, the usual late party in her room. The big celebration came at home that weekend. Many friends and relatives came to the party which started at six and ended at two a.m. Peter was there, also Arber, the Becks, Aunty Betty and Uncle Doug, Roy Atkinson, a school pal of Ian's and long a family friend. It was a super party.

As with some twenty-first birthdays, themes had been chosen for gifts. Hilary's were jewellery, travel goods, crockery. She received a lot of Green Wheat Denby ware, a silver bracelet bearing a key, symbol of maturity, began her charm collection, which was to grow and grow, with gifts from all over the world, until it held over seventy minute treasures and became almost too heavy to wear. Peter's gift, a pretty underslip, was hardly in context, but its inscription was intriguing: "A suitable gift, now that you have reached the age of discretion." She remembered briefly that this was the day they would have announced their engagement. Had Peter loved her as she loved Jim? Did he still love her? She hoped not. Mere absence was bad enough, without rejection!

Back at college came the crowning gift of all, yellow roses from Jim in Antwerp. "Congratulations. Sorry I'm late. Love, James." Late or not, she was thrilled. The poem accompanying the Interflora flowers was appropriate.

> Through the forests, over mountains,
> Over rivers, through the evening,
> Came the mighty Hiawatha,
> Seeking fire for smoking signals,
> Seeking fire to signal tepee,
> Seeking smoke for Minnehaha.
> Could not make a smoking signal,
> Could not send a birthday greeting.
> So the mighty Hiawatha
> With the wisdom of the eagle,
> With the cunning of the she-wolf,
> With the speed of rushing waters
> Kept the love of Minnehaha —
> Sent her flowers by Interflora.

"Wow!" exclaimed Hilary's diary. "My flowers were gorgeous. Oh, Jim, Jim, Jim!"

She missed him more than ever, though the mounting activities of the last weeks of college kept her too busy to dwell on her emotions. This final year she had acted as college librarian, which now entailed much extra work. This, plus preparation for examinations, the working out of displays and other final duties, caused more and more inexplicable fatigue.

However, high points emerged from the dead level of examinations, tiredness, dance rehearsals, checking books, loneliness. One was Blaenddol. Miss Morison and two other college lecturers rented an old stone farmhouse in Wales, near Corwen, about fifty miles from Liverpool. It would make a good retreat, they thought, for small groups of students. Mori asked for volunteers from the third year students to help get it into shape. The three room-mates were enthusiastic. They made the journey with Mori in her Hillman Husky several week-ends, clad in jeans, equipped with lunches, plaster, paint, brushes, pails, shears, dusters and other equipment. Ming and Tiny, the Siamese cats, accompanied them, revelling in stalking through the long grass, catching moles, or just sunning themselves.

The ancient buildings of old grey limestone were exquisite but sadly in need of repair. The gang chopped wood, pulled plaster off the walls and replastered, repaved the terrace, planted the garden. Hilary loved it all, especially the high stone steps to the door, probably built in the days when somebody wanted to mount a horse from the top. She replastered one small bedroom herself, and they called it "Hilary's room".

Wales was her Shangri-la. She loved its mountains, lakes, mists, white fluffs of sheep, and unpronounceable names. In June the whole third year went to the Central Council for Physical Recreation Hostel Plas-y-brennin in Snowdonia, for a week of canoeing, rock-climbing, map reading, mountain walking, and camping. There were lectures, films, map reading hikes, all in preparation for the climax, climbing Snowdon. Hilary enjoyed the lectures, especially one by Jack Jackson, the Everest photographer, on alpine plants. She hated the rock climbing in huge climbing boots, ropes around their waists. After days of preparation they drove to the foot of Snowdon in a truck. Climb? It was a marathon. They clambered, scrambled, scraped, clung, teetered along ghastly ridges that turned their stomachs. Hilary became deathly tired.

"Better turn back," urged Skilly anxiously. "You look all in."

No! Hilary had started for the top and she would reach it. Gritting her teeth she kept on grimly, resting frequently, crawling sometimes on hands and knees. "Got back safely, JUST!"

she chronicled. She lay down and slept while the others were
enjoying a barbecue and campfire. What was the matter with
her? Hilary the tireless, the irrepressible, the exuberent —
where had she gone? It was as baffling as it was annoying.

Miss Crabbe was surprised that Hilary had not been included
in the netball team.

"Her play was certainly good enough," explained the
lecturer, "but lately she has lacked staying power and has
seemed unable to maintain the necessary speed to the end."

During the whole last term Hilary had found games increasingly tiring, especially lacrosse. After one unusually hard game
the lecturer had said to her, "Miss Pole, you really must put
more effort in your game, you are just a passenger in the team!"
Hilary had been too close to tears to answer. Couldn't the
woman see that she had been exhausted almost to the point of
collapse? She had given up lacrosse and played hockey instead.

According to tradition third year students always did a dance
in costume for Open Day, when visitors and parents came.
Hilary's year decided to do their own adaptation of *The
Sorcerer's Apprentice*, with three apprentices instead of one,
employing chemical elements rather than brooms and pails.
There were three groups of "sprites" representing an electric
battery, a chemical balance, and some other chemical apparatus.
It was great fun. Each group wore a different shade of blue —
short, flared, sleeveless, round-necked tunics. The apprentices
wore black tights and red tunics, the sorcerer black leotard and
tights, a black cape lined with lime green. From order to wild
chaos, then back to order again — the dance was a glorious
medley of contrasting moods and movements, done to a piano
arrangement of Bach's *Toccata in D Minor*. Hilary would have
revelled in it if she had not been so tired. She had other duties
for Open Day also, having foolishly volunteered for the forma-
tion diving and getting pushed to next to the top board for her
sins!

Only three weeks more of college. Jim wrote from Port Said.
Unfortunately he had found no letter there. Hilary went for
another week-end to Blaenddol. "Started on the red room. Poly-
fixed the walls, then the beams, then we stained the beams.
Painted the walls pink. Scrubbed the floor and window sills.
Smashing!"

Two weeks. She worked furiously in the library. "Dreadfully

tired. Took ages to tidy room. Started packing." Mum, Dad, and Wendy came, and they spent a jolly weekend at Mori's farmhouse. The inter-year matches were held. "We lost the tennis, won the rounders. Cricket was fun. We came second. I took six catches and got sixteen runs off one over. Great fun."

One week. There was the traditional "chucking out" party. The third year students were entertained by the first and second years with biscuits and coffee. Then a spring board was erected in one corner of the gym. The first and second years formed in two lines facing each other, hands joined, lines reaching to the door. Each third year student took off from the board, landed tummy down on the crossed arms, was tossed down the line and on to a mattress outside the door. As they picked themselves up, they formed a single line. The first and second year students joined on behind, and all executed a noisy performance of the conga through the grounds to the swimming pool, where each third year student was unceremoniously thrown in.

Four days. "Awful to think the end is drawing near." Then suddenly, on July 9th, two days before college closed, it happened.

"There's a letter from Jim," called one of the girls as she walked down to Holmfield after lunch. "Oh, ta!" called back Hilary, and ran the rest of the way. "He's stingy," she thought noting the letter's thinness. She tore it open, stood still, staring.

"Dear Hilary, before I say goodbye for the last time . . ."

One of his foolish jokes? She read on, more and more bewildered. Then she froze. No joke — he wasn't going to write to her any more. She laughed, such a strange sound that Bunty looked up at her, alarmed. "Hil! What's wrong?" Hilary merely shrugged and handed her the letter.

"MY LAST LETTER FROM JIM," she wrote that night in her diary. "I'll survive, I suppose, though heaven only knows how. Why, why, why? Why is he so far away? If only I could see him! Still, it wouldn't do much good, I suppose."

She existed in a daze, managing very well until the last day. She had been up to college to say goodbye to the staff, students, and Mrs. East. When she got back to Holmfield, everything looked so bare and she felt so bleak that, much to her shame, she just lay on the bed and cried. Face a half-empty dining room? No! She and Bunty decided to go into Liverpool for lunch, where they had noodle soup, Cathay special, lychees and cream, followed by coffee and a cigarette. "Finished college. Said goodbyes. Felt desperately hopeless."

She went to see Bunty off at Central Station, then returned to college to wait for Mum and Dad. Must not sit and do nothing, it would be asking for trouble. She went to the pool for a swim. It was quiet and peaceful, empty of life like herself. Not even the pet mallard came to ruffle the water. She swam lazily, listening to the birds, letting the coolness drain all heat and emotion from her body.

She drove part of the way home, another surcease from pain, for she loved driving, was equally happy moving fast on good roads with a clear view or slowly along winding country lanes. Bad weather conditions, even fog, did not bother her unduly. She had often guided Dad through fog, sometimes walking in front of the car. All was clear today. The only fog was bewilderment and misery within herself.

She was about halfway home when suddenly she began seeing things double. Queer! Close either eye, her vision was perfect, but open them both, and there were two of everything. Fortunately they stopped soon for tea and Dad took over the wheel. She was not concerned. It had been a tiring week, and the shock of Jim's letter was enough to blur any one's perspective. Given rest and time, the fog would lift.

So she came home to try and start a new life.

5

"A golden girl", one of Mona's teaching colleagues had thought when Hilary had visited the Harden Infant School that spring. "That lovely corn-coloured hair, those blue eyes, that perfect skin and wonderful figure! She radiates health and happiness."

Hilary did not feel like a golden girl that summer, more leaden. True, her hair was the bright colour of corn or sunlit wheat and for once manageable with a new pin-perm. After some X-ray treatments in Liverpool her skin was smooth and

6—H • •

fresh. Her eyes were blue when she wore blue, hazel with reddish-brown, chameleon-like. Her figure had always been superb — but as for good health and happiness —

Fortunately she was immediately busy, for Edward Shelley was short-staffed, and she was asked to teach for about ten days, until the term ended. She quickly made friends with her colleagues. She was introduced to the park keeper and warned that, though excellent at his job, he could be stubborn, moody, rude. Obviously if the games were to run smoothly, she needed his good will and co-operation; so unashamedly she set about getting it. She discovered that his hobby was home-made wine — also Nan Nan's — so they had something to talk about. If anything went wrong — broken windows, crushed flowers — she made sure to get to him with an apology before he came looking for her. The strategy, devious or tactful, worked. She never had any trouble with him.

"The Edward Shelley School is not well equipped," the director had told her. It was the understatement of the century! There was a central hall, serving as assembly room, gym, concert hall, theatre, main thoroughfare. The few items of apparatus were stored behind the stage. She should have been horrified, but the situation appealed to her sense of humour. When she found a mouse's nest in one of the mats, she laughed aloud. At least, she was facing a challenge!

Mr. Lucas, the headmaster, driving her home from the year-end dinner of the staff in Worcester, was impressed with her poise and maturity. She showed no sign of awe or affectation. They discussed a variety of cultural subjects, almost as equals.

"Edward Shelley has a winner," he thought, "but we won't keep her long. With her charm and qualifications we'll soon lose her, through either marriage or promotion."

The ten days over, Hilary felt again empty and purposeless. Mum could not seem to understand the depth of her love for Jim. After all, she had been in his company little more than two months. It was just another schoolgirl infatuation. Remember Peter — and John — and others. She had no real confidante. Even Aunty Betty, happy with Uncle Doug and her new job, could not understand. Wendy was too young. There was only her diary.

"I wonder when I shall stop expecting a blue airmail to drop through the box . . . A bad Jamie day. Cried for ages in the

p.m. But — it — is — past. Buck up, Pole . . . Gorgeous dreams
about phone calls from Hong Kong. Oh, what a bloody fool
I am!"

Letters from friends did not help. The girls were angry with
Jim and thought he had treated her unfairly — but she knew
he had not. They had not been committed to each other in any
way. They had often said how much they missed each other,
how wonderful it was to be together, but there had been no real
avowal of love or talk of marriage. In fact, sometimes she
sensed with canny intuition that, since they had so little in common, marriage would have been a disaster. Still, she felt shattered and empty.

The weariness and distortion of vision persisted. Finally she
went to the surgery in Walsall, taking pot luck as to a doctor.
It happened to be Dr. Milne, young, attractive, affable. She
felt strange and embarrassed. Doctors at Halesowen and at
college had been advanced in years. She could not tell him
about Jim, only added vaguely, "Oh, I had a bit of emotional
upset, too."

"Mm," he commented after a moment. "This emotional
upset, boy friend?"

She looked up, startled, surprised that he had guessed.

"It usually is," he said kindly, with a twinkle in his eyes.

She felt instantly at ease. She was overtired and under a
strain, he diagnosed, and gave her some tablets. Tranquillisers?
"Come back in a fortnight if you're no better."

She left, both relieved and baffled; pleased, of course, that
nothing serious was wrong, but how could she have permitted
herself to get into such a state? She took the tablets, lectured
herself sternly, but still felt devoid of energy and occasionally
saw two objects where one ought to be.

The school holiday dragged. She desperately missed college
and friends her own age, even while the prospect of work and
complete independence was intriguing. She knew no one in the
community, and the neighbourhood church was in the process
of being built. Under a mask of superficial gaiety she managed
to conceal an increasing despondency and weariness. A
fortnight's holiday job with a jolly family in Wales offered brief
release. She visited Nan Nan in Sheffield, Aunty Betty and
Uncle Doug in Bromsgrove. She rejoiced with Ian over his
acceptance at Birmingham University. She went with him and

Wendy to watch Lancashire and Warwickshire play cricket at Edgbaston, with Lancashire winning by sixty-eight runs.

Alarmed by her physical symptoms, she consulted Dr. Milne again. He tested her reflexes and advised her to see a specialist. She did. "Nothing really wrong," he assured cheerfully. "Just a case of delayed shock and nerves. You're overtired."

It sounded reasonable. She was tired, yes, had to drag herself out of bed each morning, she who had always bounded to meet each day as if wound by a spring. Nothing wrong? Surely a disappointment in love could not upset her this much, a person as strong minded and reasonable as she had always been. And how could her eyes be all right when she was often seeing things double? She was even having difficulty sucking soft drinks through a straw!

One evening she really panicked. She tried to say something and was unable to pronounce the words properly. Terrified, she rushed into the kitchen to Mum, jabbering incoherently. But the difficulty passed, lasting only a few minutes. Again she consulted the specialist. "Still overtired," was the comforting verdict.

School started. She was a success at her job and loved it, in spite of the lack of proper space and equipment. She was asked to take first year Art and General Science. The latter worried her, but the physics and chemistry master went through the syllabus with her and she always checked her experiments with him before each class. She encountered problems in Physical Education. There was a battle with the first and second year students when she introduced blouses and knickers for gym; oddly enough, not with the third year. She made no attempt to change the uniform of the fourth, fifth, and sixth. In time the first three years would carry her methods up through the school. She was determined also to change into shorts herself during the day, so she arrived at school early, driven by Dad, and changed in the staff room.

Mr. Lucas was delighted when, in the absence of a Physical Education master, she offered to take some of the boys' classes. She refereed the fifth and sixth years for improvised football in the yard, and took some of the fourth year boys for gym. They were self-conscious about changing in front of her, so she left the hall and timed them for exactly three minutes. Once when she went back she was met by two boys, one clutching a bleeding head. The inch cut did not worry her. In college she had dealt with a variety of injuries on and off the field. This boy, however, was grey and shivering. His eyes looked out of focus. She bundled him into a car and took him to the Manor Hospital. Returning, she discovered that the two had been throwing shoes at each other. The steel tips had hit this lad on the head.

"If you're going to behave like children," she admonished sternly, "no more gym."

In spite of all such difficulties she was popular with both girls and boys. Her colleagues on the staff also were charmed by her youth, her vivacity, her determination to make a success of her career.

She was unable to hide all her difficulties. "Coming to lunch?" asked one, finding her in the ladies' room gazing intently into the mirror, apparently examining her hair. "No." Her voice sounded muffled. "I don't feel like lunch." Later she came into the staff room and spoke to the other teachers in a peculiar blurred speech, unintelligible, but fortunately they thought she was doing one of her humorous imitations and merely looked surprised.

She worried about her speech. It became harder and harder to make herself properly understood. Often she had to absent herself from school. It also became difficult to eat. She began to choke on food and was unable to swallow drinks. She went to the Old Girls' Reunion at King Edward's but was far too tired to take part in the usual hockey game. "You, Hil, not wanting to play hockey!"

"I feel like that song," she wrote. "'Morgen, Morgen, one more day to get through!"

But there were "ups" as well as "downs". Peter came unexpectedly one evening to take her out. She had just washed her hair and said she couldn't go, but, "It's my birthday," he insisted. "Dad's lent me the car, and I'm taking you out, so come on." She rubbed her hair as dry as possible, dressed, and went. They drove to Stratford, had a drink at the "Dirty Duck", went for a stroll by the river — beautiful, especially in moonlight. His birthday, the day they might have been married! Did he remember? If so, he gave no sign. She came back very late. It had been a lovely surprise. "He's an awfully good friend to have," she recorded. "Bless him!"

She felt well enough to play hockey in the rain. "Nice to be wet again, but, oh, my hair!" She took five fifth form pupils youth hostelling in the Peak District with the art master. "Back to school. Groan, groan. It's after a holiday that I feel so tired."

The Physical Education master came after the half-term holiday. Les was helpful, jolly, co-operative. Often when it was too wet for her classes to walk to the park for exercise, he would take them in the hall with boys for indoor games — a blessing, for she found indoor games utterly exhausting.

In November the specialist sent her into hospital for a week of tests. At least they were getting something concrete done at last. Perhaps now they would discover it was more than a case of nerves. It was not pleasant. "Good grief! Was woken at six for tea and examined by an old K.E.H.S. girl, one we used to call 'Jelly'. I'm to have a lumbar puncture." She had it. "A most weird sensation, though it really didn't hurt till afterwards. Then my back felt as though it was a victim of a hole in one."

But it was Mona who endured the greatest suffering that week. She and Wendy went to the hospital on Thursday night, by bus, because Eric had the car in London. They had visited Hilary and were returning down the corridor when the Sister in charge saw them through the door of her office. "Have you any news of Hilary?" asked Mona.

"Yes. Step inside." Wendy remained outside the open door.

Sister wasted no words. The case was incurable, she said bluntly. Hilary had myasthenia.

"What — " Mona could barely articulate the word.

Sister explained briefly the nature of the disease. Her future? Of course she wouldn't be able to follow her profession. It was doubtful if she could manage teaching at all. She had no idea how bad Hilary would get, because it was a fairly unknown disease. In a short time it could bring severe disablement or prove fatal. At best, being balanced by a specific drug, she might be able to lead a fairly normal but gentle life.

Mona left the office. She could hardly move, much less speak. As they walked to the bus terminus, they were gradually able to talk. Wendy choked. "They — they might have waited until Daddy was with us!" Only sixteen, she was bewildered but trying to help. The bus ride seemed interminable. Returning to the empty house, they made each other innumerable cups of tea. Eric returned much later to hear the grim news, and they spent a sleepless night. But next day there came a surprise. They received a call from the hospital. "When you come this evening, bring Hilary's outdoor clothes, because you can take her home." When they arrived, neither the sister nor the doctor was on duty. It was a mistake, a senior nurse explained. Hilary did not have myasthenia. She had merely developed a nervous hysteria, and she herself must wage three-quarters of the battle to correct it. They were bewildered and disconcerted. What had caused this reversal of diagnosis? Later they learned that the lumbar puncture had not revealed the deformation of cells usually characteristic of myasthenia.

Hilary plumbed a new low in despondency. Hysteria! The kind of person without strength of will to keep from going off the deep end? *No!* She gritted her teeth as on climbing Snowdon. She would show them if it killed her. It nearly did.

"This is killing me!" she soon confided to her diary. Her head felt as if it were bursting. She could hardly move in the morning without a searing, blinding pain. She tried sleeping on two pillows, then three. She felt better, forced herself to attend a school function, promised to be back teaching soon. But the improvement was only short-lived. Her condition deteriorated rapidly. She kept falling. Her speech became thick and faltering. Her eyelids began to droop.

They consulted Dr. Milne, and he in turn communicated with the specialist who had given her the tests. Presently she was given a prescription for different tablets. They got the prescription just before leaving for Brighton, to attend Uncle Aubrey's baby's christening. On the way Hilary became so weak and ill that they were frightened. She was choking and seemed unable to breathe.

"The new prescription," suggested Mona frantically. They stopped at a chemist's and had the prescription made up. Within ten minutes after taking two of the tablets Hilary showed marked improvement. Within three-quarters of an hour she was normal. Mona and Eric exchanged a look of incredulous relief. A miracle? Perhaps a cure had been found at last.

The tablets certainly helped, though their effect was temporary. Hilary had to keep taking them. But thanks be for anything that restored some of her old verve and strength, if only for an hour or two! It was not the tablets alone that sent her spirits soaring.

"A LETTER FROM JIM!" her diary carolled in late November. "My heart nearly stopped beating. Oh, God, thank you, thank you. Now I don't care what happens. He wants me to write. It'll be marvellous to be friends even if I don't see him. I could dance and shout and sing. Mum and Dad aren't pleased. They feel I'm probably clutching at straws. I suppose I am, but I haven't the strength not to write. Anyway, we can be friends. Peter and I get along very well like that."

She went back to teaching half days before the Christmas holiday, even managing a dance with her pupils. Her colleagues were as concerned over her illness as if she had been with them for years. But her voice was still erratic, and she was always tired. She went shopping, visited Aunt Betty, exulted because she learned belatedly that she had been awarded a Credit for Teaching at college. She went through the holiday motions. But even Peter's presence did not help much. "I never spent a more miserable Christmas. I felt utterly an outsider. I do so want to do something young and gay. Some day I'll really blow up."

In January she went back to school and taught for nearly three weeks. Each day demanded more stubborn strength of will than climbing Snowdon. She was drained of all emotion. "Ages since I heard from James, and I don't really care AT LAST." Then on a day in late January three things happened. She felt too fatigued to go to school. She cooked an absolutely super casserole for Dad's dinner — and dropped it! And — she went to see Dr. Milne. She did have myasthenia, he told her gravely. She was not to go back to school. She would have to give up her career of teaching. At least she would not be able to teach Physical Education.

"Well," she said, turning to Dad and speaking with a matter-of-fact calmness, "at least I can have a dog and cat and cook your dinners — that is, if I can keep from dropping them!"

She felt no shock, only a strange feeling of relief. They knew what the matter was. She was no longer shadow-boxing. There was a physical enemy to fight. Most profound relief of all, she was not a "psycho" case. She still had her strength of mind and will, unsullied and intact. Even the loss of her chosen careeer was not a shattering blow. If she could not teach Physical Education, so what? She would find something else to do.

6

Myasthenia! Being Hilary, she had to exhaust all the information available about it. Dr. Milne was helpful, although he admitted that little was known about the disease and its causes. When you want to move, the brain transmits an impulse along a motor nerve to the appropriate muscle. To enable the "message" to get across and during the time the muscles are working, a series of chemical reactions must occur. In myasthenia, for some unknown reason, one of these very important chemicals is destroyed before it has time to function. It is a kind of break-down in communication. Until the mid-1930's nothing could be done and the disease was considered fatal. Then an English woman, Dr. Mary Walker, discovered that a drug called prostigmine, although not a cure, temporarily restored the chemical balance, enabling most myasthenics to lead fairly normal lives, similar to diabetics on insulin. It was Hilary's favourable reaction to this drug which had enabled her doctors to reverse their previous decision and make a positive diagnosis. A person without myasthenia, taking the drug, would have been made violently sick.

Now began a lady's life of leisure. It was restful, fairly comfortable — and horribly frustrating. Alone nearly all day, she read; she painted; she listened to music; she watched television; she enjoyed getting Dad's dinner. But she was not allowed to leave the house by herself. There was no young company, and she was desperately lonely. Then suddenly interest quickened. A cat! Why not? She had always wanted a Siamese. She wrote to Ethel Dransfield. Could she buy one of Chakra's next litter? The answer came by return post. Chakra's family was due in early March. Of course she could have one. It was something to anticipate. Meanwhile Hilary read Doreen Tovey's books, *Cats in the Belfry* and *Cats in May*. She laughed as she hadn't done for days.

"Dad will bring you to school tomorrow after lunch," Mum said one evening. "There is something I want you to bring home in the car."

Hilary was not excited. Mum was always creating innovations, growing plants, fashioning elaborate nature studies for her classes, many of which finally landed at West Riding. A big cactus, most likely! To her amazement when she arrived, a soft wriggling bundle was thrust into her arms. Inside a black moleskin bag was a tiny beige puppy, a minute Corgi. "For you, darling!" Hilary was enchanted. A dog after all these years of yearning — and such an adorable one! She could literally hold him in the palm of her hand. Knowing Hilary's loneliness, Mona had persuaded the dog's owner to sell him at a far earlier age than was customary. Much later they acquired Shandy's pedigree when it was issued by the Kennel Club. It was impressive: Name, Shandy Galore; Sire, Rozavel Street Singer; Dam, Andy's Pet; and so on back to the sire of the Queen's own Corgi.

It was the end, thank goodness, of peace and quiet. In the middle of the first night forlorn whimpers came from the kitchen. Hilary went down. Shandy squirmed out of his bed and uttered his first bark, so surprising him that he fell over with the effort. She fed him, mopped up, popped him back on the rug by the stove and shut the door. He never disturbed her at night again.

A letter early in March announced the arrival of Chakra's family. A dog and a cat too? Why not? Ethel Dransfield and her son Peter brought the kitten from Liverpool, a fierce little scrap with long legs, a loud voice, and a fearsome spit which created an instant and welcome diversion — welcome to Ethel, for it hid her first shock at sight of Hilary. Even later she found it hard to conceal her distress. Hilary with bright eyes heavy-lidded, speech blurred, having to press her lower jaw upward in order to chew a sandwich at tea!

The little sealpoint Siamese had a pedigree as long as Shandy's, including such names as Afka Khan, Sapphira of Sabrina, Oriental Natasha, and Tschudi Buddha. Hilary's imagination was equal to the challenge. Though his registered name was Chakra's John West, she rechristened him Chiaroscuro, Chiaro for short, an art term meaning light and shadow. On encountering Shandy, he arched his back, crossed his sapphire-blue eyes and spat with amazing ferocity. She kept the two thoroughbreds apart for a few days, but they soon became friends, rough-housing like a pair of human siblings. In fact, Hilary dubbed them her "boys". Visitors were some-

times alarmed to see Shandy dragging Chiaro round by the
scruff of the neck, shrieking like a banshee.

They made the lonely days more bearable — and busier. In
between mopping up puddles and playing with the "boys",
Hilary kept house, read — novels, biographies, poetry, plays.
The family accused her of reading anything from comic strips to
government white papers. She listened to records — folk
music, jazz, musical comedies, light classics, opera, everything
but modern pop. Miss Crabbe loaned her a typewriter, suggesting that she might write book reviews, since she had excelled
in English. She sent for a correspondence course in fabric
designing. She improved so markedly on the prostigmine tablets
that in March she was able to accept Peter's invitation to meet
him in London. He met her off the eight p.m. train, admired
her suit, criticised her hat, took her to her "digs", stayed for
coffee, and explained to the landlady how to give her a tablet
if she failed to appear at breakfast. Luckily she had a good
night and managed to take the tablet herself.

On Saturday they walked round the Tate Gallery, did some
essential shopping, then started for Sadlers Wells. She managed
to get on the bus but almost fell off, and could only stagger,
even with Peter holding her up. People probably thought she
was drunk! They took a taxi back to the digs. After half an
hour she felt better and could walk again, but it was too late
for Sadlers Wells. She was bitterly disappointed as she had
never been there, and June Bronhill, a superb soprano, was
singing in *The Merry Widow*. Peter must have been disappointed too, but he did not say so, only salvaged some of her
shattered morale by remarking, "You look very seductive
tonight." On Sunday myasthenia took over again, so they just
read papers and talked until it was time for her train.

She made some new and interesting friends. Janet (Skilly),
who lived in Dudley, learned that their canon's wife, Mrs.
Monica Keith-Murray, had myasthenia, so she rang Hilary,
inviting her and her parents to meet Monica. They went.
Monica was just back from hospital and learning, successfully,
to adjust herself to the disease. She was even beginning to
participate in church work again with the aid of her balanced
doses of prostigmine. Hilary returned home both stimulated by
the new friendship and vastly encouraged. If Monica could do
it, so could she.

Soon after, Canon Tom Keith-Murray, Vicar of King Street Church, Dudley came to West Riding. Tall, dignified, nearly seventy but with serene unwrinkled features and a beatific smile, he was able to inject spiritual doses fully as potent as prostigmine. "I could listen to him forever," enthused Hilary.

The treatments, both medicinal and spiritual, were so effective that she began to feel herself a fraud. She consulted Dr. Milne. He agreed that she might try to teach, not Physical Education, of course, but perhaps younger children. She accepted a temporary post at the Whitehall Junior School teaching a class of retarded seven-year-olds and started in late April. Now the "boys" had to manage by themselves all day, but both they and the house survived. She enjoyed the teaching, but soon the old fatigue and disability returned.

"Very weary today. Hope I make it O.K. Bed, gorgeous bed! . . . Two years ago I met James! I'd hardly time to think about it all day, thank heaven! . . . Completely worn out . . . Kids noisy . . . Beginning to lose my voice."

However, the class was enthusiastic and she loved the children. One little seven-year-old brought her a four-week-old kitten, "for the nature table, Miss". They soon discovered that "Miss" got tired in the afternoon, and one would say in a conspiratorial whisper, "You take your tablet, Miss, and I'll read the story." Whereupon, often holding the book upside down, he would proceed to "read".

Hilary had been told that she could take the tablets whenever she felt tired. She was tired most of the time, and though she understood that balance was necessary, she was determined to finish the job she had started and was soon taking them in large doses. Neither she nor her doctor knew at that time that an overdose could cause stomach cramps, severe diarrhoea, even the same symptoms as myasthenia, including immobility.

Hilary stubbornly continued teaching until the Whitsun holiday. She managed to go to Liverpool for the Association of Past Students' Diamond Jubilee. As the double journey in one day would be too exhausting, she and Skilly were given special permission to stay at the college overnight. It was almost like old times except that the swiftly concealed looks of shock on friends' faces revealed how she had changed. They were the same. She was different. They watched a play on television. "The hero was just like Jim. What a jolt!" They had tea in

Miss Crabbe's flat. Dad, Ian, Shandy and Chiaro came to fetch her and Janet on Sunday, and the two "boys" were introduced to Ming and Tiny, with much swearing on both sides.

Two weeks later the family spent a weekend at Blaenddol, but Hilary could not enjoy the outing. Her condition was deteriorating rapidly. She found it difficult to turn over in bed, to breathe, and she had frightening bouts of choking. She was being poisoned by prostigmine and was rapidly going into "crisis". Twice in one week the doctor was called in the night because she could not breathe or move her mouth enough to swallow the tablet. An injection of prostigmine gave her a rapid lift. One day she went out with Mum and Dad to choose a new carpet for her room, and in the shop she became very ill with cramps and diarrhoea. When they got home Mum and Dad decided that something must be done. They rang Canon Tom Keith-Murray. What should they do? The Canon promised to ring back. He got in touch with the consulting neurologist at Queen Elizabeth Hospital in Birmingham who had performed wonders for Monica.

"Take her to the Queen Elizabeth," Tom Keith-Murray told Eric. "The consultant will come."

She went into hospital on the last day of June, which, much to her disgust, came "bang in the middle of Wimbledon fortnight". She was put on a rigid schedule, with tablets every two hours. "Nothing to worry about," they say, as I begin to choke! . . . Mad social whirl, with Dad, Mum, and Nan Nan here to visit!"

She liked the consultant neurologist. Cultured, quiet, whimsical, a bit ponderous of manner, with the mien of a university don, he was soon to become "Uncle Michael". Yet even he had doubts of the seriousness of her condition. Soon after admitting her, Sister Anne Scouse, in charge of Ward East 2B, found her sitting up in bed crying with rage. The consultant, she confessed angrily, had suggested that perhaps she was suffering from the emotional upheaval of an unsuccessful romance — in other words, he thought her a "psycho"!

Anne talked with her sympathetically. Why didn't Hilary write a detailed account of her illness from the start and give it to the consultant? Instantly Hilary agreed. In spite of the recurring weakness which made sustained activity difficult, she wrote a long and lucid record of her illness from the beginning, describing symptoms, treatments, psychological reactions in such terms as only a keen student of scientific subjects could have formulated. It was read by a decidedly shaken and far more respectful consultant.

He recommended a thymectomy, which was sometimes performed as a possible deterrent to the advance of myasthenia. Hilary wrote in her diary, "Professor d'Abreu came to see me. He's going to operate. Seventy-five per cent of patients improve, they say. Mr. Nicholls came . . ."

Vernon S. Nicholls, later Archdeacon of Birmingham, was Vicar and Rural Dean of Walsall, and Orchard Hills, the district where the Poles lived, was part of his parish. He was a good friend of the family. His spiritual counsel was constant and stimulating throughout her illness. To him also she had always been the "golden girl", and there had been rapport between them from their first meeting. Now the same dynamic energy which was sparking the building of a new church injected courage for her coming ordeal.

Removal of the thymus gland as a treatment for myasthenia was controversial as well as dangerous, its need determined by the severity of the case. It was thought that the thymus could produce, or cause to be produced, a circulating substance which interfered with neuromuscular transmission. Though definite results of the gland's removal could not be predicted, it had proved beneficial in some cases. The operation undoubtedly saved Hilary's life.

It was performed on a Friday. On Saturday she was very ill and in great pain, which was to be expected. On Sunday Mona and Eric were preparing an early lunch before going to the hospital. A telephone call came from the ward. "Hilary is very, very ill. You had better come at once — and be prepared to be too late."

Frantically Eric rang Vernon Nicholls before rushing off to the hospital. If Hilary were still alive, she would surely want to see him. "Please come now," begged Eric. "And let's hope we won't any of us be too late!"

He was there first. Mona and Eric found him sitting by her bed, holding her hand, talking in a low voice. She was so motionless they experienced a moment of panic. But the nurse standing by shook her head. "Comatose," she assured hastily. Suddenly Hilary roused, opened her eyes, took a biro from the nurse's hand, and scrawled on the sheet, "I'm O.K.," then lapsed again into a coma.

Vernon Nicholls rose. "I have a christening at three," he said, "but I'll be back." He leaned over Hilary. "You'll be O.K.," he said quietly.

Already Hilary had won the friendship and loyalty of many of the nurses. When she went off duty at four, Liz Measures, who had been helping the doctor give Hilary a chest aspiration, came weeping to Mona in the day room. "So young," she deplored, "such a shame. Can I do anything to help?" Nothing of the impersonal professional about Liz! Nursing to her meant caring as well as curing.

After his christening service Vernon Nicholls returned and stayed. "He lifted Hilary spiritually from dying to living," Mona said long afterwards.

7

Many days later Hilary emerged from a nether world which might well have been named chiaroscuro, light and shadow. She asked for her small blue diary and a biro and tried to fill in the hazy picture with a few broad strokes of memory.

Remember being taken to the theatre. Came round and felt fine. Had a good easy night. Remember smiling at every one. Couldn't speak at all because of my tracheostomy tube. Remember not being able to breathe at ten and passing out. Again at some hour in the morning begging for an injection, knowing I couldn't breathe and not being able to convince them it wasn't panic. Asking for the machine — writing *For God's sake, Sister*, and they couldn't read my writing.

Remember coming round in what I thought was a very very long bed and a huge machine clanking and thousands of people running round ... Remember them trying to get a Ryles tube down my throat for ages and Mr. Lord finally got it down ... Remember seeing Sister Simpson* and lots

* This is not Rose-Mary Simpson. "Simmy" Simpson was sister of Ward West four and became a family friend when she had had Aunty Betty on her ward for two years. When Hilary first went to East IB "Simmy" was admitted next door to her, and in a few days she died.

more people . . . Being off the respirator in the night after my jab. Nurse MacMahon kept me breathing, sent for Miss Mortell, the anaesthetist. Took them a long time to get it right again . . . Yawned and managed to help myself a bit . . . Can't move my legs very well. The machine went wrong and they spent hours trying to get it right. I'm terribly afraid of it breaking down or of being on my own . . . Can wriggle my nose! (Imagine that being a thrill!) Managed all day without the machine but in the evening felt frightened of forgetting to breathe . . . I *spoke*.

The nether world was not spawned wholly by the operation. For many days following surgery she was critically ill with pneumonia. Mona and Eric did not go home for three weeks to stay, only Eric to fetch clothes. They had the day room as their quarters and were very comfortable and well looked after. At the end of two weeks Eric returned to work, coming back each night to the hospital.

It was Canon Keith-Murray who was most helpful in dispelling the shadows of pain and delirium. Often when Hilary was plumbing the depths of fear and discomfort, she would look up to see his calm face and angelic smile.

"Think about this," he said on one of his visits. "God is love. He is always loving. He loves all the people in the world. He loves us all the time. He never stops."

"Yes," she thought, feeling his eyes draw her up out of the shadows like magnets.

"Think, 'Dear God, you love me. I love you.' Think it lovingly."

Her eyes spoke for her lips. "Dear God, you — love me. I love you."

"Think, God is calm. He is still. And quiet. And peaceful." She thought the words after him, slowly.

"Think, God is strong. I am weak. Think, 'Your strength makes me strong.' "

"Your strength — makes me strong."

"Think again and again, 'God is love. And God is in me. Keeping me calm.' These are the things you know. Say them over and over in your mind."

She did, especially in the night when she was afraid of the

machine breaking down and no one coming to set it right. *God is love ... keeping me calm ... making me strong.*

She had thought much about God before. There had been religious training in the home. Dad was a member of the Methodist Church. She herself was confirmed in the Church of England. Stories in Junior Church had made God both personal and real. There had been courses in religion at school. Miss Birch-Jones ("Church-Bones" they had called her) had not only taught her classes facts about the Bible, but she had stimulated serious thought through pertinent questions: "Who is God?" "What does God mean to you?" There had been endless discussions at Youth Fellowship, the most profitable ones not in formal meetings but spontaneous, often while groups were working in the kitchen.

College had aroused probing questions, even more serious discussions, formal and informal. Hilary had explored a variety of faiths. She had attended meetings of the Roman Catholics with Gill and been fascinated by Father Green, who came to conduct meetings once a week. (They had naughtily dubbed him "Pervert" because his name in French would have been "Père Vert".) Yes, she had thought much about God all her life, and often she had felt a deep need for faith — when Mum had been ill in hospital, when Wendy had had her serious knee operation.

With her own self-confidence and strength slipping away, the need was desperate. She *must* have faith to keep on living. *God is love ... keeping me calm ... His strength makes me strong.* "Yes," she thought, "these are the verities. These are the things I *know*."

Days passed ... weeks. July ... August ... September ... There was progress, but it was like crawling up the sheer side of Snowdon, pulling, slipping back, grimly making headway, a step at a time: "Managed the night off the machine! ... Can control a teaspoon from cup to mouth ... *Sat out* ... Only have tablets ... Tube irritated. Mr. Lord took it out. Horrible hole in my throat, but in half an hour I could swallow beautifully ... Went to chapel in a wheelchair ... Uproarious evening, knocked my carnations over!! ... Hair's a mess, gone almost straight ... I love a fresh breeze. I'd like to be out at Llanngennith in the wet bracken, in pumps and shorts! ... Went to day room to paint ... Got up to watch Brian Phelps win us a bronze medal . . . My hands are really helpless. However! . . . Peter came. Lovely surprise! . . . I shall *have* to wash my hair . . . Went for a walk. Cor! Utterly exhausted. But fresh air wonderful. Went OUTSIDE!"

She improved steadily. Her mouth drooped no longer. Her eyelids were normal. The simplest acts seemed like miracles. She could clean her own teeth. She could *spit*. She could dress herself. She could wear slacks and go for a walk. In the occupational therapy room she was able to beat sponge mixture and make a cake. "It's like being born again!"

Home again at last, October 1st. Would the "boys" have forgotten her? No need to worry. Shandy almost ate her up. They obviously decided she was not to escape again. She couldn't move from one room to another without one or the other padding at her heels. She was glad to be back — and sorry. There had been company in the hospital, nurses, other patients. Activity, excitement! Now the loneliness, the frustration began again. But she was better. Though she would never be vigorous again, she would learn to control the disease, like Monica Keith-Murray. "Jeffo" had warned her it would be slow, finding the proper balance, learning to maintain it.

But it was hard to be patient. She washed her hair. She wrote dozens of letters, responding sympathetically, often with sensible advice, to all the friends who instinctively confided to her their problems. "Letter from Bunty. She is through with Gareth. Is now madly in love with John, convinced that this is IT at last." She took books from the library and read, read, read, from light novels to the *History of Lighting*. She went to the hospital once a week by ambulance for occupational therapy. She bought records and played them. She had a reserved seat at the dedication of the new St. Martin's Church, to which the family had presented an altar cross and candlesticks. She had a new perm, bought a red cardigan by proxy. She managed short walks. "Nice day. Sort of day you'd like to be able to take the dog and go for a good long hike in the fresh air. One day!" For the present she had to take her yearning for motion vicariously, on Saturdays when the family rode in the car to see Ian play rugby. Meanwhile Shandy and Chiaro, now almost a dog and cat, were wonderful company.

Her material came from the Textile Studio in Harrow, with manual and samples. The course dealt in cretonne designing,

because draperies and upholstery materials offered a better
market than dress goods or wallpapers. She was to complete
the designs and send them for criticism within a month. Something to do at last which might lead to interesting and profitable employment. She had always loved to paint flowers like the
sample designs. In fact, one of her flower pictures, painted
when she was seventeen for Mock A Level, was framed and
hanging on the wall. Her brain swirled with fresh ideas, but
before she could get them on paper her body was limp with
exhaustion. Her hands, unable to hold the brushes properly,
simply would not execute her ideas. She did not give up.
"Going to be hard work, but once I get more strength I think
I'll enjoy it." This never happened.

November . . . Progress continued to be maddeningly slow.
"Really let down this afternoon. Absolutely helpless. Could
hardly speak or stand up . . . Better. Not too bad but not good.
Really ought to be on the way up again now." One day she fell
coming downstairs, striking her head and denting the plaster.
"As big as an orange," Dad teased, to cover his alarm and
anxiety. She could respond to his humour in kind. "Our family
never do things by halves. When they fall, they *fall*!"

Much as she longed for company, she was more thoughtful
of friends than self. "No," she said, when Mrs. Atkinson, Roy's
mother, wanted to cycle over to see her. "If I don't feel up to
it, I don't answer the door and I don't want you to have a
wasted journey."

The month crawled by. "Sick to death of all this business,"
she wrote at mid-month. "Fed up to the back teeth . . . Oh, for
some stimulating conversation! Only half the time I wouldn't
be able to take part . . . I fear it's going to be a lot slower than
I imagined, but I MUST keep going and trying."

December was like a seesaw. Up — down. The "ups" were
hours, sometimes days, of soaring hope. She filled them with
furious activity. "Saw Jeffo. Can have tablets every three hours
if I need them. Felt fine. Washed all the light shades, made
the Christmas cake. Wore a skirt! . . . Went to Wolverhampton
to watch Ian play in pelting rain . . . German record of *The
Magic Flute*. Thrilled to bits . . . On hourly feeds, feeling
better . . . Started to put up decorations. Chaos, Chiaro pulls
them down . . . Wrote Christmas cards and wrapped presents."

But after each upward thrust came the inexorable "down".

"Feeble again. Janet came. She's as amazed as I am about Bunty being engaged . . . Sick all day. Hope it's not the tablets, as I need them badly." On one Sunday she wrote, "Daddy got up at seven to give me my tablet. Bless him! Not many people have such a willing father. We're very lucky, even though we grumble now and then."

She was strangely relieved when the consultant neurologist urged that she return to hospital before Christmas. She would be with people more or less in the same condition as herself and wouldn't feel so useless. She might even have an enjoyable Christmas because everyone else would be at least slightly below par, so she could feel normal. More important, the doctors would really be *doing something*!

She went back into the Queen Elizabeth Hospital on December 23rd, 1960. She was on East 2B, her old ward. Sister Anne Scouse admitted her again, as she had the previous June, and at sight of her Hilary felt a warmth of relief and confidence. Dark, slim, vivacious, a nurse who scorned red tape and always put her patients first, Anne welcomed her with a sympathy as friendly as it was professional. It was almost like coming home. "Oh, boy," Hilary wrote in her diary, "bliss to be back and in bed!"

Though she felt distressingly weak on Christmas Day, the holiday passed happily. Everybody on the ward was jolly and kind. The family came. Nurses she had known before popped in. Restrictions on diet were off. She was allowed fruit, nuts, biscuits, and was able to swallow them in small quantities. A poor night brought an injection, which worked like magic. The doctors and nurses were super, though the registrar had not learned yet to appreciate her sense of humour. He would! On the twenty-seventh Peter came, bless him, always so devoted, so understanding. Cor! Why couldn't she have stayed in love with him instead of with Jim?

The improvement was short-lived. Her condition deteriorated rapidly. On December 31st, during the night, the doctors performed another tracheotomy. Though she was given an injection every two hours, her breathing often failed before the next injection was due. Then a nurse gave artificial respiration. The tracheotomy now made the use of a ventilator possible, but orders were that it was not to be used except in case of emergency. Often each breath was a grim, exhausting struggle.

"I know it's — cowardly," she said to her nurse, "but — could I — go on the machine — I'm worn out!"

The nurse was Pat Wyles, a "mauve" (senior staff nurse) who had returned to the hospital from midwifery. "It's not at all cowardly," she assured. "Don't worry. I'll soon fix it up." She moved Hilary to a side ward, and settled her on the ventilator.

That night the Barnet ventilator was not acting properly, and instead of going off duty Pat stayed on. The registrar wanted to change the machine to one Hilary did not like. She fought it stubbornly, and Pat also tried to prevent it. But the registrar had his way, and was quite angry with them both. Hilary became very weak and ill. Pat gave her artificial respiration for what seemed like ages, literally keeping her alive. Eventually she was put back on the Barnet, and somehow they struggled through until morning, when help could be obtained. It was by no means the last time that Pat would fight for her patient's safety and peace of mind.

The weeks that followed were another journey through light and shadow. Hilary was very ill again with pneumonia. A nurse or her parents remained with her constantly, except occasionally during the nurses' breaks, when one of the medical students would sit with her. Usually he would tell her his name, for it was almost impossible for her to see. One student always lifted her finger and rubbed it across his moustache by way of introduction.

Crises, it seemed, always came at weekends. One Sunday the myasthenia was making her feel very ill. To add insult to injury, the Barnet ventilator was not operating properly. There was a woman houseman on the ward who did not understand its mechanics but kept fiddling with it. By the afternoon, when Mum and Dad arrived, Hilary's distress was almost unbearable. She waited as long as she dared, then asked them to get the consultant. Dad asked the nurse to call him. She was shocked. Call a consultant during a weekend, on a Sunday of all times! The office would be horrified. The nurse was sorry, but she could not.

Fortunately the nurse soon went off duty. Later Hilary emerged from a haze of pain and semi-consciousness to see a pair of bright beady eyes looking down at her. With relief she recognised the face, thin, small-boned, always smiling. It belonged to Miss Griffiths, the Assistant Matron, so much like a bird in her quick, sharp movements, and so small that they called her "Mini-Griff".

"Poor Hilary, is there anything you want, dear?"

Hilary groped for a pencil. "Yes," she scribbled on the sheet. "To see — doctor."

The bright little eyes blinked, but only momentarily. Mini-Griff was not afraid of shocking the office. "Then you shall, dear," she said quickly. She left for Sister's office, returned almost immediately to say he was coming. Soon afterwards the consultant arrived. Hilary found his presence comforting, reassuring, far more than his words.

He went outside with Eric and Mona. His face was infinitely kind, but he did not spare them. "I'm afraid she is dying. The end may come before morning."

Hilary sent the nurse out to find what had been said. Eric and Mona went in, forcing themselves to smile and speak calmly. They had never told a lie to Hilary. They did not now. "The doctor says you are very, very ill, but you have coped before, and we believe you will do so now."

She did. The consultant changed her prostigmine cycle from five hours to three, which relieved the distressing symptoms of the myasthenia. He forbade anyone but the anaesthetist or the technicians to touch the ventilator. Her troubles were by no means ended, but she had fought and won another battle for survival.

A long silence in her diary was broken. "Just for fun," she recorded in March, "I've worked out the number of 'jabs' I've had — over 500 since January!"

Hilary was not discouraged. True, it was taking longer this time to find the correct balance in her treatment which would make it possible for her to return to near normality, but she was confident that it would be found. Meanwhile she was determinedly content to remain in the hospital.

"It's my home," she affirmed once cheerfully. "I've been here since December 23rd, and I'm likely to be here for several more months."

A blessing she could not know that it would be her home for almost ten years!

PART
THREE

———————

Hotel Elizabeth

Meditations during a Thunderstorm

(Written in Hospital)

Oh, how I love to hear the rain
Beat down against my window pane.
As if throughout these seven years
God-given music has taught my ears
That in the slightest, softest sound
A certain magic may be found.

Although I cannot use my eyes,
I can imagine different skies,
Sulky drizzles, joyous showers,
Despondent downpour for hours and hours;
Clad in dull depressing grey,
Or sunflecked blue throughout the day.

Rich black velvet she wears at night,
The moon and stars add silver light.
In all her moods, intense or calm,
I find some kind of special charm,
But the way I like her best
Is when she weeps and storms with zest.

Then the wind with anger howls,
Shrieks defiance, whistles, scowls;
Hail hard as bullets beats the earth,
Spoutings gush with evil mirth.
Ecstatic flashes pierce the gloom,
Tremendous thunder crashes — boom!

Treetops wildly thrash and moan,
Windows rattle, whimper, groan.
Furious temper tears descend.
Oh, will her tantrum never end?
Then suddenly the ragings cease.
The air is filled with light and peace.
At once the birds begin to sing;
The elements have had their fling.

HILARY J. POLE

I

It was the sort of marriage she had never contemplated, certainly not one of love but of convenience, and she intended to get a divorce as soon as possible. The courtship was abrupt and violent, the tracheotomy performed on the last day of 1960, and the wedding ceremony took place immediately. She had met the groom before, the previous July.

His full name was Jonathan William Barnet, but she soon knew him affectionately as John Willy, then as J. W. As his name might indicate, he was a "square", or, more accurately, a cube. To those not so intimately involved he was known as a Barnet Ventilator. He was exceedingly jealous and possessive and insisted on keeping her closely tied to him much of the time, especially at night, obviously bent on proving that she could not live without him. He was literally a wind-bag, being fed compressed air constantly from a huge cylinder, and never stopped clattering, his constant theme being "clunk-*clunk*, clunk-*clunk*". He was one of those husbands who was almost impossible to live with, yet for the present you could not live without him.

In spite of his close marital connection, he was what might be called a satellite. Like SUCKER, whose pedigree name was Haemoductor. "My particular one," decided Hilary, "was left me in Florence Nightingale's will, a relic of the Crimea. (It's a crime 'ere too!) It looks dreadful, has a very raucous voice, but it is certainly a good friend!" Anybody with a tracheotomy, especially a myasthenic on prostigmine, which promotes salivation, couldn't live without one.

Even more intimate adjuncts than the satellites (if anything

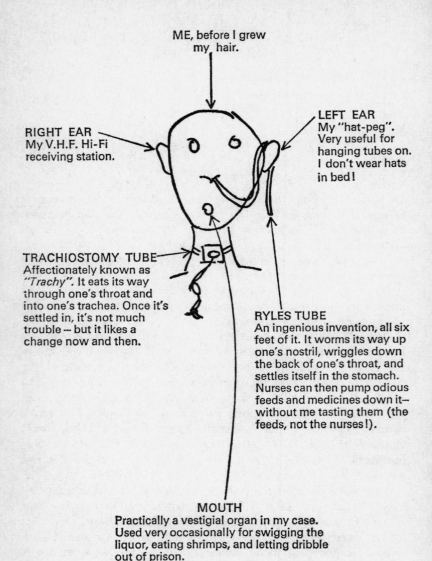

ME, before I grew
my hair.

RIGHT EAR
My V.H.F. Hi-Fi
receiving station.

LEFT EAR
My "hat-peg".
Very useful for
hanging tubes on.
I don't wear hats
in bed!

TRACHIOSTOMY TUBE
Affectionately known as
"Trachy". It eats its way
through one's throat and
into one's trachea. Once it's
settled in, it's not much
trouble — but it likes a
change now and then.

RYLES TUBE
An ingenious invention, all six
feet of it. It worms its way up
one's nostril, wriggles down
the back of one's throat, and
settles itself in the stomach.
Nurses can then pump odious
feeds and medicines down it—
without me tasting them (the
feeds, not the nurses!).

MOUTH
Practically a vestigial organ in my case.
Used very occasionally for swigging the
liquor, eating shrimps, and letting dribble
out of prison.
Is mercifully silent.

* "Trachiostomy" — normally spelt tracheostomy.

Both Ryles and Trachy have some interesting friends:

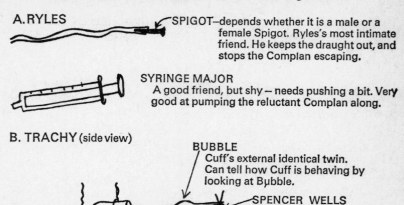

A. RYLES

SPIGOT—depends whether it is a male or a female Spigot. Ryles's most intimate friend. He keeps the draught out, and stops the Complan escaping.

SYRINGE MAJOR
A good friend, but shy — needs pushing a bit. Very good at pumping the reluctant Complan along.

B. TRACHY (side view)

BUBBLE
Cuff's external identical twin. Can tell how Cuff is behaving by looking at Bμbble.

My throat the host.

SPENCER WELLS
The aristocrat. Does his very best to clip the air in Cuff.

CUFF
A close but very temperamental friend. Very inflatable temper, which bursts now and then — most uncomfortable and inconvenient. Very tiring.

SYRINGE MINOR
Cousin to Syringe Major. Puffs air along to Cuff.

could be more intimate than a husband) were what Hilary chose to call parasites. For the educational amusement of friends and relatives she compiled some illustrated data :

It became obvious as the weeks passed that this time the balancing process was going to take many months. Six? Perhaps even a year. Hilary never had been a patient person. Now her family marvelled that she could accept her situation not only with mere resignation but with good humour and creative imagination.

"Why not?" she answered their subtle probings with firm strokes of her biro. Even if temporarily unable to speak, at least she could write in a good strong hand, especially in the hour following an injection. Of course you had to use what you had. If you had no voice, you used a biro. If you could not breathe, you were lucky to have J. W. to breathe for you. Besides, think of all the luxury and service! Somebody to give you Complan every hour through a tube, Nurse Ruth to wash and set your hair and do your nails — just look at them, orange blaze! It was like being in a hotel.

Hotel! As she thought about it, the idea grew. She took her biro and a piece of paper and began.   .

HOTEL ELIZABETH

Although I cannot recommend the City of Birmingham as a holiday resort, I can strongly recommend "Hotel Elizabeth" — all modern conveniences, personal service (Just ring if you want us), breakfast in bed and a wonderful cuisine. Endless trouble is taken with the food and all diets are respected and catered for . . .

The many windows look out on the famous University of Birmingham on the east and the residential area of Edgbaston on the west. The beautiful sound of rattling trucks, whistling engines and loudly screaming diesels filters delicately through the open windows with the still night air. During the day these sounds are obscured by the constant hum and roar of the not-too-distant traffic and the incessant whirring of a pneumatic drill, shouting workmen and dropping bricks as more and more halls are added to the educational monument of the West Midlands.

The deep silence within is broken only by the rattle and clatter of bed-pan trolleys, banging doors, the soft soothing purr of a fleet of floor-polishers, the shouts and chatter of nurses and patients, and the squeaking of a million pairs of feet.

The sleeping quarters are all that could be desired, one large room for the gregarious types — usually men — and smaller rooms for the more modest of our species. Hot and cold water, flush w.c.'s, bathrooms, and a skeleton night staff to attend to one's every need. The staff cater for many hobbies — chest aspirations, lumbar punctures, blood drips and drug peddling. There are two comfortable lounges, easy chairs and a gas fire. Television, radio, and a telephone are available."

Hotel Elizabeth! Good. Nurses and orderlies, bell hops, room service — all were highly amused. Evidently many of their guests, especially the long-stay-ones, were not blessed with a sense of humour. What should you call your *de luxe* quarters in this royal residence? Hardly a flat (one room) or a penthouse (lower floor), but something equally ritzy. Aha! Of course.

The Ritz is my own special suite within the walls of Hotel Elizabeth. It took quite a lot of hunting and organisation to find this place, but it was well worth it. I'm admirably placed opposite Sister's office. (Well, that's not strictly true, I'm really right opposite the staff w.c., with the office next door to it, but I'm not one to quibble about such minor details.) The day-room flanks my north wall and an unoccupied four-bedder my south — definitely a centre of activity. If I tune in and flap my elephant ears, I can now and then pick up a juicy tit-bit of gossip.

It's not a very big room and gradually, like a cuckoo in a hedge sparrow's nest, I've managed to push the other occupants over the edge, so to speak, and at the moment reign in solitary glory. I will follow this with a detailed, un-scaled (I never could sing!) map of the premises.

The *objets d'art* were added gradually. The hospital authorities were lenient and when it became obvious that Hilary's stay in hospital was going to be longer than at first anticipated, some of her most cherished possessions were added to the room's décor; pictures of Shandy and Chiaro, a cupboard for the tinned foods she was able to eat in tiny portions, and part of her huge collection of wooden animals, started before she was a year old and swelled by contributions from all over the world. The latest addition was a gorgeous Indian rhinoceros, which she named Rhataxes.

But she had been in hospital over two years before these first pages of "Hotel Elizabeth" and the accompanying drawings were completed. It was February 1962 when she wrote in her diary, "Managed to complete a ground plan of the Ritz using a pencil and ruler. Lovely to use a ruler again properly. Funny what tiny simple things can give so much pleasure — being able to write a letter, clean my teeth, brush my hair!"

The first year was one of slow progress and repeated setbacks, of groping and experimentation, of trial and error, for the doctors knew little more about the disease than Hilary and the nurses even less. It was also the first year of "marriage", and J. W. revealed all the temperamental vagaries of a new husband. She found this out in the first month of their union, when

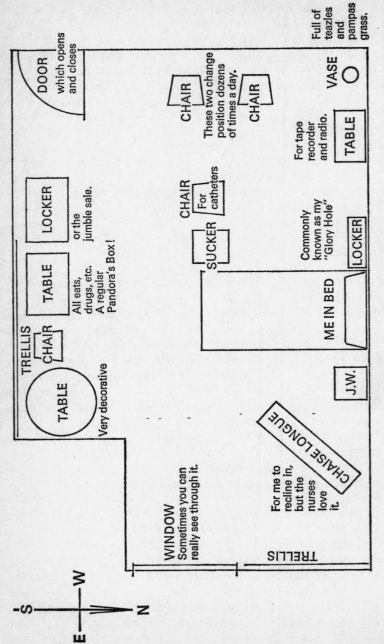

A GROUND PLAN OF THE RITZ

J. W. suddenly became agitated in the middle of the night. In panic Hilary rang for a nurse. One of the anaesthetists (a marriage counsellor?) was hastily summoned. J. W., he found, had sprung a leak. There were other nights when he became erratic. It was terrifying to wake up and find yourself gasping for breath — even more terrifying to realise that you might not have woken up at all, that the nurse who should stay in your room all night, might occasionally leave you alone. So many things could go wrong! J. W.'s valves might stick, his bellows become perforated, the air cylinders piped to him run out with no full one available. The cuff (the inflatable balloon round the middle of the tracheotomy tube in the throat which prevents air escaping back through the nose and mouth) might burst, or the tube might become blocked. Too often the nurses did not understand the life-and-death importance of such emergencies.

"Don't get mad," Hilary wrote to one exasperated nurse, "I just have a strong desire to survive in spite of John Willy." And again. "WHY get exasperated when I ring the bell more than once — you're lucky I have a bell and let you leave me. When that airflow stops — whatever the cause — so does my life begin to stop and it's not pleasant. I'm not cross, just plain petrified."

Life with J. W. would have been even more disturbing without the services of Paul Hocken, the houseman on East 2B. Always helpful, ingenious, and often blithely unorthodox, he gave Hilary tremendous confidence. Once when the trachy was being pulled by the air pipes from the ventilator Paul went outside, brought in a drip stand, bent it over his knee at right angles, and clamped it to the bedside. Then he tied the pipes over it to take the dragging pull off her throat.

"Oh," wrote Hilary on her pad, "brawns as well as brains!"

The entries in her diary those first months were as fitful and temperamental as the ventilator. "Poor night. Trachy tube was blowing back." . . . "J. W. had to be repaired." . . . "Dr. Boyles saw J. W. Not satisfactory. J. W. changed."

The pages did not reveal all the events. Perhaps the most interesting was Peter's visit. It was just like him to write, not that he was getting married, but that he *was* married. He would like to bring his wife, Jackie, to see Hilary. "Wants to show her off!" she thought, amused and delighted. She liked Jackie very much, and there was quick understanding between them.

Peter and Jackie were obviously very happy. Hilary chuckled silently when Peter announced, "We're having a baby!" with the surprised exultation of unique experience. Simon was born the following October, and twin boys two years later. When Simon started school, Jackie joined Hilary's reading rota, a group of friends who volunteered to come and read to her.

Was it providence or just happy fate, wondered Hilary, which had kept her from getting involved romantically with Peter again? Why, when she had had no idea she was seriously ill, when it would have been so easy to let him fill the void left by Jim, had a voice inside her kept warning, "No, don't get involved"? Had she been married, or even engaged, when she went into hospital, to what agonising decision might it have led? Now she was profoundly grateful. Peter was happy, and the future was her own to face.

The first year crept on. There came a spell of "ups" and "downs". It was like living on a see-saw. Sometimes she could manage five or six hours between injections, two hours off the ventilator; other times only four hours between, one hour off, occasionally only half an hour. When in an "up" phase, she could eat a bit, drink a few mouthfuls, sit in a wheelchair, even stand for a minute or two with a nurse's help. She was not at all sure, from one injection to another, how she would be. When in a "down" phase, she might even go into "crisis". Luckily she learned to recognise the symptoms — racing heart, pounding head, black and red before her eyes, clammy skin, a feeling of faintness. Then she must signal the nurse. "Jab — fast!" After the injection it would take perhaps ten minutes for the prostigmine to work.

All that spring they were trying to lengthen the periods between injections. Two hours . . . four . . . five. If she could reach the target of two injections a day, she could start on tablets again. Then, perhaps — home! But progress was slow. That first year she was prone to chest infection, leading always to successive weakness — first eyes, then mouth, neck, hands. Speech was becoming more and more impossible.

"A good suck-out, please," she wrote on April 30th, "then if I can manage just a squeak, could I have the telephone to ring Mum and say 'Happy birthday'?"

She just managed it. "Happy Birthday, Mum!" They were the last words she would ever speak.

Her diary contained only blank pages between March and May 27th. "My birthday. Opened presents."

It was Sister Anne Scouse who made possible the best present. With her help Mum and Dad were able to smuggle Shandy and Chiaro into the building through a back entrance, pass through the kitchens, and so to Hilary's room. "Don't say anything if you're stopped," she warned. "Leave it to me." The sight of Hilary's radiant face was ample reward for her defiant snipping of red tape. Shandy nearly wagged off his tail. He loved all the fuss and commotion, gaily joining in the birthday celebration. But when he started to sing his own version of "Happy Birthday", he had to go! Chiaro, looking down his nose at Shandy as if to say *he* never made such a dreadful fuss and it served Shandy right, immediately jumped on to the bed, curled up, and went to sleep. Apart from a necessary outing in the early evening, he stayed there until ten thirty p.m. when Dad had to pick him up. Then he forgot his good manners and bawled his head off, alerting the whole ward to his outrage at being disturbed.

The visit proved such a joy to Hilary that Anne adopted more orthodox measures and asked permission for the "boys" to make other visits, always making sure that Hilary had no infection which might cause them to endanger her health. Hilary hoped to see them again on Ian's twenty-first birthday, but as there was a prevalence of infection in the hospital, Matron said, "No". Of course Hilary received an invitation to the party.

Mr. Ian C. Pole requests the honour of the company of
Miss Hilary J. Pole and Mr. Jonathan William Barnet
on the occasion of his coming of age on July 22nd
at West Riding, Walsall.

It was a good sample of Ian's dry humour, so akin to Hilary's. Their letters to each other during her college days had sparkled with droll wit. Once, attempting to cheer him up before he took his A levels, Hilary had stamped across the top right hand corner of the envelope "PAR PIED" instead of "PAR AVION", and he had found the whole letter written in "mirror writing", the words as properly inscribed as if written forward. Ian was equally resourceful. One of his letters to the hospital was addressed to Miss Hilary J. Pole, E2B — or NOT 2B!

On his twenty-first birthday the family came to her. After giving Ian his present, a complete recording of Verdi's *Aida*, Hilary helped celebrate by having them pour a glass of sherry down her tube.

The roots of her buddleia tree had only twined more deeply, it seemed, with transplanting. Strange! You had wanted independence so passionately all your life — and now suddenly you wondered what you would have done had you achieved it. Thank goodness, they didn't treat you as if you were ill. In fact, you made sure they didn't! You spent half the day thinking up jokes to tell them when they arrived in the evening — not tell, because you had written them — but it was all the same. Even so, it was hard getting ahead of Dad and Uncle Doug. And Ian, of course, was always his irrepressible self. "Well, Hil, how's the old batting arm these days? Ready to knock over a wicket or two?" ... "I'm ashamed of you! Here it is late July, and you haven't got any more tan than an Eskimo in winter!"

2

Mona and Eric went to the hospital every night. It was a long trip, many miles to the other side of Birmingham. Upway, from which they had moved to be nearer their work, would have been close by. Usually it was midnight when they reached home. Wendy in her mid-teens was much alone, and it was far from a normal life for her during these impressionable years. They were torn between the two of them, but in Hilary's case, they felt, their visits were essential.

They understood her fear — not of her illness, not of her own inability to cope with all its developing complications, but of the nurses, or, worse still, the lack of any. Some, like Judy, knew exactly how to manage. They were willing to take time to communicate with her, even though the process might be slow. Hilary could tell them how to make her comfortable, where to give the injection to cause the least pain, how to suck her out properly. Others, confident in their superior knowledge, but vastly ignorant of her particular disease, proceeded without the slightest regard to her wishes, causing unnecessary pain, leaving her tubes badly congested, twisting her neck as if it belonged to a rag doll. Sometimes they even plunged a needle straight into a painful area of her hip without waking her! She dreaded to see them coming. She was merely another "case" to them, not a "person". As a matter of fact, her knowledge of anatomy and biology, certainly of ventilators, was on the whole much greater than theirs.

Her strength of mind was potent, which did not always make her a popular patient — at first, that is. Later Dr. Milne marvelled at the amount of co-operation she obtained. He discussed the matter with several of the sisters. All said that although they were originally determined to look after Hilary in their own way, making their own rules, within a few weeks they were "doing it Hilary's way". "Remarkable," he commented, "when you consider that these sisters were very determined people, and even more so considering Hilary's very great physical disadvantage."

With new nurses trying, sometimes vainly, to learn her difficult routines, Hilary was remarkably patient and understanding. The notes she wrote them reflected reassurance, good humour.

"It's not your fault — someone should show you — please don't worry . . ."

"When I can't get comfy, it's often disappointment that makes me upset — not with you — I'm so utterly helpless unless in a certain position — I can't even write!" . . .

"You mustn't worry if you can't get me comfy — it's a miracle if you can! My head's too heavy, and I can't move it a quarter of an inch when I flop!"

Even more terrifying than the ignorance of nurses was their neglect. More than once Hilary's confidence was badly shaken. The cylinder of compressed air which fed the ventilator was allowed to run out, although a full cylinder was standing nearby. Nights of course were the worst. If an emergency arose in the daytime, even though she was unable to ring, nurses were usually passing her door and would occasionally pop in. At night, though a nurse was supposed to be constantly on duty in her room, especially in the weak period before injections, she often woke to find herself alone.

Many of the nurses fully understood her needs. When Sister Anne Scouse was on night duty, if a call came from Hilary she made it her business to get there fast, knowing that it was likely to be urgent. It was usually an injection needed, the air supply gone, or the ventilator playing up. Once an argument arose between Hilary and a nurse about an overdue injection. "You're fussing," accused the nurse impatiently. Hilary wrote, "Wouldn't you fuss if your life depended on it?" Reasonable enough, thought Anne.

"All who knew her had a strong reaction," commented Anna Corser, one of Hilary's physiotherapists, "love or dislike. Those who disliked did so because of basic weaknesses in themselves : pride, inefficiency, unkindness or hardness of approach to patients, or impatience arising from the mistaken idea that they had no time. Many of them learned to care about her, and this improved their attitude towards other patients. Because they had been willing to learn from a patient, it increased their humility and understanding."

In the early days Mona and Eric knew the hospital disapproved of their staying late at night. It was suggested that their visits made Hilary overtired. They knew this was not so. They had often found her tense and strained when they arrived but markedly relaxed at the end of their visits. Under Hilary's tutelage Mona learned how to suck her out properly, how to arrange her pillows to make her comfortable. Finally Mona expressed her concern to the hospital authorities.

"Hilary's progress depends on her ability to extend the period between injections," she wrote during those crucial months of 1961. "She is on a five-hour cycle now. Following the injection she has one and a half hours when she is reasonably active and can signal. This energy gradually diminishes. During the last two hours she has little physical activity. Constant vigilance is needed to detect emergencies. Her confidence must not be shaken again, as it has been in the past."

However, most of the nurses were both competent and attentive. There was Ruth, who kept Hilary and her room immaculate and always found time to do her hair and nails. In spite of her hot temper and occasional moods, Hilary trusted her competence, admired her brilliance. Anne Morris, lively, gay, had a lot of fun teaching Hilary her native Welsh. The knowledge was useful once when an assistant matron, also Welsh, was berating Hilary, who was spared the necessity of a polite reply by retorting with an apt but slightly naughty word in Welsh, to the matron's surprise and delight.

Nurse Meredith, on night duty during Hilary's first three months in hospital, though small in build, was a tower of strength. When the porters were unable to turn the spanner that released air from the cylinders, she could do it. One night her powerful wrists rendered true yeomen service. Two neurotic patients in the ward went berserk. They knocked out a porter, shook off three or four nurses, and ran amok down the corridor. Grabbing the heavy spanner, Nurse Meredith stood on guard outside Hilary's door protecting both the patient and her venti-lator. Eventually the men were controlled by nurses with hypo-dermic syringes. All because the moonlight had shone on the face of one of the men and he had wakened screaming!

"Would you mind having a male nurse?" asked Sister.

"No," responded Hilary. "We have male doctors. If the nurse is not embarrassed, why should I be?" Many people, especially female nurses, tended to regard their male counterparts as "cissy". ROT!!! was her reaction to that. Hilary found them conscientious, dedicated, excellent lifters, great fun, good con-versationalists, a pleasant change from some of the more ortho-dox and hierarchy-conscious females.

David was her first male nurse on East 2B. They had much in common and thoroughly enjoyed each other's company. If Hilary's eating time coincided with his off-duty, he would often cook her something to eat. He brought her some of his mother's home-made lemon curd (a delicious sweet spread made from boiling together lemon juice, butter, eggs and sugar), also sweet peas from her garden. Hilary was always glad when he was on duty because she knew that nothing and no one would stop him from answering her bell even if the ward was busy. On two occasions he rescued her from dangerous situations, once when the cylinder ran out and there was no replacement, again when J. W. broke down.

"Have nothing but admiration for them all," was Hilary's comment about her male nurses.

Later there was Paul, very capable with a quiet sense of humour. One night he had just left Hilary's room to put her catheters in the steriliser, and J. W. stopped. He ran back, vaulted across the bottom of her bed and had her on the relief ventilator almost before she could ring the bell. On East Ground she met Pat, a laconic Irishman, on the ward at the same time as Terry, who was very talkative. Hilary called them

"Flotsam and Jetsam". Both had a spirited sense of humour and when they were together in her room, there was always a riot.

In fact most of the nurses found her room, homelike with its radio, pictures, and wooden carvings, a happy place to congregate. Like most people who swung into the orbit of her strangely magnetic personality — strangers and acquaintances as well as friends — they were soon confiding their problems, seeking advice, sharing their romances. Sister Anne Scouse was not immune. Hilary was thrilled to be made the confidante of Anne's wedding plans and took a great liking to her fiancé, Victor Smith. Anne naturally sent a wedding invitation to Hilary and her parents. The surprising reply delighted her.

"Sorry for the delay in answering, but it took a little checking. Now we can *all* say we shall be delighted to come."

As days of scheming, planning, and practising went by, Hilary could hardly believe her good fortune. She was really going! To be actually venturing into the world of high society again!

The day arrived — November 11th — and how! She was wakened at five a.m. by a vicious stab in her right thigh and an even more vicious sound in her ears. RAIN. Not the gentle stuff resembling "mercy" in the *Merchant of Venice*; sheets lashed against the windows by a force-eight gale! Always the cockeyed optimist, she reacted with a "Smells nice", and as they embarked on the blanket bath she was confident that the outlook would change. After a lavish sprinkling of "Blue Grass", her favourite perfume these days, she was settled down to "rest" and contemplate on the day's events.

At nine a.m. came another injection, again in her overworked thigh, a good sucking out, and she was left to read her post and inwardly curse the weather. The staff also had qualms, but at eleven fifteen when she was safely resting on faithful J. W. and airing her doubts to Aunty Betty, the O.K. came through.

The pace quickened. Clothes were laid out, make-up sorted, feeds mixed, trays of equipment set, notes consulted. At twelve forty-five p.m. the real action started. There followed a bumper feed, make-up by Aunty, injection, Ryles tube up, bed pan, off J. W., suck out, dress, more make-up, hair, ear-rings and a buttonhole bouquet from the always thoughtful Wendy. Now she really felt in festive mood! At one twenty-five she was in

a wheelchair, and the wagons rolled. Outside everything from
J. W. to a bath towel was waiting in her Red Cross carriage.

Dr. Paul Hocken who was then her houseman, and his nurse
wife Anne were her faithful attendants on the expedition.
Snuggled in a pile of scarlet blankets, she was transferred from
chair to stretcher and, in a screaming, biting wind, stowed in
the ambulance. With J. W., air and oxygen cylinders, and
numerous trays there was just room for herself, the doctor,
and the nurse. A bull-nosed, complacent-looking Morris
Oxford headed the procession, followed by the ambulance. A
nippy A40 van with a sturdy compact shooting brake brought
up the rear. The ride was uneventful for the team, momentous for Hilary. At a side gate of King's Norton Parish Church
the wheelchair was re-assembled and wheeled to the porch.
Once more a scarlet cocoon, she was carried by a motley array
of ambulance driver, attendants, and doctor; Dad and Uncle
Doug in their wake. The Sultans of Turkey had nothing to
compare with this — not even the Sultanas! Her arrival caused
great excitement and threw one usher into a panic.

"Is Hil here?" asked the bride before thinking to inquire
about the bridegroom.

Anne looked beautiful in her oyster-coloured brocade dress
embroidered with gold thread. Gold rosebuds held her short
circular veil in place. After the bridal party passed down the
aisle Hilary's wheelchair was manoeuvred into position facing
down the centre.

By the time the congregation stood to sing "O Perfect
Love", Hilary's energy was flagging. The resourceful doctor
magiced an ampoule of prostigmine and syringe from his
pocket — and dropped it. If the floor of King's Norton
Church should seem to rear up suddenly, it wouldn't be the
D.T.s! But he soon found another ampoule, and, thighs being
temporarily out of reach, she was stabbed expertly in the fore-
arm. As the couple went to sign the register, she was whisked
into the porch to be sucked out. A wonder the way the sucker
was pumped that she didn't lose a lung! Back again to see the
couple walk up the aisle. Anne stopped to kiss her and say
"Hello", Hilary was wheeled to the main door behind her,
hoisted up the steps, and had her photograph taken with the
bride and groom. An incongruous trio! The thing Anne remembered most about the adventure was that Hilary had asked the

press not to write up her visit. "It's the bride's day, not mine."

Back to the nest of scarlet blankets and her Red Cross chariot, its windows thoughtfully cleaned by the doctor so that she could get glimpses of the wide wicked world! At three p.m. she was unwrapped for the last time and triumphantly returned to E2B. A simple trip to a nearby church? No. An Odyssey, a Polar expedition, a journey into outer space! It was a rebirth to normality, a harbinger of hope.

Soon after "Operation Wedlock", as she dubbed the adventure in her account for "Hotel Elizabeth", she got a bright idea. Couldn't she go downstairs in a wheelchair and see the "boys" at the door? First they got medical permission, then Matron's.

The following Sunday morning Nurse got the wheelchair ready and put some biscuits for Shandy and shrimps for Chiaro in the lid of a transparency box. The porter rang the ward at eleven thirty a.m. They had arrived! It was heaven to see them again. Shandy did all his tricks, for the biscuits. Chiaro sat on Hilary's knee scoffing shrimps. She stayed with them for twenty whole minutes.

Two weeks later there were subtle differences. The "boys" knew where they were going. As Hilary rounded the cafeteria corner there was a great scuffling and panting, Shandy doing his best to drag Dad up the corridor, Chiaro in Mum's arms bawling a Siamese welcome, demanding to know if Hilary had remembered his shrimps. She had.

She was overjoyed when permission came to have them in her room each Sunday morning. What a performance! Chiaro, of course, had to case the joint before deigning to recognise her. Shandy barged in wriggling, wagged his tail frantically, slobbered a few kisses, and promptly drank the water out of the catheter bowl. Then with one bound he was on her knee — she was lying on the chaise-longue — panting. Already he had learned silent commands — for a biscuit. After a short game he was taken to the car. She returned to bed, and Chiaro, with a smug "Thank goodness he's gone, now we can have some peace" look, jumped lightly up, drank a saucerful of Complan, curled up, yawned, and went to sleep.

Once was enough. They had learned the routine and followed it every Sunday morning thereafter until Hilary changed wards.

After seven months' silence, her diary suddenly became "articulate". There were indications of improvement. "Was able to get up, walk to the door!... Julie washed and set my hair. Anne came and did my nails — gold-frosted rose-gold!... Listened to the *Messiah* and really enjoyed it. Had my coffee and boiled egg as usual... I CAN KNIT! Using the big Jaeger pattern which uses three balls of spiral spun at a time and Jackpin Number 1 needles, I can hold them in my fist and pull the wool around with my left hand if my right gets too tired. I like the colour, a lovely green called — Spinach... Managed two rows after my bath. It's a thrill to see it grow and know that I'm really doing it all by myself... I was never keen on egg before, but I really look forward to my daily fight. It's getting a wee bit easier, but swallowing is still practically nil... Nurse Day prepared shrimp for me. Boy, they were good!"

There were frustrations. "Was supposed to have Nurse G., but she's like a flea in a gale, in and out so fast. Most disturbing... Nurse H. attempted to put me comfy. She's so slow. It's like trying to move a ten ton weight... I only wish something could be done to teach these nurses how to suck out. It's horribly frustrating to feel all bunged up and have them poking the first three inches. I realise it must be difficult, but it's so terribly important... four thirty a.m. air very low. Couldn't make anyone hear. Very scared again."

Christmas was coming. As she couldn't be at home, there must be a big celebration on E2B. With Mum's, Dad's, and the nurses' help she began planning. The theme, after much wearying cogitation, was Christmas Carols. The main ward was to represent the Twelve Days of Christmas. There were frenzied debates as to the verity of her version, "Twelve drummers drumming." Many preferred "Twelve lords leaping", but, since she was the designer and Mum and Dad joint executors, the drummers got their way and drummed triumphantly through Christmas.

The side wards chose different carols, and the doorway of one empty two-bedder became the framework for the Christmas tableau. The Crib (a cradle and bedpan cover forming the skeleton stable) showed up beautifully against the backcloth of deep midnight blue (a mortuary sheet!) The decorations, after much hard work, were miraculously ready in time. There was great excitement when the big tree arrived; it was decorated

by the electricians with coloured lights and hung with presents.
Then into the frenzy of Saturday morning, the twenty-third,
came the Lord Mayor of Birmingham on inspection. Panic!
Caps straightened, hair tucked up, bottles hidden, cupboards
banging, nurses panting, as Matron and her followers sailed
majestically round the wards. After a hesitant "Merry
Christmas" His Worship heaved an almost audible sigh of
relief and thankfully backed out, leaving the ward to regain its
feverish tempo.

At tea time on Christmas Eve her bed was wheeled into the
corridor, all the ward lights switched off, and an expectant hush
fell. Nurses and sisters, wearing their cloaks and doctors carrying lanterns, came through, singing. Hilary was thrilled to be
asked to choose a carol. She chose "Silent Night". December
25th dawned cold and grey, but inside all was warmth and
colour. After a hurried blanket bath, once more reunited with
John Willy, Hilary settled down to enjoy being read to by her
nurse, but there were frequent interruptions from well-wishing
Florence Nightingales who had left the ward. At dinner time
she choked her way through five teaspoons of minced turkey
and sprout. The plum pudding, blazing triumphantly as it was
wheeled round the ward, was not so easy and after one teaspoon she gave up, in spite of the very spirited sauce!

More visitors streamed in and out during the afternoon, and
all spent a pleasant hour listening to the Christmas morning
service from Hilary's home church, which Dad had recorded
on tape. After her five o'clock injection (Yes, jabs, even on
Christmas Day), she was wheeled into the main ward, where
the houseman, adorned in Father Christmas robes and
smothered by a mass of curly white beard, was swimming up
and down (a kind of dolphin stroke) in a large pair of white
theatre boots, distributing gifts and tickly kisses to patients
(females, of course) and nurses alike, obviously having a whale
of a time.

Hilary's presents were legion, but three meant more to her
than all the rest. Flowers from Mrs. East. "Kind old soul!" . . .
A record of Maria Callas singing favourite French arias, from
all the girls on Smith's record counter. "I was thrilled to pieces.
Sometimes I get a wee bit frightened because I wonder if I really
am worth so much friendship." . . . A letter from the pupils of
Edward Shelley.

"Dear Miss Pole, As Christmas is coming, the form as we now are (5M) has begun to think of people in hospital, and all our thoughts have turned to you. We have decided, because of the pleasant way you treated us when you taught here, we would like to repay you in the only way we know. Please accept this small gift as a token of our appreciation, and we all hope you will enjoy Christmas as much as we shall. From all 5M."

But she did not enjoy Christmas. She confided the truth only to her diary. December 27th. "Legs just refuse to obey me. Can't understand my knees at all. Felt in an odd mood in the evening. Mum and Ian came, and I was feeling all mixed up and could have cried my eyes out. All the Christmas things going on! I was counting so much on a wonderful hospital Christmas and was too whacked to properly enjoy it."

And, what she did not bother to write, she had been in the hospital over a year now, with no end in sight.

3

Communication! Your biggest problem next to sheer survival! Your will to communicate was almost as strong as your will to live. Your receiving set was perfect. Your ears could pick up the static of a visitor's clicking heels far down the corridor, the whisper of a nurse's uniform passing your door. But how could you convey the ideas fermenting in your brain without the power of speech? In the hour following an injection it was easy. You could write fairly legibly with a biro. Then your hand grew weak. Fine writing became impossible, but you managed very well by forming the letters with your fingers on the sheet. The family was soon expert at deciphering. However, they were not always correct at interpretation! Once Uncle Doug was reading this sheet writing.

"N-o-o-n-e," he spelled aloud, then hesitated in bewilderment. "What's that? I don't get it. Noonie?"

The bed shook with Hilary's laughter. Then one by one the others in the room, including Uncle Doug, caught on. "No one"! There were bursts of hilarious glee. Noonie! Uncle Doug never lived it down. Henceforth he was known as

"Noonie" by the whole family and hospital. "Aunt Betty and Noonie came," Hilary's diary would chronicle . . . "Noonie here. What a riot. We hardly stopped laughing. Noonie in a plastic long cap ! . . . Noonie and Aunt Betty came. Died laughing over the nurse's set. (Hilary had given him a child's doctor's and nurse's set for his birthday.) Noonie wore it and went into the main ward with it on." He would still be Noonie ten years later !

Occasionally before an injection she was too "floppy" even to sheet-write. Then she devised another method — the small bell suspended on a bandage between her toe and the bedside locker. A person would go through the alphabet until the right letter was reached, when a tiny jerk of her foot would ring the bell. It worked very well providing that the nurse knew the alphabet ! But sheet-writing was usually possible.

She used short-cuts. "Ta" was "thank you", and even the slowest and newest of nurses soon learned to decipher it, for it followed every act performed for her benefit. It wasn't an ideal method of communication. Too often nurses were too busy or impatient to take time to read. They couldn't seem to understand that her case was different, demanding a special type of handling for which no conventional training could possibly have prepared them, as so little was known about it, and that she alone was capable of guiding them through the safest and most efficacious techniques.

During Hilary's second year in hospital, her diary bristled with protests, indignant, resigned, occasionally outraged and terror-stricken.

"Nurse H. at night. Never sucked anyone out before. Too timid to learn quickly. After feeling really ill after three feeds, I found she was putting three dessert spoons of Complan ! No more for awhile ! . . . New nurse specialing. Treats me like a kid . . . Nurse L. shrieking in my ear, did I want my Complan ? Yes, please. Ten minutes later she bellows in my ear again and makes me nearly leap out of bed and commences to lift my head to make me DRINK ! Imagine not knowing I was tube-fed ! . . . Nurse C. (a man) specialing. Good — but he went to dinner without giving me the bell. I was horrified. Needed J. W. Nobody came. I pulled the sucker bottles out on to the floor to make a crash, but they wouldn't break. Wriggled legs over bedside and kicked locker until Josie came . . . New physio. Fun and games started. Didn't know how to do my pillows. Hurts

so much when my head and back flops, really painful . . . Nurse
slow. Drives me crackers ! ! . . . Gave me a jab in wrong area.
I nearly leapt out of bed !' !'

As usual, Hilary's imagination was at work giving nick-
names — privately, of course. One night sister, who walked
awkwardly, was "Yogi Bear". The night superintendent on
duty when Hilary was admitted was "Flashing Amber", with
a smile to match her dashing movements. The Poles would
never forget her kindness in those early days when Hilary was
so ill. One night Dad had made Mum and the night nurse a
cup of coffee, highly illegal for the latter if discovered. When
Flashing Amber dashed into the room the nurse hastily set her
cup down on Hilary's bed. The superintendent said with a
knowing smile to Hilary, "It's lovely to see you looking better —
and *drinking*! Enjoy your coffee, my dear, good night."

Mr. Michael Lord and Mr. David Clark, two registrars
belonging to the surgical team responsible for Hilary's
thymectomy, were known as the "Terrible Twins". Hilary
came to know them well, and they were always teasing each
other. At this time a song from *The Threepenny Opera* was
popular, "Mack the Knife", so Mick Lord became "Mick the
Knife". A houseman on her consultant's team, Dr. Knight,
became the "Knight of Gravis." A nurse who had the knack of
bumping into things was "Leaping Lena". If she came into the
room and there was a clear path to Hilary's bed, she would
find something to run into. Though she was sweet of nature
and invariably kind, her presence was a bit unsettling. Then
there was her exact opposite, stout, kind-hearted, who ploughed
straight through every obstacle, sweeping all in her path to one
side. Hilary dubbed her the "Benign Steamroller".

In spite of occasional deficiencies, many of the nurses were
treasures. Though Hilary was usually friends with them all,
once they had learned her routine, certain names received an
accolade of approval.

"Nurse Grey — very sensible . . . Good to have Nurse Wyles
back . . . Lovely surprise, Nurse Gardiner to special me! Goodness knows why they haven't sent her up before . . . Judy a good
nurse ! . . . When Nurse Measures comes on, the place seems to
heave a huge sigh of relief and relax . . . Nurse Morris —
good . . . Nurse McKay — good . . . Julie." Her diary could not
say enough about Julie. "Julie put my new gold varnish on

while we listened to Maria Callas . . . Julie popped in to do my nails, each one a different colour . . . Julie passed 'State' ! I'm so thrilled for her ! . . . Julie staying on. Olé !"

Knowing that the time of maximum movement after each injection was short, Hilary utilised every moment, writing in her diary, answering letters, making additions to "Hotel Elizabeth". In February she finished what she finally called "A 'Normal' Day in the Life of Yours Truly". Starting at five a.m., it went round the clock, through injections, feeds, bath, suck-outs, letters ("*Never* have any private mail sent to hospital !"), readings ("At the moment I am fond of having Elizabeth Goudge read to me. Most enjoyable !"), a few minutes on the chaise longue, visitors. There were both good and bad moments in a typical day.

"11.20 a.m. Sitting up in bed now. A nice time, as I can usually manage to eat something — a soft boiled egg, salmon, shrimps, cheese, beetroot — anything that goes down easily. A slow business and tiring, but so wonderful to taste food."

"11.45. On Mondays, Wednesdays, Fridays, and Saturdays comes my session of 'slap and tickle'. My beautifully arranged stack of pillows is rudely assaulted and I have to lie on my right side on one pillow and one in my back and a towel under my head. The bed is then hoisted to the top rung of the elevator and the torture begins ! The physiotherapist shakes the living daylights out of me while the nurse sucks them up. When that side is really bruised and battered, I turn over and go through it all on the other side. Then, my equilibrium restored, I am put back on my nest of pillows and recuperate."

"4.00 p.m. The day nurse, early shift, staggers off duty to a welcome 'cuppa' and care of the Ritz is left to the late shift. As this is the start of the last hour before my next injection, I am at my weakest, and the nurse stays with me all the time. The bed becomes a raging inferno even if the window is wide open to the winter chill. The nurse often reads to me, if she can keep her teeth from chattering !"

"7.30. Visitors arrive. Mondays, Wednesdays, Fridays, Saturdays, and Sundays my mother and father come; Tuesdays, my father and uncle, Thursdays, my aunt and uncle. My brother, working very hard at the university, plus his friends often pop in for a few minutes."

"12.00-1.00. I am put comfortable, united with J. W., and

within a few minutes am snoring my way through the night."

"5.00 a.m. Ouch! It all starts again."

Hilary awoke one morning feeling depressed — or was it frustrated? Or perhaps a breath of spring creeping through the window? The routine was becoming deadly. She felt the urge to do something, anything. Once she would have donned slacks and sweater and taken a five-mile hike, coming back, arms laden with botanical specimens — or put on a record and executed some mad fantastic dance (*no*, better not even think of dance!) — or burst into a wild flurry of cleaning her room. Her room! As she glanced sleepily around the Ritz, the gloom deepened. It looked like a mere three-star Trust House! But it need not. All day she mulled over the possibilities. That evening Aunt Betty and Noonie came, and the drama began. If Hilary could not be actor, she could be director and production manager. Tables were turned round, locker positions altered, odd bits gleefully discarded. When they left, the Ritz looked like a new place. But action had just begun. Aunty rang Mum to report a shopping list as long as her arm — bread bin, pretty plate and saucer, attractive cruet, elegant sauce bottle, egg cup, tin opener, coloured tray, book and magazine rack.

The purchases were duly installed the following evening, but something still jarred. Sucker! Indispensable, but what a terrible eyesore! Hilary's brain started clicking, then — flash! Why not have a low trolley long enough to house the sucker, catheter, in fact the whole lot of accessories? Dad went to work. That weekend Sucker was housed on a low lime-green fablon-lined trolley and tucked under the bed.

Drugs were neatly stowed on a beautiful new coloured tray. The bread box, known as the "pantry", contained her tinned food collection: shrimps, corned beef, salmon, chicken, herrings, mushrooms, cheese, pickles, tomatoes, salad cream, beetroot, and vinegar. The table was a miscellany of bottles, Complan, syringes, meths, jab tray, feed tray, etc., dignified by a gay cloth. Operation Streamline was finished to her satisfaction.

Cor! If you didn't have a world to run in, you might as well improve the one you had to lie in. At least you could jolly well do something with what you had.

4

Divorce! Hilary welcomed the prospect — not without some regrets. John Willy had been more or less faithful. At the beginning of their marriage she had depended on him completely. Where would she have been without his constant puffing presence? Certainly not alive. It was his temper which had antagonised her. He would suddenly, for no apparent reason, start huffing and puffing fit to burst, often shouting himself to a complete standstill. She would lie in bed, frozen with terror, then, unable to bear the silence of suspense a moment longer, she would frantically ring the bell to summon artificial aid.

The successor to J. W. arrived on April 12th (a B.O.C. Beaver ventilator), whom Hilary immediately christened Eager Beaver. She liked him at once, in spite of the fact that he sounded like a constantly boiling kettle. He was a comfortable fellow, small, compact, and very charming; easy to open and had no expiratory pipe, just a valve, so that any time she felt like breathing on her own, she could have him disconnected without fuss. So divorce proceedings started in earnest. A very dejected Jonathan William Barnet was wheeled out of the Ritz, muttering dark threats about certain people, hopefully to take up residence in the next door day room for several days, but to no avail. Hilary had finished with him (she hoped) for good. So the wedding of Miss Hilary Pole to Mr. Eager Beaver was finally solemnised on Monday, May 14th, 1962.

Eb, as she affectionately called her new husband, was gay and dynamic. He needed no separate air supply and if necessary was easy to hand-pump. Though they both had much to learn before he became a steady and reliable companion, they were happy together most of the time. Now that she had got rid of Jonathan William Barnet, she thought her anxious nights were over. Ha! Not a bit of it. Men! She was all set for a peaceful sleep one Thursday night. After the eleven thirty injection she was all ready to dispense with Eb's services for a short while when — puff! The silence was eerie. Eb had just "walked out" on her. Luckily at the moment she was feeling independent. As always, right after an injection, she could breathe on her own. But the independence was tempor-

Hilary with Ian her brother.

Feeding the ducks, 1943.

Hilary, aged 10.

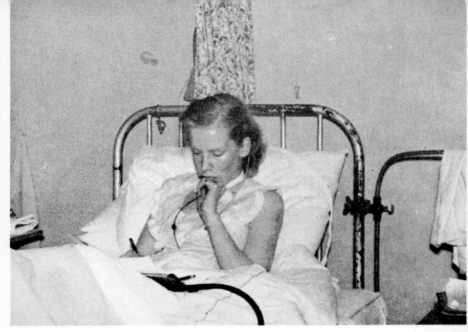

When first admitted to hospital, 1961.

Bridesmaid by proxy.

Goodbye to Hotel Elizabeth. Hilary is lifted into the ambulance supervised by Dr.S. who travelled home with her.

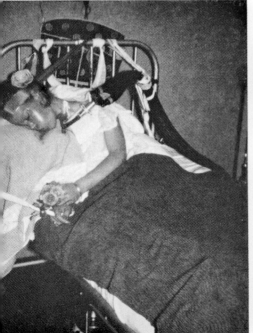

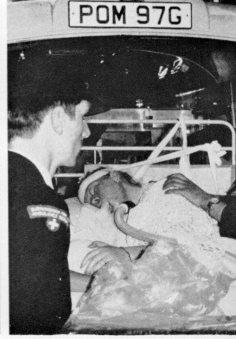

ary. She tried coaxing Eb into action. Not a murmur. She had to ring.

Night Sister made several attempts to bring life back into the old boy, then summoned the anaesthetist. Even the cajoling wheedlings of seniority had no effect. Poor Eb had a vicious heart attack. The room gradually filled with people, two night sisters, two anaesthetists, two night nurses, and a doctor.

She couldn't possibly manage a night on her own. One of the Barnet brothers was fetched from West 4. He was all right till he caught sight of poor Eb. "Phew! If she's done that to him — !" He refused to help. Several minutes and many grey hairs later in rolled Jonathan William II and she was soon merrily breathing. What a night! J. W. II was eating air at a tremendous rate, and the night porters were not too clever at finding full cylinders.

The next time Eb failed it was not his fault, nor Hilary's, though she had always been afraid of thunderstorms. At the first darkening of the sky her head would begin to ache and as the preliminary rolls echoed round, her stomach would turn to water. She felt almost as sick as at the prospect of going to the dentist. Thursday, May 3rd, was no exception. Neither was her nurse a heroine. At the first flash Dot giggled helplessly and admitted she hated storms. They exchanged gruesome reminiscences and were desperately vying for supremacy when Mum walked in. More lightning, more stories, more laughter. Hilary whipped off her copper friendship ring. At seven forty, with forced gaiety and some chitchat about the attraction of cutlery for lightning, Dot departed for supper.

"Hope it gets your spoon," Hilary jabbed on the sheet.

At seven forty-five it happened. A flash, a crash that defied description, and the lights went out. Then realisation dawned. Eb — no batteries! Panic? Never. Cool, calm, and disconnected, Hilary rapped out terse instructions to Mum on the sheet. There was still enough light outside to see dimly. "Screw out, pump bellows." Mum jumped to attention, and a moment later with a mighty whoosh a current of air that could have launched a space module surged into Hilary's lungs. Luckily a passing staff nurse came to the rescue and set Eb on his proper rhythm. At first Mum had to glue her eyes on Hilary's time-beat. Up, down. One, two, three. Up, down. Then, the beat firmly in her head, she could concentrate on the pressure dial, muttering the count to herself. But it's humanly impossible to pump a ventilator to a definite rhythm, eyes straining to read a tiny dial in the dim light, AND read letters on a sheet. Conversation was limited.

As her chest rumbled threateningly, the shadow at the back of Hilary's mind took grim shape : no power, no sucker. Someone was dispatched to East Ground A to borrow the foot-pump contraption used in "Operation Wedlock", and Mum tackled the job of running Eb and Sucker simultaneously. Try to jerk your foot vigorously up and down on a pump pedal and at the same time smoothly and gently twist a catheter down a tracheotomy tube. Either the catheter will go down beautifully with no suction or waggle up and down half an inch inside the tube, with enough suction to water a herd of elephants! Add to the confusion the contortions of a patient who, suddenly seeing the funny side of the whole fiasco, was shaking the bed with her silent hysterics like an aspen shaken by a whirlwind!

A torch finally appeared and was set on the locker, while Nurse groped to the table to prepare the long-overdue feed. As the torch's glimmer of light was needed to illuminate the pressure dial, she had to fumble in the dark for the Complan. Her hands fell on the right box. The feed was completed without mishap, except for a soggy drip of Complan down the patient's neck. Then, exactly an hour after the plunge into darkness, came the sudden burst of light. Like the world of Sleeping Beauty, all sprang into life. Eb bubbled again under his own steam, the sucker roared like an army of pneumatic drills, and everyone sighed with vast relief. Later Hilary recorded the incident under the title, "Calamity Fair".

Strange how even a journey outside the four walls of the Ritz could assume the magnitude of a great adventure! Like "Exodus for Spring Cleaning". E2B had to be emptied by Friday. Demolition started on Wednesday evening when Mum and Dad arrived with a myriad of boxes, into which disappeared beer mats, china and wooden ornaments, pictures, nail varnishes, tins of food, spare toilet requisites, books, papers. The room looked more like the blitz than the Ritz. By lunchtime on Friday Hilary was the only patient left in E2B. They left her long enough to hear the dedication service of Coventry Cathedral on the radio. She heard Richard Dimbleby describe the arrival of the Queen at the new-old cathedral.

(Did she really remember that night of its burning in 1940, or had others' accounts created that seeming memory of a frightening lurid glow against the sky?) She listened with an artist's appreciation to the commentator's description of the new edifice combined so skilfully with the ruins of the ancient : the ineffable colours of the John Piper window, the huge magnificence of Graham Sutherland's controversial tapestry, the wrought-iron crown of thorns, the stark simplicity of the font (a boulder hewn from a hillside in Bethlehem), and finally the solemn service of consecration. How soon would she be able to see it, she wondered, and would she like it? She admired modern architecture, yet she loved old churches, especially small ones, like St. Kenelm's, Llangennith, Dunster. Yes, she had a split personality where tradition was concerned. Easter and Christmas wouldn't be the same without the old traditional hymns and ceremonies. Neither would Harvest Festival, Remembrance Sunday, weddings, coronations, investitures. Yet she was an ardent believer in Church unity. She had visited many churches, Methodist, Catholic, Baptist. She was a keen student of other faiths, Jewish, Muslim, Hindu. She liked the cadences of Bible English, yet she was entirely in agreement with bringing services, hymns, Bible up to date for better understanding. Yes, she knew she would like Coventry Cathedral, with its strange and symbolic marriage of ancient and modern, tradition and surrealism. She couldn't wait to see it.

As the Archbishop of Canterbury's sermon ended, nurse unobtrusively gave her an injection. The radio was switched off. She was transferred to a wheelchair and pushed to her temporary abode, Eb meekly following. The new room seemed like a foreign land, smaller but pleasant, with a large French window and yellow counterpane and cloths, a welcome change from her native green.

The following Sunday was her birthday. On Saturday Sister Gordon brought a huge pile of post, but, despite temptation, nothing was opened until Sunday morning. Barely. At twelve fifteen a.m. her night nurse, Barbara, attacked the pile with gusto. Sister Wyles popped in to say "Happy birthday" and bring a lovely "witch" carving. She was "jabbed" awake at ten thirty a.m. and was all glamoured and on her chaise longue when the door burst open, propelled by a sandy creature that bounced to her lap to deliver a wet kiss, sedately followed by Chiaro. Then a wonderful surprise! Not only Mum and Dad, but Nan Nan and Grom and Wendy! More presents, more visitors, more laughter. Sister and Julie came from E2B with a gorgeous nylon nightdress from the staff. Ian and his digs mate popped in. Into the midst of the chaos walked Matron, who promised that Hilary would be home for her next birthday and fell in love with the blue-eyed Satan lying on her bed. Hilary rested in the afternoon, while Aunty Betty pinned up all her cards and arranged her presents for "Lord Noonie Snowdon" to photograph.

Having Wendy there was one of the highlights of the day, a rare surprise, for in recent months their meetings had been few. In July, 1961 Wendy had finished at the Joseph Leckie School, near the new home in Walsall, where she had won a prize for being "the pupil who has given the best service to the school". Domestic arts had finally won over horticulture, and, after working for several months as a student teacher at the Croft Street Secondary School, she had entered the Ilkley College of Housecraft in January. Hilary envied her the glorious locale of the college — right on the edge of the wild, beautiful, windswept Ilkley Moor in West Riding of Yorkshire! She even greeted her by spelling on the sheet the famous song:

> Where has tha' bin since I saw thee
> On Ilkley Moor baht'at . . .

Gaily Wendy returned the appropriate line, "I've bin a courting Mary Jane . . ." and they enjoyed a wonderful tête-à tête, Hilary listening eagerly as Wendy described the fascinating courses which the college offered — home economics, flower arranging, dress-designing, interior decorating. Wendy needed no course in personal charm, thought Hilary, though college had given her poise and maturity. As always, her clothes were dressmaker-smart, blonde hair smooth and shining, make-up faultless. All this, plus a sweetness of disposition which the more tempestuous Hilary had always envied! No wonder young Peter Dunn, who lived a few houses further up Fallowfield Road from West Riding, had developed more than a friendly interest since their first meeting in 1958! Of course — a Wendy must have a Peter. He was attending Hull University and, like Wendy, planned to become a teacher.

While Hilary's temporary quarters were the scene of all this excitement, E2B was undergoing a thorough metamorphosis: beds stripped, mattresses and pillows piled on trolleys and carted off for stoving, lockers collected, curtains down. Sister, in charge of operations, a slave-driver in gown and red gloves, set her squad scraping, scrubbing, polishing. Six days after Hilary's exodus came repatriation. She was almost sorry to leave her temporary quarters. There was a beautiful balcony outside the French windows, and she had put crumbs out for the birds, gaining a regular family of sparrows and two pigeons that she christened Bert (the grey) and Gert (the brown). Once there had even been a pied-wagtail. So lovely to see one again!

The sucker, Eb, and the drug table went first. Then she was bundled out of bed into a wheelchair and trundled along the corridor. Surprise! Instead of entering the Ritz the chair swerved to the right, and again she was in a balcony room. She did not even grimace when the physiotherapist walked in and started her excruciating punishment. To add to the perfection of homecoming, the time was eleven-thirty a.m., and the first ball of the 1962 Test match, Pakistan v. England, was being bowled at Edgbaston as she tuned in the radio.

The balcony offered untold possibilities. Soon Dad struggled upstairs with a table-box and two cardboard boxes full of soil. She had a garden! Aunty and Noonie brought plants — geranium, dwarf fuschias, French marigolds, trailing nasturtiums. Dad became official gardener. Bert and Gert followed her to her new room, so did the sparrows. She spent hours watching "her" birds. Nurses were forever robbing the kitchen of slices of bread, and the balcony got very messy. More work for Dad! Clad in a bed-pan gown, armed with mops, pail, dustpan and brush, he offered onlookers a weekly half hour of merriment.

Three hot days in June beguiled her to the balcony. After the eleven thirty a.m. injection she was settled on the chaise longue and dragged out with Eb — bless his sleek compact form! — for an afternoon of sun-worshipping. Needless to say, the acquisition of a lovely bucket-shaped sun hat in orange and white straw, a pair of Grace Kelly sun glasses, a tin of Elizabeth Arden's protective spray, and a pretty wrap to cover her legs, meant one thing only — the sun went into hibernation for many weeks.

No matter. Wimbledon fortnight and the second Test match were due. A television set was hired, and the nurses spent ages trying to arrange her pillows so she could watch. Then it was discovered that with the pillows arranged normally (for her) a Cassell's French Dictionary wrapped in cotton wool propping her head up, and the television on the floor, she could see everything — cricket, tennis, horse jumping. She had it on one night at twelve thirty-five a.m. to watch the first Telstar attempts, and she even saw the Duke of Kent's wedding. It was near injection time and her eyelids were heavy, but a physiotherapist stood behind her and held her eyes open.

But it was sport, especially tennis and cricket, which interested her most. She became just as excited and just as frustrated, as if she were actually at Edgbaston or Wimbledon. "Cricket was dull," she wrote in her diary in July. "RAIN. England was 16 for 1 when rain stopped play ... England still batting. Getting far too big a score. Pity!" Perhaps some of this frustration was already crystallising into the words of a poem she was to write later.

THE MAGIC GAME

Cricket is a magic game which excites
The god of rain,
Who, banishing the cowardly sun,
Comes along to watch the fun.
At first
He drops a gentle shower,
Then releases all his power.

Torrential rain, a howling gale,
Thunder, lightning, even hail!
But suddenly
The god seems bored, and calling off
His demon horde, allows the match to start
Once more;
The batsman settles down to score.

Eagerly they try to please, but soon the god again
Must tease.
This time he robs them of their sight.
The commentator sighs,
"Bad light!"

Trooping off the field again, disconsolate,
Unhappy men, to stand
Frustrated at the bar, discussing
How they've done so far.

But being a philosophic race,
They understand the odds they face,
And smilingly
They drown their sorrow.
There may be time for play —
Tomorrow .

5

The balcony room was temporary, a summer holiday resort.
Presently she was back in the Ritz again, cosily enclosed in
her four-walled cocoon, a recumbent creature waiting as
patiently for rebirth into the world of glorious MOTION as
a butterfly.

Not that life for Hilary Pole could ever assume the
boundaries of four walls! The world came to her — through
television and radio, through books read in snatches by the
nurses, through letters and cards and parcels, but, most of all,
through people.

She was as deeply involved with the family as ever, more so,
for she could immerse herself in the concerns of others without the diverting absorption in personal activities. She followed
Wendy's first year at Ilkley with as much zest as she had
tackled her own study at the I. M. Marsh College, watched
with approval the developing romance with Peter Dunn, went
with her in fancy on a summer holiday in Holland and Denmark
(it inspired her to write an account of her own holiday in
Corsica, with Mum's help), and welcomed her back with as
much excitement as if she had taken the trip herself.

"Wendy and Peter came. She's put on weight. And the
things she brought! Clogs from Holland, a gorgeous butterfly
in Brussels lace, and a little angel from Denmark!"

She rejoiced in the triumph of Ian's graduation in Civil
Engineering from Birmingham University, where he took second

class honours. She was as proud of his half-blue in rugby as of any athletic honour she had won at college. "Ian has his Costain's job in London," she noted in April. "The one he wanted. So glad!"

She studied with dispassionate and appraising eyes Ian's attachment to Val, his romantic interest all through university, and a frequent visitor to the hospital. Val was lovely, gay, elegant in appearance, a skilled musician and linguist, a perfect complement to Ian's six-foot rugged leanness and scientific brilliance. They made a handsome couple. And Val shared his love of the outdoor life and sports, had been hockey captain in university and was much like Hilary in energy and temperament. (Too much? It was a wife Ian wanted, not another sister.) They seemed perfectly matched, yet — Hilary sensed rather than observed that in their fine relationship there was something missing. She was not surprised when, with Ian in London and Val in Sheffield, they slowly drifted apart.

She was as interested a participant in the lives of her college friends as when they had chattered half the night on the top floor of Barkhill. When Bunty was married to John, she was bridesmaid by proxy. Her bouquet was sent from Blackpool by train and Dad picked it up at the station. "Letter from Bunty and John," her diary recorded. "They are settled in their new home." . . . On April 24th Janet (Skilly) married Peter Shaw, an England basketball player, lecturer in Physical Education at Loughborough Teacher Training College. (Another Peter!) "At three forty-five p.m. in walked Janet and Peter all ready in their going away clothes! Jan brought me her bouquet, white carnations and lilies of the valley. She had on a lovely red hat." . . . She was delighted to hear that *Anne Tsoi-a-Sue*, one of her college "daughters", was expecting a baby in July. "Thrilled to bits about my prospective 'grandchild'." And when photos of the baby finally arrived, "I'm getting quite a family by proxy. So far all boys. High time I had a 'daughter'!"

She was by no means immune to ideas of romance for herself, as she once confided to her diary. "J— came. I'm afraid I'm heading for trouble in that direction. He's beginning to mean too much to me. That's a big menace with this. Physically I look a total wreck, my face really is dreadful, but emotionally there is no dullness at all. Quite honestly I can't ever see anyone wanting to marry someone in my condition, that's the worst part. I'd love a family of my own. Oh, well, not to worry."

Students came from I. M. Marsh with news and photos of the new buildings. One was named Judy. ("She sleeps in my bed at Holmfield!") Jan Walker, a pupil at Edward Shelley, came to visit Hilary. "She could read my fingers extremely well. So lovely and happy. We chattered away about everything under the sun."

Yes, the world came to her, as it had always come — relatives, friends, shopkeepers, porters, fellow travellers — and now nurses, orderlies, residents, other patients. What was it about her that invited confidences, the unbaring of emotions, the sharing of problems? Whatever it was, she had always had it, perhaps by inheritance, for Nan Nan and Grandad had possessed the same magnetic power of drawing strangers' confidences. Call it response to lively interest and curiosity? Call it recognition of an indomitable spirit that gave evidence of ability to cope? Better, call it empathy, for she was somehow attuned to the needs of other people.

Curiously, her elders often came to her for advice. Aunty Betty and Noonie would consult her about opportunities offered in the teaching profession, sensing that she possessed an astute knowledge of their capabilities coupled with rare common sense. "That's not the right job for you, Noonie," she was to say once without equivocation. "It's the thing for you to do," she was to tell Aunty Betty when the latter was debating the wisdom of taking a diploma course in education in London.

Nurses were always people to Hilary, with names — Jane, Judy, Julie, Pat, Mary, Miriam — never professional automatons. She was interested in all that concerned them, new clothes, romances, tiffs, what they did in their off duty time. She knew what went on in the hospital better than many of the staff. A nurse might rush into Hilary's room with a red-hot bit of gossip, and she would be much amused because she had heard it days ago. In fact, she congratulated herself on having helped promote some of the romances.

"Nurse Cousins came up," her diary noted. "John Cookson proposed on Thursday and she said 'yes'. My marriage bureau is working very well . . . Pat woke me. She's walking on air about Alan, so I'll keep my fingers crossed and hope it works out all right . . . Nurse Jones is going to London to see her boy friend, a painter just beginning to be recognised. I must watch for his work . . . Letter from Dot Morgan. It's all definitely off between her and D. Pity! I know just how she must feel."

Not that Hilary was an easy patient! "When one first had dealings with Hil," one nurse commented, "she certainly was not always popular. However, as you gradually got to know her and realised she was a person with a definite outlook on life and a rare sense of humour, you became her admiring friend. If any of us had problems, we knew we could go to Hil for a perfectly unbiased opinion. She was always ready to listen."

Though almost ruthlessly demanding when she felt her safety was at stake, at all other times she was patience and thoughtfulness personified. The continual salivation attendant on the disease was doubtless disagreeable but not dangerous. To make her more comfortable she had a mackintosh, covered with a towel, on her top pillow. Once when a nurse was busy tidying the room, she looked round to find a large pool of saliva on the towel. "Why didn't you ring your bell and I would have sucked it up for you?" she reproached. As she hastened to apply the electric sucker, she was struck anew by what must be her patient's constant discomfort. "Dear me, Hil," she blurted, "don't you get tired of your mouth being continually wet?"

Hilary's beautifully shaped and lacquered nail flew across the sheet. "Better," it spelled out, "than being continually dry."

Another nurse once saw a fly settling down for a good old scratch on Hilary's nose. Luckily she was there to shoo it off. "What do you do if there's nobody here?" she asked curiously. The answer came. "Oh, just a case of mind over matter."

Her humour was swift and pungent. "Will you miss me terribly?" chaffed one of the nurses who was leaving for the weekend. "Like arsenic!" was Hilary's quick response.

"Might have been doing the twist," she scrawled when one of the nurses was trying to straighten her nightdress. "Should have sat that one out."

Jane Cox was one of the nurses who at first found Hilary difficult. They were not on the same wavelength. In the first few weeks she had to keep putting herself in the patient's place. "Hasn't she a right to be difficult?" she asked herself. "Wouldn't I be much worse?" But as days and weeks passed, she realised that Hilary's brain was so active it made up for most of her disability. Her admiration grew. Jane became quite adept at "putting Hilary back", adjusting her in a comfortable position on her pillows after a blanket bath, sucking her out, restoring her to Eb, but she was not skilful in taking the lead. One day she was the only person on the ward who understood Hilary's case and she had to "put her back" with a new nurse to help. Everything went wrong. Jane was soon making bitter comments and Hilary was jabbing terse accusations on the sheet. They were both in tears when the work was finished and Jane left, ashamed to leave her patient looking so uncomfortable, yet vowing never to go back into the room again. When Hilary sent for her soon and apologised, she was even more ashamed, knowing that her own. incompetence had caused their quarrel. But the incident drew her even closer to Hilary.

"We never felt it was a ward with a patient," she remembered, "but a family group talking with a friend. Hilary's father once told me that they liked to feel Hil was living in a flat of her own, and they were calling to visit her."

The room was a small oasis of homelike comfort in the desert of hospital sterility. April Townsend, who was wheeled into Hilary's room one day in June with severe polyneuritis, found it so. Feeling strange and frightened, she was cheered by a hand flapping upward in encouraging welcome. The small room's décor was startling but as friendly as its occupant — postcards all over one wall, flowers, plants, books, wooden figures — you name it, she had it. They conversed in a strange fashion, April taking a gasp and talking until her breath was gone, Hilary writing the reply on her sheet and a nurse reading it, often convulsed with laughter, as when she interpreted, "Tell April she has the wrong idea. In a place like this there's no need to make up her face. She'd be more noticed if she made up her bottom!" When April said something funny, she would see the foot end of the other bed shake with Hilary's silent laughter. When she recovered sufficiently to sit up, she would talk Hilary to sleep, relaying the news of what happened outside the window. After her own visitors were gone, she would listen to Eric or Noonie reading the stories of Monsieur Hulot and his holiday, or learn to appreciate Beethoven on the tape recorder, and revel in the peaceful climate of a happy family.

"On my first morning at breakfast," remembered another room-mate, "I had no egg, but immediately Hilary gave me one of hers, which, she said, came from hens in the country. I felt touched by her thoughtfulness."

She learned to read the sheet writing and they chatted together gaily, for both were fond of joking. After being told a story of her room-mate's husband, who had done a ballet dance in his long underpants, Hilary dubbed him Panton. "And you must be Yellow Bird," she decided. "After all, don't you have jaundice?" Panton and Yellow Bird they would remain, during a friendship which has lasted more than a decade.

It was from talk of the nurses that Hilary learned about another patient on E2B, Clifford Medhurst.

"You should hear him," they grumbled. "Too bad his voice box isn't paralysed like the rest of his body. He certainly makes that work overtime."

"What's the matter with him?" Hilary wanted to know.

"Polyneuritis. He's heard about you and thinks his trouble is much like yours."

It was not, Hilary well knew. Myasthenia could only be controlled. Polyneuritis could be cured. "I must go and see him," she decided.

Immediately after an injection, when she could transfer for a few minutes to a wheelchair — the precious time she usually spent writing — she had herself wheeled to his bedside in the main ward. Cliff stopped bemoaning his lot and regarded his visitor with interest. He saw a blonde young woman who must once have been very attractive, head propped on one hand, elbow resting on the chair arm, eyelids heavy and drooping, a bright scarf wound about her neck, as he soon learned, to hide the tracheotomy tube. Her golden hair was swept to the top of her head and tied with a bright ribbon to match her nightdress. He watched with fascination as a lacquered and perfectly manicured fingernail made strange gyrations on her blanket.

"She says," translated the accompanying nurse, "that it's a beautiful day and she is glad to see you looking so well."

There were more of such visits. Cliff was at first unimpressed and a bit resentful. Trying to boost his morale, was she, this woman who could sit in a wheelchair while he lay paralysed flat on his back? But as he came to realise the seriousness of her condition, he became another of her sincere admirers. Largely because of her unselfish concern and her stubborn determination to live, he emerged from despondency and began to fight his own comparatively minor misfortune. During the many months that he was in the hospital Hilary reached a stage where the drug became less and less effective, and she was unable to leave her room in a wheelchair for such visits, but they maintained contact through messages via the nurses, swapping notes, small gifts, flowers.

"Six absolutely gorgeous roses from Cliff," wrote Hilary one day in 1962.

The day came when he could sit in a wheelchair, and his first request was a visit to Hilary's room. Progressively he visited her on crutches, finally on sticks. He became adept at reading her finger writing and they conversed at length about cricket, a subject of passionate and mutual interest. Then he was transferred to another hospital with better physiotherapy facilities. But the friendship with both him and his wife continued.

"Anne Medhurst came," wrote Hilary after he had left. "Cliff's wonderful. Only using one stick to walk with. Even strikes his own matches!"

6

It was cricket that brought many of the hospital staff into her room at odd times. When Test matches were in progress, her radio and television were never off. Nurses would creep about talking in whispers and doctors would come in to ask, not "How is the patient?" but "What's the score?" Orderlies and porters would find errands in her room when sporting events were scheduled. One of these was Khalil, a young Pakistani acting as an X-ray porter on E2B in 1962.

At first he was timid and tongue-tied, knowing little English and more fascinated by the awesome puffings and clonkings of the ventilator than by radio or television. Then, "Hello," he began to greet her shyly, and gradually he learned to read some simple finger writing. She asked Mum and Dad to bring some English language books from home and began teaching him English. Like many Pakistanis, he was an ardent cricket fan. He would come to her room during his lunch hour, sit cross-legged on the floor and watch the matches. He was quick to learn the alphabet method of communication, and sometimes the sister would use him to help her converse by bell with

Hilary. "Ah, be, cee," he would pronounce carefully, proceeding until the little bell tinkled.

He soon adopted himself into the family, calling the Poles "Mum" and "Dad" with great possessive enjoyment and filial affection. "Hello, Mum, hello Dad," he would shout when he saw their car across the car park, somewhat to their embarrassment. But they were as interested in his exuberant outpouring of confidences as Hilary, learned all about his family at home — his mother and father, who was a tailor, his five brothers and married sister, his promised wife Zarina — and his dream of earning enough to bring them to England.

When Wendy was admitted to ward West 5 of Queen Elizabeth Hospital during one of her college holidays for an appendectomy, it was Khalil who acted as delighted "go-between".

"She can't talk, cough, move, or laugh," he reported gleefully after the surgery, "but she is doing very well and sends her love to you."

Khalil was only one of Hilary's many human concerns. Though energy flagged often during that year of 1962, her mind was superactive. In February she began planning a holiday for her parents (the first in three years, a twenty-fifth wedding anniversary present). She and Aunty Betty decided on Alfriston in Sussex. Noonie began scenting out the best hotels. Less than three weeks later a room was booked for the Poles at "The Star Inn", August 21st to September 1st, morning tea and coffee after meals included.

July 28th. "Have to tell Mum and Dad about their week in Alfriston." . . . July 31st. "Told Mum and Dad about their holiday. They were a bit overwhelmed at first."

All went smoothly, Noonie and Aunty substituting for Mum and Dad at the hospital. But there were more surprises to come. Ian, before starting his job with Costain's, planned to go on holiday with nine other university graduates. They would drive across Europe to Greece in a second-hand army lorry which they had bought and put in superb condition. Wendy also was going to Europe with Peter and his family. Before they left, plans had been discussed for an anniversary party. By the time Wendy returned Hilary had sent out forty invitations, rushed a letter to Uncle Aubrey, Mum's only brother, in Australia asking him to propose a toast on tape, and one to Ian in Trieste telling him to ring up and reverse charges, even giving him the French for "Please reverse call". Then she had another daring idea. She tackled the houseman. She approached Uncle Michael. She contacted the St. John's Ambulance man. Every move turned up trumps. *She was going to be there herself!*

There was excitement at Hotel Elizabeth. They had planned a small party in Hilary's room on Tuesday, September 4th, ostensibly to celebrate the anniversary. Nurse Porter came in at four p.m. and started to move furniture. All the nursing paraphernalia was hidden under the bed and in lockers. Wendy and Peter staggered in at six o'clock. Fruit was put into bowls, cream whipped, glasses arranged, their combined present (a stainless steel carving dish) wrapped. Aunty and Noonie arrived next, then the happy couple with Nan Nan. The highlight of the party was Dad's opening a bottle of champagne which Wendy had brought from Holland. The cork hit the ceiling with a mighty pop. Hilary joined in the fun by taking a few spoonfuls down her tube. But the pièce de résistance was still to come. Preparations for her outing were Herculean.

It could not have been managed without Derek, who assumed charge of the expedition. Dr. Derek Sampson was houseman on the team of Hilary's consultant, therefore one of her attending doctors. Gay, always cheerful, he had soon become friend as well as an exceedingly competent medical adviser. "Do you think you could do without sparine?" he had once asked her. "Yes," she had agreed hopefully, always wary of sedatives. With the consent of the consultant he had removed it from her drug sheet, with beneficial results.

Not only clever but seriously committed to his work, Derek inspired confidence in his patients by his relaxed and easy manner. His pretty, petite fiancée Elise, a dental surgeon, had also become Hilary's friend. They were to be married in another couple of weeks, and, oh, how Hilary wished she could go to the wedding! "A super couple," she rated them.

The team rehearsed the whole drama on Wednesday. Julie came in at four p.m., laid out clothes, feeds and ampoules, fetched a wheelchair. At five fifteen everything started. Hilary had her injection and dressed, finding to her delight that a pair of beige courtelle slacks and a yellow blouse brought by Wendy fitted. Julie and Anne Smith, who had also been roped in, lifted her into the wheelchair, and she was trundled to the lift, then returned to bed. While Julie dutifully hand-pumped Eb, Hilary kept her in time with the bell. This represented the journey home. Having arrived, so to speak, and had her injection, she had her hair washed during the time she would spend at home. Again to the lift and back, and the rehearsal was completed.

The tape from Australia arrived on Thursday. Hilary had written to Grom in Sheffield. Dad was supposed to be fetching her on Friday night as a surprise for Hilary, so when Mum arrived alone, glibly saying, "Dad needs the car for business," Hilary had silent hysterics. Grom was ready and waiting and hopped into the car like a two-year-old. Later while Hilary slept, Dot Morgan, her night nurse, made a trachy cover, an oval of velvet with a hole in the centre and ribbon at either side, to hide the untidy rubber tube.

Wendy got Mum and Dad away for the whole of Saturday morning and lunch. There was a new elegant hair salon near Aunty Betty's in Bromsgrove. Mum would have her hair done there at nine thirty, meet Dad for coffee, then they would go to Betty's for lunch. They arrived back at West Riding in mid-afternoon to find the tables beautifully set and the guests arriving. It was a perfect surprise — with more to come. Nonchalantly Noonie announced that he was going to the hospital and no one was to leave. He would phone Hilary's message from there. Many people had to move their cars to let him drive Ookie out, then complied with the huge sign which Aunty had pinned on the pear tree : "Visitors please park cars in side road to keep drive clear."

Since five thirty a.m. the Ritz had been a hive of activity : blanket bath at five thirty, injection at nine. Nurse Wootton assembled the props : sterile receivers, catheters, drugs, syringes, spare trachy. Julie arrived at twelve o'clock, Noonie at five fifteen p.m., just as a dose of prostigmine was being shot into the patient. He began loading the car. Hilary had a bumper feed of Complan plus an egg, a thorough suck out, Ryles tube up, etc. Then — near disaster. She had spent so much energy getting dressed that Julie had to shout for an orderly to help lift her into the wheelchair. At six fifteen p.m. the ambulance men arrived. At Casualty Entrance she was lifted on to a stretcher, wrapped in a pink blanket and hoisted into the ambulance. Derek and Julie literally squeezed in beside Eb. The other nurses and Elise went in Ookie. Swiftly Julie attached Hilary to the ventilator, and with a few creaks, groans, and manoeuvring of feet, arms, and knees, the hand-pumped ventilator puffed into action. They were away. Next stop — *home*!

Hearing the commotion, Mum and Dad appeared, first bewildered, then speechless with delight. The ambulance men carried Hilary halfway to the porch before the truth dawned. Stretchers do not bend. She was marooned outside her own house. However, they marched her round to the back of the house and in through the French window, then set her in a chaise longue. Chiaro hopped on her knees. Shandy bellowed from upstairs. Two minutes later he was there, a seething wriggling mass of red fur.

A glass of champagne appeared in all hands, and Uncle Aubrey's voice boomed over the tape, followed by Aunty Madelaine's and their three children's. Uncle gave his toast. Hilary managed a sip of champagne and puffed gleefully at a cigarette perched jauntily inside her trachy tube. The large three-tiered cake was brought in, with gay shouts the anniversary couple cut the first slice; then laughs as Noonie and Aunty cut the top tier, plain sponge for Noonie, who always refused to eat currants.

It soon ended. Like Cinderella, Hilary was lifted on to the stretcher, into the pink blanket, jogged through the back garden and hoisted into her waiting pumpkin. Shouts and waves, and the ambulance bell clanging! At eight forty p.m. she was back in bed, no more tired than after climbing Snowdon and even more triumphant.

Only forty minutes, yet a sip of champagne contains the same effervescent zest as a full goblet. She could imagine the rest — the telephone call (it came five minutes after she had left!) "Please, will you accept a reverse charge call from Venice?" then Ian's "Hello there!", forging the final link with the family; some of the sixty or more guests staying till the early hours of the morning.

Thanks to her loyal cohorts, Hilary had another zestful sip in November when she went home on the Saturday following Guy Fawkes day. There were fireworks, a bonfire, baked potatoes, chestnuts. Ian, back from his European trip, hair bleached and skin bronzed, was his usual chaffing self, sparing no punches. "Hiya, Hil. Looking rather pale, aren't you? Want me to rub some of my tan off on you?" He had brought her some beautiful shells that he had dived for in Cyprus. After her injection at six thirty p.m. she was able to sit up and look round; then Wendy poured a glass of gorgeous Cypriot wine down her throat.

"Fabulous day!" Hilary's diary recorded. Even the death of Grom a little over a week before did not dampen their enjoyment too much. She had died suddenly, with her usual direct approach, just as she would have wished.

"These outings were very exhausting for us all," remembered one of the nurses involved, "and they took much organising, most of it done by Hil. But for her sake they were abundantly worth it."

Yet these brief sorties, though pleasant, did not signify improvement in her condition. No one knew this better than Hilary herself. She studied her own case dispassionately, keeping careful records of each stage of her illness, anxious to provide knowledge which might benefit future myasthenics, for all — doctors, nurses, patient — were more or less groping in the dark. She knew, even better than the doctors, that she had passed the point of no return. Other myasthenics might be able to control the disease on a proper balance of drugs. Not she. Already it had gone too far.

"Dreadfully floppy," she recorded one day in December. "Have to write odds and ends whenever possible." They were almost the last words she was ever to write in a diary.

Curiously, the knowledge did not bring depression or resentment. She was too busy making sure that she stayed alive, preventing foolish mistakes by nurses, yes, even by doctors, to take time for useless emotion. Besides, there were too many things to plan and do. The worst danger was apathy. She would resist it with all the vigour of a stubborn, indomitable will. Moreover, she knew that she was indescribably lucky. She had a love of music and of being read to and of people. She had been given a good education, with a knowledge of the body, its functions and its needs, which could help her understand her condition. She had shining memories of the past and no fear of the future. Best of all, perhaps, she had an irrepressible sense of humour. In other words, whatever happened, she would be able to *cope*.

7

"The Warwickshire County Cricket Club have made special arrangements for an invalid woman to watch the third Test match. She is Miss Hilary Pole . . ."

Hilary, along with excited nurses, heard the announcement over the B.B.C. Midland News at eight fourteen a.m. on Thursday, July 4th, 1963, and realised it was actually true. *She was going to see a Test match.* Further proof came ten minutes later when Khalil burst in wildly waving the *Birmingham Post.*

"Here, Hil, your name's in the paper!" Sure enough it was: "Girl will see Test from Iron Lung." Iron lung, indeed! Poor Eb was looking most disgusted. Throughout the morning people brought her more papers with varying headlines. Some had her *in* a respirator, some in an iron lung, some with a muscular disease, and without exception all had her paralysed. (She was *on* a ventilator, not *in* a respirator. Eb was not an iron lung. Myasthenia was not a muscular disease but a failure in the connection between the nerve endings and the muscle fibres. And, since there was no damage to the nerves or muscles, except some flaccidity of the latter due to lack of exercise, she was not truly paralysed.)

But they had one thing right: her lifelong passion for cricket. The present excitement all started the previous summer during the match between England and Australia, when she spent her early morning being blanket-bathed to a background of squeaks, fizzles, and cracks from a protesting radio. When the last battle for the Ashes was on, Khalil came early and from seven a.m. sat glued to the radio, helping Hilary fill in her home-made score card. She was both disappointed and disgusted with the unsporting attitude of the Australian batsmen and had never been so bored.

"When the Test match is at Edgbaston," she vowed, "sometime, somehow, I'm going to get there to see it!"

There was irony in the rash avowal. She had always been in the right place at the wrong time, in Liverpool when the test was at Edgbaston, at home when it was played at Old Trafford.

"*Achcha*! Good!" agreed Khalil. She recognised the exclamation, for he had been teaching her some Urdu. "I will push the bed, and Mr. Khan will push Eb."

It was a vain boast, of course, just a dream. But a year later Mr. Sanderson, captain of her St. John ambulance team and his crew came in one evening to see her, and of course the talk drifted to cricket and the impending Test match.

"We're on duty at the Test match," said Mr. Sanderson suddenly. "How would you like to go with us?"

Would she! Immediately her mind started clicking. The old "excursion gang" was now scattered, Derek to the neurological depths of East Lower Ground and Julie to the Midland Nerve Hospital. However, Derek popped in two minutes later and enthusiastically agreed to co-operate. Sister was approached, and the following week the now shock-proof "Uncle Michael" gave his permission. Meanwhile Dad rang up an old cricket friend, Cyril Goodway, then vice-chairman of the Warwickshire County Cricket Club and chairman of the Ground and Buildings sub-Committee. He was enthusiastic and suggested it be mentioned to Professor d'Abreu, Medical Officer for the Club. What a coincidence! He was the surgeon who had done Hilary's thymectomy in 1960! He said, "Yes, by all means," and came to see her.

Newspapers sprouted headlines. "Paralysed, but she will see Test." . . . "Six people, including a doctor and nurse, will give up their Saturday afternoon so that a paralysed woman can see the Test match." . . . "The bravest member of the public at the Test match between England and the West Indies will be Miss Hilary Pole, daughter of a former cricketer, Eric Pole, who will arrive by ambulance."

The match started on Thursday morning, with Hall bowling Richardson when only two runs had been scored. Hilary's radio and television were both on, and several male patients came to watch. Khalil was a permanent fixture. When just after tea with a score of 157 for 5 bad light and rain stopped play, England's hope seemed as murky as the weather. Friday too was gloomy. Dodging rain and bad light, England only managed a total of 216, in spite of Brian Close's 55. Next morning hope dwindled. It had rained in the night and light was atrocious. At eleven thirty a.m. "no play at Edgbaston," though hope glimmered when it was announced that umpires hoped for play later.

Preparations went ahead. Nurse Farron collected the para-phernalia, Julia arrived to manicure nails, and Khalil gave quarter-hour weather reports. At one thirty Hilary had her injection and Mum fed her Complan and two eggs, as she had no intention of appearing in public with more tubes than necessary. Mr. Sanderson and his crew arrived. Hilary was lifted on to the stretcher and into the ambulance. Dad went ahead with Ookie, a card on the windscreen admitting bearer's car to Car Park X and a letter in his pocket for the gate attendant at Constance Road instructing him to admit car, registration number OOK 984, with ambulance in attendance and to direct the occupants to the special enclosure in front of the Thwaite scoreboard.

They turned into a "back stage" entrance and came to a halt just behind the score board. The "gang" soon had the stretcher hitched up, foot end on the fence and head end on boxes. Eb was at one side, plugged into a special external socket installed for Hilary's use but made permanent, so that any other disabled person needing power would have it available. The sucker was on the other. Professor d'Abreu came to see if she was comfortable and to offer all kinds of help. Cor! Here she was at last, seeing her first Test match!

Hunte and Carew were batting when they arrived and to her great joy Trueman was bowling at one end supported by Shackleton at the other. Carew hit a gorgeous six off Shackleton. At the score of 42 Hunte was bowled by Trueman and Kanhai came in, causing some rude *sotto voce* remarks from Cliff, seated on her right, and unfavourable remarks from Khalil as he sucked her out. Noonie was on her left telling her who was who, and she had a portable radio on her lap. They saw Carew caught and bowled by Trueman when the score was 79. After an appeal for bad light by Butcher and Kanhai they put on 29 runs before Kanhai was beautifully caught by Lock off Shackleton. As he left the field, the drizzle became heavier. She had to have an umbrella held over her head, a rubber sheet spread over the blanket.

At three thirty she had half an injection, and twenty minutes later, Butcher and Sobers having added but two runs, the players left the field. So did Hilary. She stayed in the ambulance, Derek, Julie, and Khalil manfully taking turns at the hand pump, hoping for good news, but the rain got heavier and heavier. Not all was lost. It was the first rain she had felt in two and a half years. Delicious!

A thrilling adventure! At the hospital there was a bouquet of red roses from Mrs. East. "Hilary Stays Tuned In," Monday's *Evening Mail* proclaimed. Of course she did, to every ball. Now she had a mental image of the ground, flanked by 20,000 spectators, among them colourful and vociferous West Indian supporters urging their team on, throwing their hats into the air with joy or grief. Trueman ("Fiery Fred") soon had the remaining West Indian wickets down, giving England a lead of 30 runs. Hopes began to slide again as they lost 4 wickets for 69, but Dexter and Sharpe played England back into the game with a determined stand of 101. Close of play Monday left them in the interesting position of a ninth wicket stand by Sharpe and Lock having already produced 37 runs. Would Dexter declare? The next morning, despite an all-out attack by Hall and Griffiths, Lock hit his first test 50. Still no declaration! Sharpe seemed all set for his maiden test century when Lock was bowled by Gibbs for 56.

"Declare, you fool!" Hilary ESP's frantically.

Dexter must have heard, for at 278 for 9 with four hours and forty minutes left for play, he called his batsmen in.

In the break between innings Nurse opened a parcel. It contained a ferocious looking wooden figure, face masked by an unruly mop of coarse black hair, grimly clutching a murderous battle axe and glowering so like Trueman that Hilary's bed shook with laughter. It must have been an omen, for immediately after play started the real "Fiery Fred" soon had the West Indian batsmen trooping disconsolately back to the pavilion in rapid succession. By three o'clock they were all out for 91, Trueman ending with 7 for 44. A perfect match with a perfect result!

Letters began pouring in from people who had seen Hilary on television. Apparently A.T.V. had filmed her arrival from the top of the wall by the score box! She even received a letter from a girl in British Guiana, Ann Changle. Please would she be Ann's pen friend?

There was another interesting aftermath of the episode. Later Cyril Goodway and his wife went shopping in Barbados for a gift for Hilary. Their taxi driver, realising they were English, asked if they knew Birmingham. Yes, they replied, it was their home. "Oh!" he exclaimed. "Do you know about a girl named Hilary?" He had read about her going to the cricket match. Since then he had asked every English tourist if he knew her. When he learned that they were on their way to buy a présent for her he was delightedly incredulous. Could he suggest a gift? Indeed he could — a record of real West Indian music, and he would show them where to get it. His name was Gordon, and he sent a message to Hilary. What a coincidence — smashing!

8

It was becoming harder and harder to write with a biro. Her hand refused to hold it properly. When words became impossible, she resorted to the old habit of drawing little animals. They were easier to fashion than letters, and gay little cartoons appeared in the pages of "Hotel Elizabeth". They threw the nurses into gales of laughter.

As the months passed the routine continued with few changes: six-hourly injections; five teaspoons of Complan every hour in 150 cc. of warm water, followed by 20 cc. of water to clear poor old Ryles (Food by mouth was becoming next to impossible, even the beautifully smooth and delectable shrimps!); the "put-back" on mountains of pillows; the increasingly long periods on the ventilator; but here there was a change.

Hilary thought her conjugal bliss with the streamlined and dapper Eager Beaver was for the duration (hopefully, not "until death do us part"), but no such luck! One day "Uncle Michael" came in, admired her décor of wooden animals and hundreds of beer mats, and informed her that the Beaver ventilator was not intended for constant use, only for occasional service. If on twenty-four hour duty he was inclined to over heat. Regretfully she returned to J. W., who fortunately seemed to have improved in disposition and dependability during his ostracism. Eb remained available for emergencies and the momentous sorties into the outer world. She was doomed to the life of a bigamist!

Faces under the nurses' caps changed also. There was Ro

Darlington, whom Hilary christened "Silverstreak", because she did things well and quickly. Plump, with a perfect figure that Hilary could lean against, she was so expert in the "put-back" that they dubbed her the B.B.P.P.I., Best Bottom Pillow Putter Inner. Hilary's personal hygiene was A plus when Ro was on duty. There was Roz (Rosemary), gay and volatile, who was engaged to a boy who made ceramic jewellery and who enthused over Hilary's beautiful hands and rings. Priti, an Indian girl as attractive as her name, slim and graceful, especially in the saris which she always wore off duty, was gentle and compassionate as well as competent. Like Khalil, she was soon calling Hilary's parents "Mum" and "Dad". She rarely worked on the ward with Margaret, an English pen friend with whom she had started training, but they visited Hilary together in their off-duty time. In spite of her prejudice against men in the kitchen, she eventually allowed Dad to make coffee for her but never to move away her dirty cup or wash up. She was willing to do menial jobs for a staff nurse but would stand no nonsense. Once a senior consultant with whom she was working threw something on the floor. "Pick that up, nurse," he ordered. "Oh, no, sir," she replied in her soft deep voice. "I will fetch and carry anything that you need or drop, but you threw that down, and I am not here to do that." She won the prize for being the best surgical nurse of the year and invited "Mum" and "Dad" to see her receive the medal.

Khalil continued to haunt Hilary's room in his off-duty hours, especially during cricket matches. Partly because of Hilary's encouragement he was attending technical college in the evenings and studying electrical engineering, still in the hope of bringing his family to England. In his superior knowledge of the situation he was known to correct the nurses. "Not like that! Hilary not like it like that!" During his many years of visits to Hilary's room he aired his increasing familiarity with English in lengthy discussion, if incorrect in terms.

"Oh, oh! Sorry, Mum and Dad," he apologised once when the Poles arrived. "I was just disgusting with Hilary."

His habits of pronunciation, especially the reversal of "v" and "w" were also occasionally misleading. Once, after he had been promoted to theatre attendant, he inquired of the theatre Sister, "Please Sister, what means Wee-Wee?" The embarrassed Sister finally replied, "That is what little children say when they want to use the potty." Khalil looked equally embarrassed. The Sister saw his frown as he continued to study the theatre list. Then the penny dropped. "V. V." — code for varicose veins!

An ever-growing number of visitors, many regular in attendance, relieved what for anyone but Hilary might have been monotony. The Edward Shelley staff set up a Hilary Pole fund and when any of them was in Birmingham, he would call at the hospital with flowers or some other suitable gift for Hilary. Mr. Lucas, Gladys Wilson, Roy Atkinson, Elsa Freeman, all became regular visitors.

"The first time I went I thought I would feel awkward and embarrassed," confessed Elsa Freeman, "knowing that she could not speak and realising how hard complete immobility must be for one who had so loved motion. But she put me at ease at once in a 'biro' conversation. Her first questions when I visited her were always, 'How are you and how is your mother?' Then would follow inquiries about members of the staff or concerning my own comfort. 'Would you like the window closed?' I used to come away better, refreshed after a day's teaching by her sense of humour, outward concern, lack of self pity, and sound philosophy."

Anne Smith and her husband Vic always visited on her birthday, Christmas Eve, and at other times when the duties of a growing family permitted. (Hilary had sent a card on the birth of their first daughter which said : "1 plus 1 equals 3.") Though Anne sometimes felt guilty at not coming oftener, she never heard Hilary say, "Long time no see." "I don't care when you come," Hilary told her once, "as long as you don't stop coming. It's always nice to see you." Vic was terrified when Hilary asked him to do the crossword puzzle with her. She could write out the answer, or spell it out by bell, before he had even thought of it, making him feel stupidly slow. But somehow Hilary was able to sense his anxiety and slow down.

There were new friends also, some of them patients. Olwen Strange met Eric in the kitchen when they were making the evening coffee. "Would she like me to visit her?" she asked. While in the hospital, she saw Hilary at least once a day. "Never did I feel I was with a sick person," she commented. After she left she visited her as often as possible, found her amused and interested in all her problems with her business staff. Jim Adey, in hospital for a brain operation, was asked if he would like to meet her. They established instant rapport through an interest in cricket, Hilary's favourite team being Yorkshire, Jim's Warwickshire. "She has an electronic brain," he was heard to comment.

Another new friend was the Rev. Arthur Mawson, curate of her home parish. "I believe her difficulties have been made more acute," he once observed, "by her intelligence and yet this is the very weapon she has used to devise the means of combating them."

"You didn't invite me to tea," he complained when she was being fed Complan.

"Give him some," scrawled Hilary instantly. She had a plastic shoe tidy over her bed, the kind with many pockets. In it she kept all sorts of odd articles, including bottles of beer for male patients.

The time came when she was unable to hold a biro, even for drawing animals, though she was still adept at sheet-writing. Her slender index finger with its shining oval nail, manicured each week by Aunty Betty and polished with one of her numerous varnishes, would outline letters so expertly that even new nurses, frightened and awed at first, soon learned to read them. If the finger-writing was illegible, there was always the small bell, suspended on a bandage between the bedside locker and her big toe. By ploughing through the alphabet and getting a "ding" at the right letter, a person could arrive at the intended word — usually.

At one time there was a male nurse from Ghana on the ward. Herman's command of English was faultless until it came to repeating the alphabet. Hilary would ring her bell and he would begin cheerfully in his deep rumbling voice: a, b, c, d, e, f — pause, frown, then continue — g, t, h — frown more deeply — q, r, s, v — sigh heavily, then end up with a rush — w, y, z. Often he would miss the correct letter completely.

Herman was of huge build, could almost have picked Hilary up in one hand. If things went wrong, he would always see the funny side and roar with laughter. At the time he was on duty in the ward Hilary had a very painful shoulder. Since her muscles did not hold her skeleton firmly together, her limbs became easily dislocated. Herman knew exactly what to do. His huge but gentle hands were adept at massaging away the pain. When he had finished putting her comfy he always lifted her forearms on his one hand, then with his other hand smoothed away all the wrinkles on the pillows, saying with a smile, "No wrinkles." Though his father was a chief with five wives, Herman was a firm believer in monogamy and the education of women. After finishing his general, then his psychiatric nursing training, he intended to go back and serve his people. His deficiency with the alphabet was somewhat mitigated when he and Hilary discovered a mutual knowledge of French.

The inability to write brought many new problems. No more diary entries, no more stories for "Hotel Elizabeth", no more letters to her large family of correspondents! Dependence — hardest of all trials to bear! It took long laborious hours for relatives and friends to translate into written words even such little articles as made up the text of "Hotel Elizabeth". Yet there were ideas milling about her brain clamouring to be expressed. *How?*

One answer came : *poetry.* She had never written a poem in her life. But she had painted pictures. She had conceived sequences of dance in flowing rhythm. She had lived with ears attuned to every sort of music. Now, as she lay motionless, pictures began to take shape in words, in rhythmic iambics, in flowing harmonies. She would store them up, repeating them over and over in her mind until she knew them by heart. Not difficult then to communicate them to Mum or Dad or someone else for transcription on to paper! Just a few words, yet what economy of substance, like oceans of calcite condensed into a single pearl!

Not that her creations were pearls. Often they were mere baubles of humour. But wasn't humour one of the primal instincts within her most clamouring for expression? She seized on the most mundane details of her surroundings, taking potshots at her own problems :

THE MONSTER
A noise resembling distant drums
From just across the passage comes,
Increasing as it nears my door
To thunderous, clattering, rattling roar.
It shrieks and hisses, raves and rants,
Coughs and wheezes, puffs and pants;

Convulsed with anger, mad with rage,
Defiantly hostile in its cage.
But when I say my prayers tonight
I will plead with all my might
That Biffin in his basement lair
Will stir himself, and fast repair
My injured sucker, politely mute,
And rid me of this bellowing brute.

And perhaps it was as well to poke fun at your frightening struggles with new nurses as to worry. At least, it made the nurse laugh, if you couldn't!

LEARNER'S LAMENT

Nurse come here, nurse go there,
For goodness' sake, nurse, watch that air.
Lift her head, but mind the neck,
What, not like this? Then how the heck?

Sit her forward, up the bed,
Now, nurse, remember what I said,
Shoulders first, head back last,
Steady does it, not so fast.

Twist her hips, shoulders too,
Look at list for what to do.
Even pillows, press them down,
I know that's wrong, no need to frown.

Can I lift head? Well, yes, I'll try,
What's that you said? Far too high?
Wrong again, please don't shout,
I'll push ribs, you suck out.

Oh, Hil, you cause me such concern,
I'm sure I'll never, never learn.

Some of them did learn. Some did not. Either way the apprenticeship was harassing, dangerous, often painful. But she lived through each one and usually made another lifelong friend. Not always. Some including doctors, never did understand her.

Sister Anne Scouse Smith, the nurse who had admitted her, was one who understood better than most. As she explained it, "Hilary proved to be a patient of the type that a lot of the medical profession are incapable of coming to terms with, one who needs to be consulted about her treatment, because she knows more about herself than the doctor does. At all stages one got full co-operation from Hil as long as she understood the reason for her treatment. She demanded a high standard of nursing, which I felt at all times she deserved and required, but not everyone else in the hospital felt the same, I fear. She always wanted to take an active part in her own treatment, and this didn't go down well with some."

But few could resist her humour. It was worth taking time to read her sheet-scrawls, even to labour through the alphabet, just to find out what she would say. Like the time when a humourless doctor tried to put her on a ventilator which she had tried before, unsuccessfully. Even though she could hardly breathe, she managed to scrawl the one word, "ROT!" More eloquent by far than a whole string of oaths from another patient! Her jokes were pithy, earthy, and even at times a bit indecorous, like one piece of doggerel which any nurse could appreciate and which was quoted with glee from one end of the hospital to another:

BOTTOMS

Bottoms large, bottoms small,
We poor nurses get 'em all
To rub and polish, keep 'em clean,
It's surprising what we've seen.

Bottoms fat, bottoms thin,
We poor nurses cannot win,
Fetching bedpans, changing sheets,
We perform most menial feats.

Bottoms young, bottoms old,
We nurses do just as we're told.
Treat 'em gentle, treat 'em rough,
We often feel we've had enough!

Bottoms clothed, bottoms bare,
We nurses know it's rude to stare,
BUT the thought unbidden comes,
What funny things are people's bums!

9

Thanks to her loyal and long-suffering coterie, Hilary was able to make three sorties from the hospital in 1964. Each one entailed feverish planning on her part and more feverish activity on that of her team. One Monday morning she received a letter from Wendy saying that she and Peter Dunn were announcing their engagement on his twenty-first birthday that weekend. There followed five hectic days of rounding up ambulance crew, getting in touch with Derek, finding nurses. But she got there in time to drink the toast, admire Wendy's ring, appear in the photographs, and roll happily back to hospital.

Wendy's twenty-first in March was better organised. The crew started wangling their off-duty time early. Sister Wyles was on holiday, Pat Powell had the weekend off. The others were not so easy. Priti and Margaret were on nights, Khalil and Khan on theatre duties. But she arranged to leave as soon as possible after her ten a.m. injection, with Derek, the two Pats, and the ambulance crew. Dad would pick the others up at four o'clock. What to wear? Would her white nightdress be too immodest? Aunty thought not, with a slip underneath. Mum made her a white velvet trachy cover, and she used her pink candlewick counterpane. Aunty Betty did her nails, madly gay in five colours, found two large white ear-rings for her hair and painted blobs on them, the same five colours as her nails. Mum wrapped Wendy's present, a wood carving of two ducks in flight.

It was a marvellous day. Peter and Jackie Tetley brought Simon and their nine-month-old twins. Arber was there. Khalil expertly pushed Sauterne down her Ryles tube with one hand, vainly trying to hang on to his sherry with the other. She waited just long enough to see Wendy cut her cake before gathering her clan and heading Ritzward.

She was planning her second visit to Edgbaston in 1964 when her eye mysteriously swelled and refused to open, the eye with which she watched television, for she always lay on her right side. It remained an enigma for weeks; then the eye specialist suggested that if she kept her head up all the time, the swelling might disappear. So her head was tied upright to the bed frame, and, sure enough, she was able to see once more.

It was the year of weddings. In August she was bridesmaid "by proxy" to Polly Perkins. In September came Pat Wyles' wedding at St. Mary's Church, Selly Oak, with a reception afterwards at the Longbridge Hotel, Rubery. Recklessly Hilary accepted both invitations and put her brain to work. Derek called and she booked his services. Permission was obtained by Pat from "Uncle Michael" and the "office". Pat Powell was available. Khalil would ask for the day off. Sue Pegg volunteered to be second nurse.

Now for a suitable costume that would not look like night attire. She finally decided on a jazzy striped nightie with a green bed cover, nails raspberry red to match one of the stripes. Mum bought a ribbon of the same colour to tie her head, and they found a pale pink towel. On Friday the hair washing squad moved in with their new streamlined technique: just cover her and the floor with rubber sheets and pour water over her head!! Her brain hummed: how to keep comfortable on the journey and still arrive at the church in a presentable state? Bright idea: If the nurses could "put her back" on the stretcher just as in bed, tie the various pillows to it and her head to the back rest, she could travel "pre-packed"!

Hitch Number One: Tina was off sick, so Sue had to go on night duty. They had to find another nurse. Pat Jones agreed to come. (The Pats were almost as ubiquitous as the Peters!) Hitch Number Two: when all seemed ready, it was discovered that Eb's bellows had perished! Nurse Bashford and Khalil frantically searched J. W.'s drawers for spare bellows, but to no avail, so they patched Eb with Sleek. While Pam and the two Pats arranged her carefully on the stretcher, Mum applied brush and comb, Blue Grass spray and face powder. Time was short. Pat finished tying her hair with ribbon, pinned on her white orchid, and she was galloped down the corridor. Baulked — no lift! Finally it was located on the fifth floor, with the door left open. Once in the lift they clanged to the ground, sped along that corridor and simply charged through the casualty entrance. As the ambulance careered along the Bristol road, its theme song might well have been, "Get me to the church on time."

It did. As she was hauled out of her chariot the bells began to ring. Pat and her father had been sitting in their car waiting for Hilary to arrive. She was safely on the camp bed in the aisle with Eb plugged in when the vicar and choir filed in. Eb made far too much noise, so Derek squatted at Hilary's feet and hand-pumped him. They heard every word of the ceremony. After the reading the choir sang a beautiful setting of "God Be in My Head". (A good theme song for me, thought Hilary!) During the signing of the register she was rushed outside for suction and rushed back in time to see Mr. and Mrs. Alan Westwood walk triumphantly down the aisle.

Then to the hotel. It was well they had brought J. W., for Eb conked out again, and Pat had to push Hilary's ribs as she was transferred from ambulance to hotel. J. W.'s pipes were tied to a convenient hat stand, and the bell was fixed to her foot. She had her injection, her hair was combed, the orchid pinned on, "Blue Grass" applied. Eb had been coaxed back to life, and she was taken into the dining room to hear the speeches and telegrams. Pat and Alan came to talk to her before going to change, and she was able to examine the beautiful brocade wedding dress. She waited just long enough to see Pat in her going-away outfit and to share in the shower of confetti. Worth all the Herculean labour and vigilance? Not a single participant who did not think so!

There could be few more such special events. What might be called Hilary's version of the "dark ages" was already closing in. In subsequent weeks and months she gradually lost all use of her hands. The sheet-writing ceased. Her only means of communication became the small bell suspended between the locker and her big toe, operated by a somewhat streamlined use of the alphabet. "Beginning," one would say to instigate a two-way conversation. If the letter she wished was in the first half of the alphabet, she would twitch her foot, then one would patiently repeat the alphabet from A to K; if the second half, there would be no movement, and one would start with L. It was surprising how fast and efficient conversation could become with practice.

Home at last: her mother opens the outside door of the purpose-built extension as Hilary covers the final few yards. The faithful Possum environmental control unit, to the right of the picture awaits installation in the new situation.

Hilary's room at home. Dorothy Clarke Wilson is reading what Hilary types with her Possum typewriter unit.

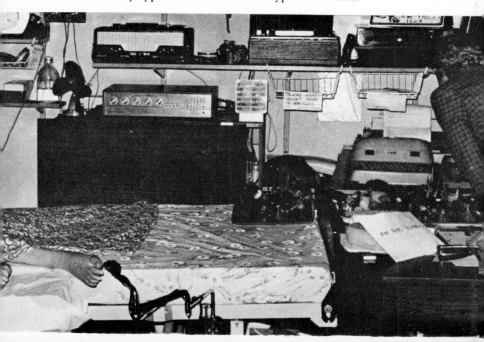

Roger chats with Hilar[y]
Her new respirator is [on]
the right.

The vital link between
Hilary and her Possum
unit—the sensitive micro-
switch especially devel-
oped by the Burgess
Microswitch Company
exclusively for Hilary.
Note the widely adjust-
able mounting assembly.

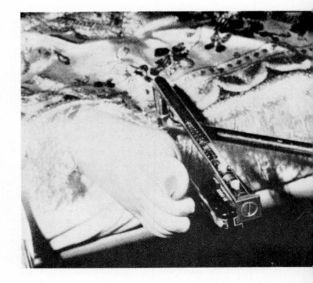

The major difficulty, Hilary felt, was in lack of *inflection*. So much of one's feelings was expressed in emphasis, quality, the rise and fall of one's voice, all of which were impossible in physical communication. She could express anger and impatience through sharper foot movements, though it took extra effort and energy. But gentler emotions like love, sympathy, so eloquent in the timbre of one's voice — how communicate them in mechanical A, B, Cs? It was like sending a kiss by mail with the letter X!

As voluntary movement of her eyelids became impossible, her vision was impaired. She could see only if someone lifted her eyelid and held it. So for all practical purposes she was blind. Not technically, not enough to become a candidate for "Books for the Blind". For all practical purposes she was almost completely paralysed. Not technically, for her muscles, except for disuse, were as healthy as ever, her nerves as keenly sensitive. She could feel — how she could feel! — discomfort, the soothing softness of "Blue Grass" lotion, the excruciating pain of being mishandled. She could smell — perfumes, flowers, food being wheeled on trolleys, cool mists in the air, the coffee Dad brought from the kitchen.

And, thank God, she could hear! She learned to know footsteps in the corridor, the different nurses', the family's, occasionally visitors', and sensed human presence. One evening when Mrs. Wyn Dingley, who came regularly to read to her, brought her husband with her, he came into the room but did not speak. "Who else is here?" asked Hilary.

The world flowed in through the senses left to her — hearing smell, touch. Friends brought her wild flowers, told her about their walks. "Hilary wants an autumn collection," reported Miss Halstead to her teachers at Olive Hill School, and that week came acorns, conkers, ferns, leaves, models of squirrels. "Bluebells please for Hilary," came another directive, and on her birthday morning, with a terrific thunderstorm lashing the windows, the ledges were massed with heavenly blue. No matter if she couldn't see them. She could picture bluebells.

She saw through her friends' eyes. One day Norah Deakins, wife of the Secretary of Warwickshire County Cricket Club, was admiring the dress the librarian, Mrs. Ashe, was wearing. "Describe it to me please," said Hilary. Later Mrs. Ashe came back into the room, and Hilary asked Norah to show her the dress. Lifting the eyelids, Norah wondered, "How accurate have I been?" She was inordinately pleased when Hilary said, "A very good description." It was a lesson to Norah. From then on she looked more closely at postcards, pictures, clothes, objects about which Hilary might inquire, knowing she might be subjected to severe testing.

Hilary enjoyed holidays by proxy. No harassing preparations to make, no headaches about passports, finding a good hotel, puzzling over exchange rates, saving money for months! She spent most of them in the British Isles as letters and postcards poured in — pony trekking in Exmoor, rock climbing in Snowdonia, aqualung diving in the Lake District, hill climbing in Derbyshire, botanising in the Wye forest, sailing on the Broads, swimming at Tenby, fishing in Scotland, sunbathing at Brighton and moonbathing in Cornwall. One friend described in detail an expedition to Swildon Caves in the Mendips — dank coldness, frightening tunnels, narrow ledges, forty-foot drops, rope ladders. Swallow Caves in the Peak District by boat had been enough for her!

Within her own cavern of silence she waged a constant battle for survival. No one knew better than she that her life hung, if not by a thread, at least by an old bandage, an electric wire, or an air tube. She was determined, with all the stubborn strength of an indomitable will, to *live*. She well understood the problems of the hospital. It was desperately short of staff. But she understood her own condition, too. If she were left alone during the night or in the last hour before injections, she might not be able to signal in case of emergency. Once during the day she heard a "pop". No one answered her bell. Matron happened to be passing her door and called a nurse. The tube in her throat had burst. The bedside manner of some nurses infuriated her. "Now don't panic, my dear, don't panic." "It's not me that's panicking," Hilary would respond if they would take time to listen, "it's you." "We must learn by trial and error," another would reason. "Yes, your error," was Hilary's rejoinder, "but my trial."

The error sometimes resulted in the frightening condition of her "passing out". It was a complicated process "putting her back" — that is, restoring her to the ventilator, readjusting her pillows, her body, head, arms, legs in the easiest position, making her comfortable for the next two or three hours. If her head was thrown forward in a certain way, she was sent completely "out", unable to communicate, and might remain so for hours. On several of these occasions new nurses were on duty who knew nothing of the procedure, and Mona was hurriedly sent for, even called from school. She knew exactly what to do and was invariably able to put Hilary's head in the correct position to restore communication. She tried to teach the inexperienced nurses, often unsuccessfully.

"I don't expect nurses to know all about the disease and the machines," Hilary explained to her parents, "but I feel it's essential that they know my normal air pressures, what sends pressure up, where leaks can occur, how to put Eb on if J. W. fails, how to hand-pump me on Eb, how to regulate the wall air supply and cylinders, how to change from one to the other." One good nurse, who knew her and the whole situation, could cope with one "groper", but not two of them. And sometimes all were "gropers".

She was able to make one more sortie, to Edgbaston in 1965 to see the Test match, New Zealand v. England — no, not see; feel, hear, sense with every tingling nerve the colour and motion and excitement. Unable now to write, she dictated a poetic account of the trip, partly in sheet talk, partly in toe talk, to Mum or Dad or Noonie.

It was soon after this last trip to Edgbaston in 1965 that the bombshell exploded. The Ritz was no longer to be her home! This was a teaching hospital, Hilary was told, and practice in dealing with this unusual disease must be distributed among as many nurses as possible. Moreover, the nurses on E2B were becoming too personally involved with her case.

Mona and Eric were stunned. Where had it all gone — the friendship, the *camaraderie*? They had suddenly become strangers in their second home! They went to question her consultant. Yes, he admitted, the Administration had made a change in policy for which he was not responsible. He promised that the air would be piped to her new room and nurses she knew would accompany her.

"East 5A," Hilary was told, would be her next port of call. Stunned, helpless, Eric and Mona went to make the acquaintance of the senior nurse on that ward. She was pleasant but looked terrified at the prospect of her new patient. No, Hilary learned later, it was to be East 1B. The ward sister came to prepare her. All this extra paraphernalia — wooden animals, beer mats, pictures, decorative shelves, personal gadgets — must be discarded. For years Hilary's room had resembled a home more than a hospital — not any more. She could not even take Anthony her goldfish, which had lived in a tank on her table for three or four years, good company in the night, for she could hear him plopping in and out of the water. All must go.

Eric and Mona saw the Matron and tried to emphasise Hilary's three minimal requirements : a nurse for her last hour, put-back by people who knew how, constant nursing at night by someone familiar with her condition. By and large, yes, agreed Matron, but she would talk to Hilary herself.

Hilary made no protest. What could not be helped must be accepted. Mum promised to help with the move but asked that a certain fortnight be avoided because she was committed to an education course in Devon. "Next Monday," came the verdict. It was the day before she had to go ! The sister in the new ward sent nurses to watch Hilary's routine. No nurses except the night nurse would be allowed to go with her.

The dismantling of the room was sheer torture. What if she *was* unable to see them, the animals, the beer mats, the pictures of Shandy and Chiaro ? She had known they were there and exactly where each one was. They were anchors holding one fast to beloved reality. It was like the buddleia tree, like the monk's bench . . .

Mona still remembered Hilary's utter dismay when she had casually broken the news about that. "Oh, by the way, we sold the monk's bench today. A decorator came to the house and admired it. You know it never really fitted into our new décor."

"But you could NOT !" Hilary's shock had been instant and furious. "Its always been there, it's older than I am. Why, I can't remember home without it. I can remember it with winter flowers on it. I can remember it with dandelions in a blue bowl . . ." She had gone on and on. "You must get it back !"

"But, darling, we can't ! It's gone. The man paid for it."

"No, no, it can't have. You must get it back."

The next day Mona had rung the decorator and explained. "Of course she must have it." It had been returned that very day. Strange ! Hilary would probably never see it again, but just the knowledge that it was there brought happiness, security.

Monday was a ghastly day. The Ritz was stripped, her treasures taken away. She was allowed to keep a few books, some flowers, her linen. Her room must henceforth be kept more clinical, more like a ward. Worse, the relatives must be more moderate in their visiting. "Adapt yourselves, please, to as near normal visiting hours as you can."

"Mini-Griff" was almost as distressed as the family. She kept coming to the room and giving all the help possible. Mum was there for the move, which took place mid-morning. The Sister on the new ward came to inspect. A few of Hilary's possessions were still left in the locker — her cosmetics and nail varnishes, a few spare pretty nightdresses. "Take them all home," directed Sister firmly, "except one nightdress, one varnish, and one general purpose cream." Mum tried to explain to her how Hilary loved all the different colours. "But she can't see them!" was the Sister's blunt rejoinder. At this bleak prospect of callousness Mona almost dissolved into tears. Miss Griffith came to her rescue, insisting that she came back to the old ward for a cup of tea.

However, Sister was not the only one who could be adamant. Hilary kept her nail vanishes and perfumes.

When the time came that afternoon for Hilary's injection and put-back, Mona was sent out of the room. She waited in the corridor, certain that with new nurses performing the complicated routine, she would be called in to help. What seemed an age passed, but no one came. It was the beginning of a frightening period for both Mona and Eric. Mona went on her scheduled assignment but kept in touch daily by telephone. Never did she completely unpack her bags.

The period was even more frightening for Hilary. Nurses were with her at night, yes, but she felt no security. Her cuff burst; the pipe fell off J. W. She passed out and was unconscious for a few minutes. She was more upset and terrified than when she had first gone into hospital. She felt she had to fight for sheer survival. She knew also the rumours and gossip that were being bandied about. She was fussy, demanding, a veritable ogre of a patient. Her parents were busybodies. It was painful, but she made no apologies. She felt her life was at stake.

She discovered that she was being sedated, to make it easier for the nurses to "put her back". "Easier, when she was extra

limp!" She wrote to "Uncle Michael via Mum, violently object-
ing to sedation. "My life is mental, and if you take that away,
I am lost. I tell you it's no good your trying to fool me!" ("And
my goodness, it isn't!" commented Wendy.) "Uncle Michael"
immediately forbade sedation. At least she had gained some
ground.

At the end of the first fortnight Matron put a notice on the
notice board in the nurses' hall asking for volunteers to help
care for Hilary. Now at last Mona was allowed to help again.
Evidently the new ward did not relish its responsibility.

It was a new life. Apart from the clinical nursing, Hilary
would be alone for many hours. Not that she minded this much
of the time; but in the last hour or so of the injection cycle
when she could not ring the bell, it was risky. Eventually since
they were so short of staff, the hospital allowed visitors to sit
with her during her weakest times, and Mona arranged a rota
of friends. In subsequent months they became very important
to Hilary's care. Mona and Eric still took responsibility for
every evening, plus Saturdays and Sundays from noon to mid-
afternoon. Noonie took Tuesday evening with Eric; then Mum
would come in about nine thirty to "put Hilary to bed" with
Dad and a nurse. Noonie and Aunty Betty did the same
on Thursday evenings.

Girls from King Edward's High School came on Wednesday
afternoons. Hilary had a grand time with them. Helen sometimes brought her 'cello and played. Angela and Pixie brought
their guitars and sang folks songs and carols. Angela, who had
a beautiful voice, later went to Oxford University and sang
with the Bach Choir. Val, Jackie, and Sue learned to feed and
suck Hilary and adjust her pillows. They read to her, played
tapes, brought concert programmes. After they left the high
school Sue and Jackie would bring their boy friends. Later they
did her a beautiful brass rubbing which became a prized
possession.

Stella, an Austrian Jewish widow doing Red Cross voluntary
work on E.I.B. asked to be permitted to help with Hilary: she
came on Saturday from four p.m. to six. They talked of music
and painting, and moved with Hilary from ward to ward.
Hilary loved her delightful Austrian lilt. She got Dad to tape
Stella's favourite Beethoven's Pastoral Symphony, and they
listened to it together.

Mrs. Lloyd, who had taught Hilary at Olive Hill, came Tuesday at dinner time, and they read poetry together — Andrew Young, John Betjeman, Ogden Nash. Another Olive Hill teacher, Mrs. Taylor, came every week after school, a long journey by two buses in the rush hour. She could "talk the hind leg off a donkey", as she said jokingly about herself, so there was always entertainment during her visits.

Rikki, an old Edwardian (ex-pupil of King Edward's High School) came Thursdays at lunch time, to read fascinating letters from her son James, a civil engineer in Swaziland, and other parts of Africa. Even more fascinating were her experiences as leader of a handicapped scout troop. Later on Thursdays came Wyn Dingley, fond of jokes and horses, who brought her snowdrops, primroses, cowslips in gorgeous bunches from her weekend cottage near Bibury in the Cotswolds.

There was Norah Deakins, who came on Fridays, learned Hilary's bath routine, and often helped the nurses. She shared Hilary's love of cricket and short stories.

A new friend was Perrin Radley, who usually arrived about eight-thirty in the morning. After getting his theology degree at Cambridge, he was doing post graduate work at Queen's College, Birmingham University. Janet Smith, another friend of Hilary's, had met him at a working community in France and told him about her.

"Hello, Princess," he would invariably greet her. Strange, Cliff Medhurst had also called her that!

Perrin was an American, and Hilary loved to tease him about his vagaries of speech, like saying "zee" in their alphabet talk instead of "zed". Later, when he returned to America, took a church, and married, Hilary remained in close contact with both him and his wife by correspondence. He always admired her different colour schemes of dress and once, when ill in bed, made and sent her three beautiful folded bows in narrow velvet on small combs — blue, emerald, red — for her hair.

When Perrin left Queen's College, he asked another student to visit her, Adam Smith, who always brought a notebook so that he could write down the letters spelled out by her little bell. What fascinated him most was the fact that she knew exactly where everything was in her room. One afternoon he searched through drawers and cupboards to find something she wanted — in vain. But it wasn't Hilary's fault. She knew where it should have been. Someone had moved it. When Adam Smith left Birmingham and went to Durham, he introduced her to another theological student, John Wilkinson, so during her years of moving she had a succession of visiting theologists.

Of course she made new friends among the sisters and nurses. Some not only became adept at her routine but introduced helpful innovations. Sister Matthews on East 5A suggested changing Hilary's trachy tube from a Harris with the very heavy MacGill connector to a Radcliffe, which was much lighter, with a magnetic connection, and it also relieved the constant menace of a bursting cuff. East 5A, dubbed "mental, dental, and confidential", was supposed to be haunted by the spirit of a nurse who, blaming herself for a patient's death, had committed suicide on the ward. Hilary never saw or heard the ghost, though the wind, whistling and howling about the fifth floor ward on a stormy night, did sound like a lost soul.

There was Joyce Green, who had a wonderful knack of making Hilary comfortable even from an impossible position and was always quick to act when things went wrong. On East 1B there were two nurses known as "Handle Bars" and "Apple Crumble", always good for a laugh. Later there was an auxiliary, Jennie, a slim attractive Jamaican, who envied Hilary's "tall" nails and beautiful varnishes and was very quick to learn.

Later there was Iola. Hilary had met her first during the halcyon years on East 2B. Iola had lacked confidence, and it had taken all of Hilary's persuasive powers to convince her that she was doing well with the routine. They had rejoiced together when Iola passed her examination, though the nurse had cried. With both parents dead, there had been no one to tell who thought it important. Iola had gone to Zambia on Voluntary Service. Now, returning with a husband, happier and more confident, she came back to the hospital part time with special responsibility for Hilary. At least Matron was doing her best to meet Hilary's needs in spite of her desperate problems with staff shortage! The coming of Iola created a bright thread of continuity in the tangle of constant moves.

Hilary's first encounters with another nurse, Rachel, were discordant. Rachel treated her like a naughty child. But as they came to understand each other, they became staunch friends. Homely, motherly, extremely competent, Rachel studied to become adept at nursing Hilary. She came to learn her routine at ten p.m. in her own time so that when Hilary should make the next move she would be able to take charge. True, there were occasional clashes of will, but they did not last long. Hilary could discuss the most intimate subjects with the motherly Rachel without embarrassment, and she became interested in the nurse's four children, as excited as Rachel when Jimmie gained entrance to King Edward's School and Robbie was accepted for the Cathedral choir. It was Rachel who first thought of using sheepskin under Hilary's heel. She bought a little piece for her birthday and a square bowl, much more convenient, for washing her feet. She would leave her own ward at any time to help with Hilary, coming early and staying late — when the hospital would let her.

Such was the pattern of life during the great migration, changing of wards every six months, each January, each July or August, only occasionally retracing the path. 1B...2A... 5A...2A...G.A...G.B...2B...1B...1A... a pattern that was to last for the next five years.

II

"Well," wrote Ian in 1966 from Lusaka, Zambia, where as civil engineer he was helping to build an airport, "and how's big sister there? Bet you're not half so brown as I am. So Wendy tells me you're on the move again, E2A this time. I'd better send you an ace photo of myself so you can show all the nurses what a thrill they've got in store for them!"

He hadn't met any interesting females on this expedition, he was still fond of a girl back home named Anne. He was playing rugby. In fact, his Lusaka team had travelled over two hundred miles one Saturday to play. He expected to be home soon but probably would not make it before the New Year, which meant that he would have to miss Wendy's wedding. What a disappointment!

They could not wait for him. Both Wendy and Peter were teachers, so they must arrange to be married during a school holiday. They did not want to wait until Easter. Of course they sent him an invitation.

No trials of her nomadic existence could mar Hilary's excitement in the coming event. Her invitation from Mum and Dad read :

Mr. & Mrs. E. Pole
request the pleasure of the company of
Miss Hilary J. Pole
and E. B., etc. at the marriage of their daughter
Gillian Wendy
with
Peter John Dunn
at St. Matthew's Parish Church, Walsall
on Wednesday, December 28, 1966
at 12 noon
and afterwards at Moor Hall, Little Aston

No safari this time for Hilary and her loyal cohorts, though the family had hoped she might make it. She could not have managed it even if the Administration had let her. Uncle Michael thought it unwise for her to go out at that time of year; the church could be cold and the weather inclement. Naturally she was disappointed, but it was sensible advice, so — she would again be bridesmaid by proxy ! However, she was included in all the plans and took an active part in the arrangements and preparations, discussing with Wendy colours and styles for the bridesmaids' dresses and hats, flowers, table decorations, menus — even music. Wendy did not want to walk up the aisle to the march from *Lohengrin* ("Here comes the bride"), and Hilary was thrilled when she chose "The Grand March" from *Aida*. When Wendy told the organist of her choice, he asked cryptically, "What are you coming in on — an elephant ?"

The other bridesmaids — Edwina, a college friend of Wendy's, Janet, Peter's only sister, and Anne, Ian's girl friend — shared with Hilary all the excitement of choosing their outfits. They eventually decided on empire line dresses of blue tweed flecked with gold and matching "bomb" hats. Wendy chose a pale honey-coloured dress of heavy crepe with a guipure lace bodice and train. A flat "pill-box" hat of the same lace would hold her long three-tiered honey-coloured veil. Her bouquet of leaf skeletons and seedpods would be sprayed with gold. The men were to be handsome in morning dress and grey "toppers" (a pity Ian, handsomer than any of them, could not be there!)

The wedding luncheon was booked for one-fifteen p.m. When it was certain that Hilary could not attend, they decided that of course she must see the wedding party. With the ceremony at noon, there would not be time to visit the hospital between that and the luncheon. The hotel booking could not be changed, so they brought the service forward to eleven a.m. Then the whole party would go straight to the hospital to see Hilary, cut a small cake just like a tier of the wedding cake, and toast the bride and groom with champagne; then move on to the hotel in time to receive the guests before the meal. The guests were to be taken to West Riding for cocktails before going to the hotel. Naturally Ian was not notified of the change of plans, since he could not be there.

However, his own plans were rushing to culmination. He hoped to make the wedding but did not want to tell them for fear of disappointment. He hired a car to be waiting for him in Southampton and drove straight up from the ship like mad. In spite of heavy fog he would have arrived in time had the original noon hour been kept.

The service was over. Wendy, Peter, and the wedding party had left for the hospital. Mona, Betty, and Noonie had stayed to see all the guests into cars for West Riding and were just getting into Noonie's car to go themselves when the Rev. Vernon Nicholls came towards them waving. Mona did not notice his companion. She thought she must have left something in the church and was getting out of the car when — Ian! Her face when she saw him! The bride had not been more radiant. She flew to him. Leaving Noonie and Betty to take care of the guests at West Riding, Mona and Ian rushed off to the hospital to share with Hilary and the rest of the wedding party this marvellous surprise.

The day was proving equally exciting for Hilary. Ro Darlington — "Silver Streak" — came at six a.m. to wash her hair, bath and dress her. A telegram arrived: "Everyone sends greetings to chief bridesmaid. God bless. Love from everyone." Even the usual morning routine — Complan, suck-out, put-back — had a festive air. At ten o'clock the final preparations began. Hilary was dressed in a pale blue nightdress, and her bedspread was of the same material as the bridesmaids' dresses. Her hair was arranged in a "bun" on top of her head, round it a bandeau made from honey-coloured satin and covered with motifs of the same guipure lace as Wendy's train. Her bouquet was of leaf skeletons, dried natural fruits, berries, flowers and tiny cones, an exquisite harmony of browns. Ro arranged the room, covering a table like an altar with flowers.

At last the big moment came. Festive in her bridesmaid's apparel, the bouquet in her hand, Hilary received the wedding party. However, the climax was yet to come. When Ian's old familiar knock sounded on the door, she shook with excitement. Not thousands of miles away in Cape Town — not even on the high seas — *here*! The party gathered about her bed, a dozen strong. Cameras were cocked, bulbs flashed. It was the first time the family had been together for two years. The cake was cut, with enough left over to share with the nurses. Champagne was passed and a drop poured down the Ryles tube. Hilary could almost taste it! At least she savoured to the full the flavour of joyous excitement.

It was soon over. Mona and Ian left for a gents' outfitters, for Ian had come straight from the ship and was not only dishevelled but travel-stained. Armed with a new shirt and other accessories, they rushed home for him to change, then hurried to the reception, arriving JUST in time. In Hilary's room the excitement lingered. The party had brought a tape of the wedding. Ro stayed until four thirty listening to it with her. Together they admired the beautiful bracelet, a present to the chief bridesmaid from Peter. Nurses came in to sample the wedding cake. Bridesmaid by proxy? The real thing could hardly have been more exciting!

The following month, January, Ian telephoned West Riding from Scotland, where he had gone on a skiing holiday. "I'm bringing home a friend, Mum — O.K.?" he announced cryptically.

"Yes, of course, but which sex?" returned Mona. "I want to be able to plan properly."

"Female."

"All right. Name? Do I know it?"

"No. You haven't heard it. It's — Beth."

She was beautiful, warm, outgoing. From the moment she arrived she might have been Mona's own daughter. Mona exchanged an excited surreptitious glance with Betty. "Don't you think this is it?" They had liked the others, but somehow, seeing Ian and Beth together, they could see harmony, they belonged.

Beth and her friend String had boarded Ian's ship in Durban, South Africa, their home country. The two girls had trained and qualified as teachers, taught for a little while in South Africa and saved to come to Europe for a year of travel, planning to get themselves jobs in England or on the Continent if their money ran out. At one of the ports Ian and a friend hired a special cart to go sightseeing; and they had overtaken Beth and String, walking. "Hello, Funny Face," Ian had called. "Want a lift?" An acquaintance had started, ripening swiftly into what seemed like friendship plus. Of course Ian took Beth to see Hilary. Seldom had he embarked on any important new relationship in recent years without sharing with her its details and seeking her approval. There was no doubt this time. From the first moment Hilary and Beth were on the same wave length.

During the following months Beth came home with Ian, first for a weekend or two, then whenever he came from London to West Riding. When Mona and Eric went to London to see Ian, Beth always joined them. That summer Beth and String travelled on the Continent for three months, as they had planned. Ian and his flat mate Bob would have liked to go, but they were committed to work, with only a fortnight's holiday due. However, they arranged to meet the girls in Jugoslavia in August. Ian had intended coming home for Mum and Dad's thirtieth wedding anniversary in September, but a rugby match prevented him. He came the following weekend . . . with Beth.

The night they arrived Ian and Beth went straight to the hospital. Hilary was on Tatty's ward — one of her happy ports of call in the successive migrations. Mum and Dad were already in Hilary's room. Ian grew more and more restless as visitors kept coming in. After Hilary had been "put-back" for the night, he sent the others out. "I'll meet you in the corrridor."

"Look, Hil," he said when they were alone. "I want to show you something."

He lifted her eyelid so she could really see. It was a beautiful engagement ring.

"Oh, Ian — wonderful! When —"

"I haven't given it to her yet," he said. "I wanted to tell you first."

For a quarter of an hour they talked together, and he told her of his plans. (Somehow one always said "talked" about a conversation with Hilary. "But she can't speak!" someone had once commented when Mary Alcock, a nurse, had remarked, "Hilary said —" Mary had only smiled.)

"S — m!" the little bell spelled vigorously, Hilary's abbreviation for "smashing". "She's just the one for you."

It was only after this intimate interchange that Ian gave the ring to Beth. Then they told Mona and Eric.

Perhaps only Ian, who had known Hilary so well, tested so often her physical strength and fierce independence, shared her insatiable thirst for adventure, could fully understand what the loss of sight and movement must mean to her. No more nature walks, cricket, dance, swimming, climbing, running with short hair unbound, face into the wind. What did he feel as he entered her room and saw her lying sightless, motionless, voiceless? Bitterness? Rebellion? Sympathy? None of them, least of all sympathy. Perhaps he had known some such reaction in the beginning, had consciously put it out of his mind. If so, he could not remember when. He never, never thought of her as being ill. She was the same Hilary he had always known, a fully competent human being.

"When I am on leave and go to see her," he once tried to explain his feelings, "I don't come out thinking, 'Oh, what a shame! If only Hilary could this or the other.' I think, 'Oh, jolly good fun, that! Must remember to tell her so and so when I go back.' It just doesn't occur to me that she isn't 100 per cent physically — mentally she is so alive. Others have come to me saying the same thing. Instead of 'Oh, what a terrible thing, what a tragedy!' they come out saying, 'What a super half hour! I must go back and see her again soon.' You don't even seem to notice that she is bedridden, her personality so oozes all over the room. I think she must have decided early in her illness that she wasn't going to dwell on what she had lost, but on what she had left. Thinking, hearing, feeling. She can learn. She can listen. She can teach and help others. That's Hilary!"

PART
FOUR

World of Possum

My Answer

I'm often asked if I am bored,
Frustrated, lonely,
My life abhorred.
And so I answer,
"I am not." —
That now I can accept my lot,
Remind the sadly shaking head,
"It is my body, not my mind, in bed."

I'm rarely frightened or in pain,
For this
I thank my God again.
I have many loyal friends,
My joy in them despair transcends.
There's music too,
Books to read.
Discontentment cannot breed.

Although I can no longer play,
I can listen
Every day
To football, rugby, tennis, cricket,
Imagination has no limit.
Add to this
A sense of humour
Killing that "depression" rumour.

Now I have my Possum too,
A miracle
In all men's view.
No longer do I have to wait.
My poems and letters to dictate.
Just flick my toe
And type myself,
I have no time to brood on "health"!

HILARY J. POLE

I

It was Roy Atkinson, Ian's school friend, who introduced the Poles to the idea of Possum. Roy, a physicist studying at Oxford for a teaching diploma, was friendly with an occupational therapist who knew Reginald Maling, founder and director of the P.O.S.M. Research Foundation and who had seen some of the project's early work. This young woman saw the possibilities of the electronic device for Hilary and felt that perhaps it could be adapted to her needs.

"Have you heard of a thing called Possum?" Roy asked the Poles one day in 1964.

"I think I read something about it lately," said Mona vaguely. She and Eric listened with interest to Roy's enthusiastic description of the work of Reginald Maling, an engineer inventor who had applied his mechanical genius to the problems of disabled people.

While working as a research chemist for a phonograph record company in Aylesbury, Reg Maling had become involved in working with paralytics at Stoke Mandeville Hospital. One day he saw a young man in a side ward who had broken his neck at such a high level that it had left him paralysed below the neck. Because his breathing was restricted, making him unable to call effectively, the nursing staff had hung a whistle over his lips, his sole method of attracting attention. Reg Maling had a startling idea. Why couldn't severely handicapped people use the mouth to amplify what little residual control ability they might possess, perhaps even to operate machines?

Working with a colleague and experimenting on this patient, he invented an electronic device which could be operated by "sucking" and "puffing", giving two effective switching actions, making it possible for even a person on a ventilator to operate a mechanism which could open doors, turn on lights, heat, radio, television, control an intercom, and connect a telephone. And, for a person unable to speak, it could even be adapted for use with a specially modified electric typewriter!

Eric and Mona were excited. What a boon it would be for Hilary to be able to summon help when necessary, to say nothing of all the other benefits the device might make possible!

"Do you think one of those new electronic devices could help Hilary?" they asked her consultant.

He forcefully rejected the idea. Oh, no, impossible! If she had had enough movement they had all the best available resources for treating her right there in the Queen Elizabeth Hospital. They would not need outside help.

But Roy, imbued with the missionary zeal of a person who has seen a miracle, persisted. "You should see some of the people whose lives have been changed by this Possum thing. I say — why don't you let me make a date for you to see this Mr. Maling? How about during your October holiday?"

He made an appointment for them, but Roy's friend had to change it. They would come the following month. But by that time the friend had left the project. Eric and Mona disliked going without an introduction and especially without hospital recommendation. Three years passed. They kept seeing references to Possum in the newspapers and on television. Then Eric read an article about it in *Responaut*, a magazine written by and for people on ventilators.

Meanwhile conditions at the hospital had been deteriorating. Hilary was making her twice yearly migrations from ward to ward. The whole hospital was becoming desperately short of staff. Although her visitors came regularly for the last hour before injections, she was completely dependent on the bell and often could not ring it, either because she was too weak or because it needed adjusting. Inevitably she was in the care of many "learner" nurses. Though the Sisters on the different wards tried to arrange teaching sessions for learners with nurses who knew her "put-backs", she had some harrowing experiences, literally narrow escapes.

One night Eric and Mona were reduced to desperation. Communication by toe talk was a grim business. Hilary was being attended by new nurses without adequate instructions. Several times no nurse had been with her during the last hour, and she had found it impossible to ring her bell. Sister Brown was doing her best, but lack of staff caused insuperable difficulties.

"I'm just terrified," Hilary confessed with unusual candour, for she seldom expressed criticism of the hospital. "Something may go wrong, and before help can come, I may pass out."

Eric and Mona returned home in a nadir of despair. "Oh, what can we do?" wondered Mona. "Possum?" suggested Eric. It seemed a faint hope, but they were desperate. The article in *Responaut* had emphasised the benefits of an alarm system, which was Hilary's greatest need. After all, the hospital had had plenty of opportunity to cope with the situation. What if it were an unorthodox action? Hilary's well being, perhaps her life, was at stake. In a few days she was due to move to another ward, a prospect of even greater uncertainty. Eric wrote to Reginald Maling.

The following Saturday Reg Maling telephoned requesting more details. He and Eric talked for an hour. "I'm sure we can do something," he assured. "We never give up." He asked Eric to get medical permission for one of the Possum team to come up and visit Hilary immediately. They would try to come Monday. Eric wrote at once to the consultant asking for permission and gave the letter to Sister Brown to pass on to the doctor. Monday night came, and there had been no reply.

It was Tuesday, July 11th, 1967. Hilary was in the middle of her blanket bath when Sister Brown ushered in a stranger. "This is Mr. Jefcoate," she introduced him.

"Hello, Hilary," said a quiet voice. "I'm Roger."

With Rachel interpreting, Hilary answered his many questions, listening to his brief but lucid explanations of Possum with the intense interest of a curious and agile mind trained to scientific perception, together with an almost unbearable emotional excitement. She could tell by the erratic pressure of the fingers on her ankle that Rachel was equally excited. While calmly giving information about the limited residual movement existent in her toes, Hilary's mind was cavorting like a dervish, leaping, gyrating in imaginary sequences. A miracle! Could it really happen? A door opening in this wall of insecurity? To be certain you could operate an alarm system? A bit of independence? To express yourself again without a slow lumbering intermediary? But she

must not hope. No one knew better than she the bitter aftermath of vain hopes. She knew also her limitation of movement
and the unlikelihood that this young man could adapt this
scientific miracle to her use.

"Of course I can't promise anything," said Roger, as if reading her thoughts, "how, what, or when. But no one has ever
beaten Possum yet, so — we'll think of something."

Hilary knew something else too : the impossibility of his even
trying without the full co-operation of doctors and technicians.
The medical profession was not receptive to innovations. Look
how many decades it had taken it to acknowledge that Semmel-
weiss's theories of cleanliness as a prevention of fever were not
the babblings of a "heretic" !

Again Roger Jefcoate seemed to read her thoughts. "I wonder
if I could see one of Hilary's consultants," he suggested.

Sister immediately got in touch with the consultant neurologist,
who said he would come down later for an interview. In the
meantime Roger went to telephone Eric.

"Where are you ?" came the swift inquiry.

"At the Queen Elizabeth Hospital. I have already seen Hilary,
and I am to have a conference with her consultant."

Rachel was more able than Hilary to express her excitement.
Wasn't it wonderful? And he actually sounded as if he could do
it ! Such a fine looking young man, too — tall, slim, good looking ! If only Hilary could have seen him !

Hilary had not needed to see. Looks were unimportant. She
already knew what Roger Jefcoate was like by his air of quiet
authority, his understanding, his immediate grasp of her situation.
Whatever happened now, she knew she had made a new friend.
In spite of his assurances she tried to quell her excitement. Nothing to do now but wait. She was used to waiting. Already she
had had seven years of it.

Meanwhile there was excitement of a different, less pleasurable
kind. The very next day Hilary was moving to a new ward,
East Ground A. A new move was always hectic for the Poles.
They spent a fortnight previous to it sorting post, sending home
books, extra nightdresses, everything that could be spared. The
move to EGA was especially dreaded, for rumour had it that
Sister Tatlow was a martinet. That Tuesday evening Eric got a
trolley, loaded it, and went down in the lift with Hilary's belongings to meet Sister. She was off duty, and Hilary's new room

was locked. No one had a key. Phew! Was this a sample of the next six months? Hilary, having tasted hospital gossip before, was determined not to judge — yet even she had butterflies the day she moved. The only reassuring feature was the presence of Rachel, taking competent charge of the move and promising to come to her aid any time she was needed, yes, even in her off duty hours if the authorities would let her.

The gossips were wrong. Sister Tatlow — "Tatty" — had locked the door only because she wanted no one to upset the room. There was a comfortable chair for visitors, a vase of flowers to welcome the newcomer. Sister proved to be a skilled and inspired nurse, often missing meals in order to help patients and going off duty late. She was understanding in dealing with Eric and Mona. "There is no such thing as a difficult relative," she often said, "only a worried one!" With Hilary she was not only considerate but imaginative. She tried to make her food more interesting — egg-nog with sherry, liquidised tomato from her own greenhouse. She lent her books and records, arranged to do her work in Hilary's room during the low times before injections. On Saturdays and Sundays she would set two lunch-trays in the room for Mum and Dad. "Only fair, you're saving staff!" They often went to her flat for a relaxed half hour. Coming to the car park they might find a cryptic message under the windscreen wipers or through the door handle — "Baked last night, call in." . . . "Apple pie will be done by three."

Best of all, she had a sense of humour. Once when her ward was very busy, a consultant came to examine a patient just as "Tatty" had started the drug round and there was no other nurse on duty. Dilemma — no one to stay with the trolley. She placed it in the middle of the ward, rolled her eyes upward, and said, "Please Lord, look after the drugs till I get back." He did.

Yet not even the most competent Sister could eliminate all the dangers and difficulties encountered on a new ward. The feeling of constant insecurity and fear persisted. The tiny bell was such a frighteningly frail link between peril and safety! The hope of this miracle called Possum — an alarm, a buzzer, dependent on just a flicker of movement — was like a light at the end of a dark alley. Hope? No, she must not hope. But, being Hilary, how could she help it? It was like telling a bird not to sing at the first hint of dawn, for fear the sun might not rise.

2

In 1967 the P.O.S.M. Research Foundation in Aylesbury was a lusty youngster under ten years of age with clothes bursting at the seams. Still housed in the pre-fab building next to Stoke Mandeville Hospital where they had moved the previous year and a few outlying shelters scarcely bigger than sheds, the team was experimenting, manufacturing, publicising, distributing, servicing — all in a space which seemed hardly sufficient for a single department. But, like their brilliant founder and director, Reg Maling, and their deputy director, Roger Jefcoate, the entire team was adventurous, sacrificially loyal, totally dedicated to an idea which was transforming human life.

In fact some of them, like David Hyde, chief demonstrator and later sales executive, had had their own lives transformed. Back in 1955 he had broken his neck playing rugger at school and been almost completely paralysed. Depressed, no future in sight, he had met Reg Maling at Stoke Mandeville and been used as a guinea pig to test the new blow-suck equipment. He had gone on a trip to Copenhagen to demonstrate Possum at the International Congress for Rehabilitation of the Disabled, where the new invention had won the Bell Greve Memorial Award. Since then, with Margaret Perry, an occupational therapist, he had demonstrated in Wiesbaden, Prague, Rouen, Heidelberg, Budapest, Zurich, Paris, Dublin, Moscow, and, this same year of 1967, in Australia. Whipping about in his electric Possum-operated wheelchair, brilliant dark eyes aglow, lips alertly smiling between neat moustache and beautifully clipped short beard, he was a perfect example of the renewed energy and activity which the remarkable service could engender.

Joy Wakefield, both a highly qualified occupational therapist and a trained nurse, was another efficient worker who had joined the project in its early years. She had become its first secretary in 1962 soon after the electro-mechanical laboratory was set up at Stoke Mandeville Hospital by Action for the Crippled Child (then the national fund for research into poliomyelitis and other crippling diseases). But she was far more than a secretary! She carried out a wide variety of tasks with utter dedication and selfless disregard of required working hours —

keeping accounts, estimating costs, performing occasional demonstrations as the project rapidly expanded.

Like David, Stan Cross was a team member whose own disability had led to an exceptional degree of skill and service. Severely paralysed when only nineteen by an attack of polio in 1946, he had spent six months at Stoke Mandeville in an iron lung and two and a half years in the hospital. He had met his wife there and after marriage had started a small printing business in his garage. Then he had obtained a position as a wire-man at a leading firm of manufacturers of flight-simulators, thanks to the efforts of the Government Department of Employment. Despite his very limited mobility, he had risen rapidly to a position of prototype wire-man. In 1964 he had jumped at the chance to work for Possum. Though still in a wheelchair and with limited use of his arms, he proceeded not only to contribute his own superb technical skill to the project but to train up to a dozen others to reach his high standard of workmanship.

Aided by grants from the National Fund for Research into Crippling Diseases, the team had adapted the original basic unit to a variety of purposes, enabling disabled persons to operate not only this, but typewriters, adding machines, dictation machines, tape recorders, telephones, industrial machine tools; also to read micro-filmed books. Then the grants had run out. The project might well have foundered, since research was expensive and funds very limited, had not the Department of Health and Social Security been persuaded to issue basic units to all handicapped persons who could be proved to benefit from their use. Though the cost of the basic unit, about four hundred pounds, was considerable, it was a profitable investment for the government, since Possum users, rendered remarkably independent, often no longer required hospitalisation at a cost of up to seventy pounds a week.

Though Reg Maling was the original laser brain of the project, Roger Jefcoate might well be called its voice, arms, legs — with a brain second only to Maling's. He had joined the Possum Foundation early in its existence, had worked closely with its founder for the past five years, helping to devise units for a variety of purposes. It was usually his task to make the initial visit to the patient, conduct a case conference, prove the need to the government, devise the necessary electrical equipment, install it, and thereafter help keep it in good repair. His work demanded almost constant travel to all part of the British Isles and sometimes to the Continent, intense mental and physical energy, phenomenal electrical know-how, a vast supply of tact, and unqualified devotion. His young wife Jean, a gifted concert singer, was as committed to the cause as he, enduring his long periods of absence or driving the van so he could save precious time by dictating memos and letters to his tape recorder as they travelled.

Never yet, it was P.O.S.M.'s boast, had they been unable to supply a disabled applicant with equipment which would increase his independence. Would this, wondered Roger, be their first failure? For Hilary Pole was by far the greatest challenge they had ever faced. How were they to give her the two things she needed most : security, the ability to summon help effectively and, equally essential for that keen imprisoned mind, COMMUNICATION!

The problems were not all technical, though the erratic flicker of residual movement, varying from a maximum of an eighth-inch to next to nothing before an injection, seemed at the moment insurmountable. Equally formidable were problems of tactics. With Hilary moving every six months, changing consultants, nurses, sisters with each move, there was a host of people in the hospital who, having become involved with her case, had to be approached and their co-operation won. A herculean test in diplomacy for a young whippersnapper in his mid-twenties, his boyish looks belying even that degree of maturity, to convert professional sages, many of them twice his age, to an idea so novel as to be devoid as yet of professional blessing! It was due undoubtedly to Hilary's courage and sense of humour as much as to his own delicate tact that without exception everybody who was approached or took part in the joint project co-operated to the hilt in the difficult provision of equipment.

Roger proceeded swiftly but with his usual punctilious attention to detail. The consultant was sceptical but promised to be co-operative. A week after his visit a copy of Rogers case report was sent to Eric and to Mr. Dearden, the hospital Administrator. In an accompanying letter Reg Maling asked for formal agreement by the medical and administrative staff for the investigation to proceed, formal permission for access to the patient for a study of Hilary's possible controllability, by a department of

Birmingham University, and made suggestions as to possible methods of financing the provision of a typewriter control unit. Eric and Mona made an exciting trip to Aylesbury to observe Possum users, examine the equipment, and talk with Reg Maling and Roger in greater depth about Hilary's case.

Roger worked furiously, realising that in Hilary's situation the time element was crucial. One failure of that tiny bell to call help in any emergency could well be fatal. In response to his solicitations for help many activities were set in motion. Tests were made under Professor Prime of Birmingham University's Department of Electronics and Electrical Engineering to measure Hilary's residual movement. Professor Prime visited her often on EGA, and his right-hand man Conrad Lewis spent hours making the tests with a sensitive tension gauge resembling an electrocardiograph. It was found that with her right toe, the stronger, she was able to maintain a pressure of ten grammes for periods up to ten seconds. With the other she could only manage, at the end of her four-hourly prostigmine cycle (just before an injection) a flicker that was barely measurable. Because her prime need was for summoning help, it was decided that her stronger input, the right toe, should be linked to a microswitch, provided one sufficiently sensitive could be found. *Provided* —

"Must not hope," she kept reminding herself.

The Burgess Microswitch Company at Gateshead set to work on the development of a switch. Mr. Walker of the Dental Department of Queen Elizabeth Hospital directed the making of a very light-weight splint of dental plastic, shaped to her lower leg, in an attempt to keep the leg comfortable but sufficiently rigid to support a transducer, a small coil arrangement about an inch in diameter which would form the vital link between her toe and Possum. Reginald Maling visited her, trying out two microswitches on her thumb and finger. Hilary marvelled at his skill in holding her hand, giving her maximum movement in her weak fingers. However, though he had hoped to find two input movements, toe and finger, that in the latter was not strong enough. It was to be toe or nothing!

Roger made the eighty-mile trip between Aylesbury and Birmingham innumerable times that summer and early autumn. He would have made it every day if necessary. By now he was so personally involved in Hilary's case that no sacrifice for the success of the project seemed too great. It was no longer a business of mere life or death, but of making a rare life worth living.

On September 26th he conducted his Case Conference, always a preliminary procedure for obtaining the Possum environmental controller under the National Health Service. This was the unit intended to provide Hilary with the ability to summon help, also to control a number of items in her room. In a conference the night before with her parents it was decided that the proposed indicator should include : START, BELL (S.O.S.), BUZZ (AID), RADIOS 2, 3, and 4, TAPE, AIR, FAN, BOOK, SPACE, TYPEWRITER. All the officials in any way interested attended : Professor Arnott of the Department of Medicine, Professor Bishop, nominally in charge of her case on EGA, the consultant neurologist, Mr. Milnes, Deputy Administrator, Mr. Walker in charge of the Dental Department, Mr. Bradshaw the electrical engineer, Mr. Prince, the hospital mechanical engineer, Mr. Mowbray in charge of the Carpentry Department, Miss Currie, the medical social worker, the Deputy Matron, Sister Tatlow, and Mr. Ray Miller, technical adviser to the Ministry of Health and Social Security, who came to all the conferences. Roger once more explained the project, using his demonstration unit, and pointed out Hilary's special needs for the various inputs.

"Because she seems quite unable to provide anything more than a single impulse," he outlined the difficulties, "we will need to provide, together with each microswitch, an impulse-latching relay so that the first impulse will start the selector scanning and the next impulse will stop it."

The P.O.S.M. Research Project, under the National Health Service scheme, he further explained, would provide the basic unit, together with the alarm unit and a remote indicator, so that the nursing staff would know which equipment had been switched on and off. The three radio sets would be provided by Hilary's family, also the tape recorder. The fan would be furnished by the hospital engineering department. Vic Currie, who had taken an avid interest in the project from the first would explore the possibility of a talking book from the Listening Library.

The co-operation of the group was amazingly unanimous. Mr. Milnes agreed to provide the administrative co-ordination at the hospital, and it was decided that, because of the twice-yearly moves of Hilary and all her possessions from ward to ward, her

Possum equipment should all be mounted on a mobile trolley which could be chained to a wall. The trolley would be built by the engineering and carpentry departments at the hospital.

October . . . November . . . The application to the National Health Service was approved. Slowly pieces of the intricate puzzle began to fit together. Some had to be discarded. Careful investigation by the Dental Department showed that a leg-mounted splint to hold the input transducers would prove unsatisfactory. Help was then sought from Mr. Brian Jarvis, chief technician in the radio therapy mould room at the hospital. He devoted hours of work to the problem and when Burgess's produced a hypersensitive microswitch, a masterpiece of delicate mechanism, Mr. Jarvis built a versatile clamping arrangement which gave firm support to the switch providing the input to the basic Possum unit and to the solid state coil transducer that Birmingham University produced as the input to the typewriter control. It was a prime demonstration of almost incredible co-operation in technical skills.

3

Hope! By mid-December, when the transducer invented by Birmingham University actually became a reality, hope had long since become expectation, almost unbearable suspense. Roger's confidence and optimism were contagious. Already Hilary felt as if they had been friends for years, partners in a great adventure. Curiosity finally won. She asked someone to lift her eyelid so she could see what he looked like. The result was satisfying — a keen-eyed, smiling, unusually boyish face topped by a shock of straight, slightly unruly hair. But of course she had known what he was like before, very much like herself, in fact, possessed of the same stubborn will, driving energy, determination.

The transducer, comprising two small electric coils, finally arrived. One coil was clamped to the bedside, the other attached to her big toe. The IBM typewriter adapted by Possum was the first "thing" to come. Fittingly it arrived on Christmas Eve, certainly the best Christmas present she had ever had; the most expensive also, for it had cost the hospital over five hundred pounds. The reality of it was almost a surprise. Foremost in her hopes through all the months of planning had been the possibility of means to summon help. All the other benefits of Possum — control of radio, tape recorder, fan — had seemed just bonuses, good but unimportant. The typewriter had been only a vague dream, beautiful but hazy, doubtless a mirage. Now that it was actually here, its possibilities sprang into dazzlingly clear perspective. Communication again! Christmas that year was the happiest and most triumphant she had ever known — yes, even better than the nostalgic memories of childhood. For what could release mean then to one who had never been in prison, freedom of expression to one who had never known silence? It was a day of impatience, too, for she couldn't wait to get on with the business of learning how to use the miracle.

Already Hilary was attempting to learn the new code, aurally, since she couldn't see. She had the lines read to her one by one, and by the time her visitors arrived she had a rough idea of the grid and was ready to practise. They invented a new parlour game, "Typewriters", as hilarious as the old guessing games and treasure hunts of childhood Christmasses. Her victim would sit at the side of the bed, paper and pencil in one hand, a layout of the grid in the other. When Hilary rang he would emulate the typewriter, intoning slowly, "Click, click, click . . ." For the second ring he had to stop clicking and start clonking, and so on until she had finished a sentence.

It was really quite simple. The first flick of the coil made the typewriter click. The second flick made it stop clicking and start to clonk. The third flick made it buzz, which signified the printing of the letter and return to "START". She merely had to count the clicks and clonks and flick the coil in the appropriate places. "A" was two clicks, two clonks, "z" six clicks, seven clonks. Carriage return was accomplished with six clicks, one clonk, and so *ad infinitum.*

Fortunately the door was closed during these practice periods. If anyone had overheard the hilarious noise, the whole family would have been packed off to the psychiatric unit! But the scheme worked. Mr. Jarvis, who had volunteered to instruct Hilary in the use of the typewriter, as well as to brief the nursing staff on how to set up the equipment, was amazed to find that, merely by the use of audible clicks, she had committed the grid to memory in a few hours!

She could actually type! Communication again, not through

laborious, often frustratingly slow intermediaries, but all on her own! However, the new medium could be frustrating too. The coils proved so sensitive that the slightest extraneous movement — a jarring of the bed, a cough from John Willy, or an unwary nurse's feet — would send the typewriter careering off in strange aberrations, and some weird and wonderful language it managed to turn out! The era of experimentation had not ended.

The new year promised not only another move but more pleasurable excitement. Ian and Beth were getting married. They wanted Mum to go with them to South Africa, but she was hesitant. Time off from her school might be managed, but — leave Hilary when she was just getting adjusted to a strange new ward with nobody knew what dangers? Then came an unexpected stroke of luck. Sister Shelagh Churton on East Ground B, a good friend of Tatty's, offered to take Hilary on her ward, the male medical corresponding to Tatty's female — not the ward where she was scheduled to go, of course, but the move could be arranged. The offer was a god-send. Sister Churton was familiar with Hilary's case, and Tatty would be near enough to render assistance. Mona could feel safe in leaving. Hilary moved in January, and Mona flew with Ian and Beth on February 3rd.

They received a grand welcome in Johannesburg from Hans Pfotenhauer, Beth's father, after which they all drove to Bergville, a small town in the foothills of the Drakensberg Mountains, where Betty, Beth's mother, and a friend, Peggy Smithers, awaited them. The wedding day, February 10th, was perfection — weather, ceremony, guests, garden reception. Beth's relatives arrived from hundreds of miles away. Ian too was modestly represented. Alan Brown, one of his university friends, was his best man. Vera and Derek, friends working in Zambia, were present, also a South African who had played rugby with Ian's Hampstead team and who happened to be spending a holiday in Johannesburg.

Thanks to Sister Churton and her nurses, Hilary attended the wedding as chief bridesmaid by proxy. At nine a.m., the hour of the wedding British time, she was dressed and ready for the ceremony. She wore a soft yellow nightdress, its top layer floral nylon over a plain lower layer. Her bedspread, made by Beth, was of the same dull gold satin as the bridesmaids' dresses. In her hand was a bouquet of soft yellow flowers. Dad, Wendy and Peter joined her. Sister had arranged for the padre to come and read the marriage service at the exact hour when it was being read in South Africa. When he had left a nurse brought in a tray with champagne and glasses with the compliments of Sister and her nurses. A telegram came from Ian and Beth, a letter from Sally, Beth's sister in America, another from a second sister in Germany.

For Mona there came an equally climatic moment on February 20th, when an air mail letter arrived typed by Hilary — her first! She ran excitedly to show it to Ian and Beth, Betty and Hans. She and Ian clung together, both laughing and crying with the surge of joyous emotion. That Hilary had burst out of her long dependence at last!

The wedding party arrived home on March 1st and came almost immediately to the hospital. Next day a reception was held for them at West Riding. There were other visits before their return to London two days later. It was almost as satisfying as attending the wedding, listening to all the exciting accounts.

"Look in the top drawer," she was soon telling all her visitors, "and see those perfectly gorgeous photographs of Ian and his bride. Smashing!"

Angela Bennett, one of her old high school friends, found herself looking at them through tears, indescribably touched by Hilary's enthusiasm, when she could not even see them herself.

It was in March that the second miracle arrived, the basic, device, Possum Selector Unit Type One (PSU 1). Hilary learned the layout of the indicator in minutes.

"It's uncanny!" exclaimed Roger. To his utter amazement she needed no second reminder of the correct number of clicks to activate the unit for any one function. At the very first attempt she operated the bell and immediately cancelled it again without panicking or losing control. If Roger's reaction was near incredulity, that of Mona and Eric was a mingling of awe and inexpressible rapture. They were overcome with emotion. For the first time in years they were able to leave her without worry for her safety, wondering if in case of emergency she could produce enough flicker from her toe to set the little bell hung from the bandage in motion, if the clapper would eventually hit the gong, if — hopefully — there might be a nurse in the corridor outside her door, near enough to hear the warning tinkle.

Here was independence such as she had never dreamed of

having again. A whole world of music, of sport, of SECURITY,
at her — not fingertips, but toetips! And the operation of the
mechanism was so simple — a mere flick of the toe to activate
START, then by counting the clicks she could exert just enough
pressure to sound an emergency BELL, create a less urgent
BUZZ, turn on and off her RADIO, turn on her Fan, be
read to.

For Vic Currie, the medical social worker, was able to procure for Hilary a talking book. After learning about the Listening
Library, she wrote to the Spastics Society to see if they could
help with the subscription costs. Since Hilary was not a spastic,
they could not use Society funds, but — they would be delighted
to donate the collection from their carol concert. They sent a
cheque for twenty pounds! Since her tape recorder was only
a two track machine — books were on four tracks — the Listening Library lent her one of theirs, and Vic brought it from
London. She was as excited as Hilary when the first book arrived,
Gerald Durrell's *My Family and Other Animals*. It was one of
Hilary's favourites. She and Vic had more in common than a love
of books. They both loved music, theatre, birds, cooking, people.

Even though one understood its intricate mechanism, Possum
seemed a miracle. Hilary had two inputs, one from each foot.
The stronger, from her right, was used to operate the typewriter control system, interlocked with PSU 1. The other foot
was used to trip the microswitch which in its turn fed the manual
input of the PSU 1. With equal rapidity she mastered the technique of transferring from one to the other, using the coil input.
At all times she maintained direct access to the basic unit, using
her microswitch. Because of "toe-talk" she later decided to use
just one output for Possum, for both selection and typewriter,
leaving the left foot free for the speedier alphabet conversation.
There were two alarm units, one mounted on the trolly itself,
the other outside the ward sister's office, so that a wide range of
calling could be provided. However, this combination of direct
access and the provision of an alarm unit was not an unmixed
blessing. Like many other people, she "talked" in her sleep! Set
up with direct access to her PSU 1, the slightest flicker of her toe
caused the bell to ring while she slept on, happily unaware of
the ensuing pandemonium. More work for the inventors.

Roger re-labelled socket number seven, previously AIR, S.O.S.

2, and wired the alarm so that the bell would not ring unless both S.O.S. stations were selected. So far, so good. Still problems were not all solved. Owing to the extreme sensitivity of the coil, switching on the sucker would often send the whole unit into action — alarm, tape, radios, talking book, fan — a medley that the Sorcerer's Apprentice could not have emulated! The nurses began to look strained. Visiting her in June Roger felt that the principal difficulty was the seeming inability of the nurses to set up the coils and switch correctly. It was little good to try to educate this group of nurses, for Hilary was to be moved again in two weeks, this time to East 2 B. Mr. Jarvis agreed to give the new nursing staff a demonstration.

Hilary dreaded this change more than any other in her migrations. The two ground wards had offered a homelike atmosphere, security. Shelagh Churton, cultured, quiet spoken, artistic, full of Irish humour, had become as much friend as Sister. She was dedicated to helping others, not her patients alone but humanity in general. She had continued Tatty's practice of giving Mum and Dad their lunch at weekends. Her love of travel had given her wide experience, and the four of them had many long serious discussions in Hilary's room. The last twelve months had been almost as happy as her five years in the "Ritz". Hilary confessed her reluctance to leave in a bit of humorous doggerel:

LOOKING BACK ON BEING HERE

> I'd rather like to stay
> On East Ground B and East Ground A.
> Although I do not wish to roam
> From this place I now call home,
> The powers that be do not approve
> Of staying put, and so I move.
> In this sound environment
> I have felt safe, secure, content.
> My gratitude is greater far
> Than can be said by one word "Ta".
> When I'm upstairs upon East Two
> I shall often think of you.
> And when at last I've done the round,
> I shall return to East Floor Ground.

The change resulted in more than the usual agonies of adjustment. Of course the new trolley with all its equipment went along and was chained to the wall of the new room, but even the miracle of Possum was powerless to combat ignorance and inexperience. What good to be able to summon help if the person summoned did not know how to give it? Worse, how summon it if you were thrust into a state of non-communication by inexpert handling? When you had your put-back, it was very easy for the nurse to put your neck in such a position that you could not move to communicate. You were not unconscious. You could hear and feel discomfort, often pain. As long as there was someone nearby who could read J.W. and knew how to put you on E.B. if necessary, you were safe, but the minute you were left alone you were in danger.

The Sister on the new ward was kind and friendly but very strict, so fair and conscientious that she found it difficult to absorb Hilary into the situation with extra care and privileges. Permitting her to send a message home by telephone in case of emergency seemed to Sister favouritism, even though other patients were allowed unrestricted use of a telephone trolley. New methods prescribed for Hilary's routines were excruciatingly painful. The adjustment was as traumatic for Mona as for Hilary. Once when she found no one on duty who knew Hilary or could communicate with her, she stayed all night, going straight to school in the morning. At other times she stayed until midnight, knowing that Hilary felt insecure.

Possum continued to present difficulties. The solid state transducer arrangement which was her input to the typewriter was not satisfactory. Not knowing this, Roger one day made the observation, "It would be nice to have a letter from you sometime".

Stung by the suggestion that she was not utilising the new device to the best of her capabilities, she dictated a poem to Dad to post at once "To Roger".

> I know you're waiting pensively
> Frustrated
> By no word from me.
> I do assure you
> It's not true
> To think that I've
> Forgotten you.

Every dawn of each new day
I lie in bed
And hope and pray
Someone will
Release the power
Which could be mine,
And in one hour
I would be
Typing good as new
That letter
I have promised you.

Alas,
I have no lusty shout
To summon them
From all about,
But thought that you
Might telephone,
Bark a bit,
Even groan,
Stir them up and shake them loose
From offices,
And thus produce
Some action up on East Two B,
Which would perhaps enable me
To leave alone
My tinkling bell,
And use my Possum
Really well.

Roger was conscience-stricken. He had been blaming Hilary
for something which was not her fault. Immediately he phoned
Birmingham University and asked them what the trouble was.
It was recommended that in place of the unsatisfactory coil
arrangement a single ultrasensitive microswitch be provided, to
be clamped to the bed. The new clamp unit was constructed in
the hospital's own workshop by Mr. Robert Edge, who had
taken an active interest in provision of the equipment. Later,
when Mr. Jarvis left the hospital, Mr. Edge took over the technical responsibilities for Possum.

Soon a beautifully typed letter of appreciation was on its way to Roger.

"This is fantastic! Did you bark hysterically, or is it mere coincidence? Anyway, this week has seen action with a capital A. Possum had been chained down and is working well. The second microswitch is easier to control than the coil . . . Now I can work these exciting gadgets, I've a new problem for you. Do you think P.O.S.M. could invent a time machine which would give me at least thirty hours a day? . . . P.S. do you need a private secretary? P.P.S. I even typed the envelope!"

It was slow work, of course. It might take ten or more clicks and clonks to form even one letter, but compared with the old bell or heel method it was going like wildfire — at least for talk with strangers. Best of all, she could do it herself.

"Wonderful piece of good fortune, your typewriter," wrote her preacher friend Perrin from America. "No marathon memory contests, remembering poems to be put on paper by a nurse. Has the bell been retired? One thing you must really like: you can write in private, without any nurse saying 'oh ho' or 'ah ha'. You can be risqué without the whole hospital hearing about it!"

However, the old toe-talk was usually employed with intimate friends and members of the family. Even this was sometimes too much effort, as on one morning when Ian was up from London. Fortunately he was willing to do all the talking. He had been chosen captain of a new rugby team which had managed to persuade officials to let them use part of the sacred grass of Regent's Park and Hampstead Heath. The next week they were playing their inaugural match against a team comprising a majority of international players, the first time rugby would have been played on the Heath for over a hundred years. Ian was both nervous and exhilarated over the prospect with not only the game but the success of his club at stake. Hilary listened to his excited chatter for half an hour but without her usual eager responses. "Scat," she spelled.

Ian returned that evening and, as usual, placed his fingers on her ankle as he prepared for conversation. "Beginning . . ." There was no flick of the muscle, so he started with "l". At "s" there came a sharp jerk. "Shut up," she spelled with more than her usual vigour. "Find a pencil and take this down." Letter by letter, without the slightest hesitation, she dictated the following poetic tribute to "The Hampstead Rugby Club".

A thrilling fight, a free for all, centred round
An oval ball.
A field where mud replaces grass as quickly as
The minutes pass.
At either end the tall white posts,
Looking down like
Aerial ghosts
On thirty men
Careering round
The Hampstead Heath new rugby ground.
Whistles,
Shouts,
Claps and cheers
Not heard here for a hundred years.
Wild with excitement spectators go
Urging their men
To beat the foe —
This international fighting team,
One of the best
In the rugby scene;
So — set them off on a game career
Of wins and losses,
Songs — and beer!

Ian looked at her, astounded. All this from his half hour of
chatter, when she had seemed half asleep! She had dictated it
straight off without any reading back or hesitation. "And some
people think she needs pity!" he thought with humble admiration.
Later the members of the team sent her a copy of the poem,
beautifully engraved.

It was almost time to move again. In spite of all difficulties
E2B now seemed like home. Many of the excellent nurses had
learned her routines, and most had become loyal companions.
Though she and Sister had differed sometimes in opinion, they
had remained friends. When Wendy went into the hospital in
November for the birth of her first child, Sister could not have
been more considerate. There was long labour with difficult
complications, and Hilary was in constant anxiety. Sister kept
ringing the maternity hospital for news. One night she came in
announcing gaily, "Baby is born, all is well," only to find to her
chagrin that it was a mistake. They had thought she said "Lunn"

instead of "Dunn". There were two more agonising days before the baby finally arrived by emergency caesarian. Sister joined in the celebration.

Even Possum had not thrilled Hilary like this second miracle, when Wendy's tiny daughter Joanne was placed beside her on the bed, the baby flesh warm and velvet soft against her hand. A void within her seemed suddenly to be filled. She felt all the creative joy of vicarious motherhood.

4

Thirty-hour day, had she wished for? One twice that long wouldn't have been enough for all the things she wanted to do. She could have spent the whole of it, yes, and the night too, just letting this World of Possum enfold her in its magic.

The radio alone could consume hours. Late in 1968 Dad secured for Hilary a new radio, modified internally so that each of the three stations was connected to a separate power plug and pre-selected. Now with a flick of the toe she could choose any station she wished. She enjoyed almost all of the programmes, from "Housewife's Choice" to politics, Bach to Jim Reeves, Slim Whitman, and Tex Ritter. Being able to choose just what she wanted, to switch from one station to another without help — smashing! For a long time she was on the B.B.C. Audience Research Panel and filled in detailed questionnaires about the programmes. It was fun, but during one of her low periods on a difficult ward she had to give it up. The joy of radio was enough to inspire her to poetry for a B.B.C. Competition.

> I have no power of speech or sight,
> T.V. for me has no delight.
> I have no power to move my limbs,
> I cannot follow fashion's whims.
> But as I lie in bed all day
> You keep me happy, cheerful, gay.
> I always know the latest scores,
> I get the news from foreign shores.
> Plays and quizzes, lively tunes.

Then there's 'Home this Afternoon'.
Politicians blow their gaff,
Then "Round the Horn" to make me laugh.
Long live the voice of B.B.C.,
For radio means LIFE to me.

So did all the other instruments which sprang to attention at the slightest flick of her toe. Sometimes she felt like a maestro conducting an obedient orchestra — if a toe could be likened to a baton! Her tape recorder could be even more sensitive to her whims than the three radio stations, especially when she felt like listening to opera. She had not always liked it. Though she had seen *The Marriage of Figaro* and *The Bartered Bride* in Birmingham, two excellent performances, and had enjoyed helping to stage *The Magic Flute* and *Dido and Aeneas* at school, a disastrous performance of *Carmen* in Liverpool had quite spoiled her appetite. The tape recorder, acquired since coming to hospital, had changed all that. A biography of Joan Sutherland, plus a record of excerpts from her *Lucia*, and Hilary had really been hooked. Now she could listen to opera on tapes to her heart's content.

Yes, and teach others to like it too. When Anne Smith came back to hospital each Monday night in 1968 to do her weekly hair wash, Hilary gently initiated her into the intricacies of *Aida* or *Carmen* or *Lucia di Lammermoor*. She would encourage Anne to choose a tape, then tell her everything she knew about it.

"I felt I must try to listen hard and learn to appreciate it," confessed Anne, "since I never knew if she would ask me something about it!"

The talking book from "The Listening Library", secured by Vic Currie, was a new miracle. Hilary was delighted with its wide variety of choice. That year she enjoyed some fascinating reading : the biography of Mrs. G. B. Shaw, autobiographies of Nevil Shute and Charles Chaplin, some of her favourite children's stories — *Wind in the Willows*, *Heidi*, *The Secret Garden*. She became a Mary Stuart fan, revelling in *This Rough Magic*, *Airs above the Ground*, and others. Another favourite author was Anya Seton, whose *Katherine* she liked best. Thanks to her talking book, she was able to devour at least three books a week. She did most of her "reading" at night, after being tucked up for a sleep. Very cosy !

The tape recorder brought a new bonus. In August 1968 John Allison, a teacher at Olive Hill School, wrote to Mona. He knew about Hilary, had made tapes of children's voices at Olive Hill to send her. He was a member of the Birmingham Hospitals Broadcasting Association, in charge of Cricket Commentaries from Edgbaston, and covered every home match. A pity, he thought, that Hilary was not linked to their network, as were standard ward beds. "Would Hilary like to have recordings of their commentaries?" he asked Mona. He had a large number of tapes, containing highlights of matches back to 1961. Would she! John came himself to bring the first of these cricket tapes. He was very shy, but definitely on Hilary's wave length. The next day he sent her a poem he had composed about their meeting:

DEAR OCTOPUS

From your hospital bed
With twitching toe
You spread your tentacles,
Your cricket-lively spirit leaping far
    beyond the barrack walls
    and echoing corridors.
Awhile you pause, applaud
    a lusty hit for four;
Anon you cheer an England win
    at Wimbledon.
These are your pleasures, but not
    the confines of your realm.
Let Armstrong and Aldrin prate —
    Too late!
Already you have danced upon the dusty moon,
Pierced Venusian clouds,
    Trod Martian deserts,
    Sped to and through the galaxies
        To Beyond.
That Beyond which hides within,
Flesh-clothed, but not of flesh,
Mind-making, but not of mind.
From your hospital bed
With twitching toe you spread
    your messages of cheer

Grasping the hands of gropers;
General of shock-troops,
  You lead,
Not from the rear,
But from the front with flashing
  blade of undaunted wit,
Lifting the hearts of laggards.
This is your magic;
No idiot's tale (though full of sound and fury),
Your piece in the Great Mosaic.
Beloved of the Pattern Maker
You forge your pattern-part
From your hospital bed.
You spread your tentacles
And cannot tell how many seize the ends.
Some you know, who give you all they can;
  But none can give as much
  As you give them.

John was a real poet, and his inspired tribute was humbling.
Beside it her own poor attempts were usually nothing but doggerel. Yet as she listened to the tapes, the greater became her
sympathy for the poor commentators, and finally, doggerel or
not, she had to express it in words.

A commentator's life is hard. He has to be a cricket bard.
When the game is fast and gay. He rattles on about
  the play,
But when the game is dull and dreary
He must assure us he's not weary.
He must *ad lib* to fill the gap, and that is when he takes
  the rap.
Some people seem to sit at home
Just waiting for a slip,
To phone and tell him he is wrong,
That he had better curb his tongue.
Oh, how thankful he must be
For mice and sparrows,
Cups of tea,
An agitator in the crowd,
A drunkard shouting extra loud,

For anything his eye might catch
To subsidise a boring match.
A commentator's life is hard. He has to be a cricket bard.

During Test matches she missed Khalil, sitting crosslegged on the floor and keeping score, for the ebullient little Pakistani was no longer a hospital employee. Study at technical school, where he had excelled in mathematics, had won him a job in an electrical engineering factory. He had realised his dream by helping to bring his mother and father and five brothers to England — also his lovely Zarina, whom he had married by proxy while she was still in Pakistan. Khalil, the eldest, felt duly responsible for them all and shared his worries with his adopted family.

"Hi, Hil, Mum, Dad —" he would begin on his frequent visits to the hospital — "about my dad — about my brothers —"

His father, a tailor, whom he set up in business, had to give up his shop because of poor health, so Khalil gave up his own job and helped his parents buy a small store, running it with them. "Goes very well," he reported happily on one of his visits. "Have a van." He was inordinately generous, had given Wendy a beautiful set of china for her wedding and would have showered presents on the whole family had they permitted. He had never forgotten the birthday party they had given him in Hilary's room, with a real cake and candles, plus a greeting managed by Hilary in the Urdu he had taught her, traced by Wendy in icing. Hilary had blown out the candles with her trachy. It had been one of the high points of his life. There was no preventing him and Zarina from bringing gifts to Hilary for Christmas, New Year, birthdays. Thanks to Zarina's delightful taste, they took the form of the most beautiful shorty night-dresses in her collection : white nylon with pink rosebuds, grey over pink, and, most gorgeous of all, black nylon lace over flame.

Khalil, Gladys Wilson, Anne Smith, Uncle Leslie and Aunt Joan, Rikki Arthur, Roy Atkinson, or whoever . . . Hilary was always glad to flick off the second-hand visitors when a human one appeared. For what were music, books, plays, quizzes, even cricket, compared with the actual thrill of person to person en-counter? Eagerly she would switch on her typewriter, revelling in a click-clonk of repartee that made a genuine two-way conversation. She worked on continuous paper and stopped her letter-writing to "chat".

Naturally there was publicity about her remarkable emergence into a world of independence. Visitors kept coming, to watch, amazed, while she conjured a host of sounds, created words, apparently out of thin air. Her new equipment was a source of great curiosity, not only to hospital officials, but to university professors, to county magnates, even to national dignitaries. One of those who had expressed interest in Possum was Mr. David Ennals, Minister of State, Department of Health and Social Security, who himself had suffered an attack of polio in childhood and had a remarkable sympathy for all disabled people. Mr. Ray Miller of the Department had taken some excellent pictures on one of his visits to Hilary and had shown them to Mr. Ennals. Also, Roger Jefcoate had written him a full account of Hilary's case history, so Roger suggested that Hilary write to Mr. Ennals.

Hilary did so, a casual friendly letter telling about the miracle of independence Possum had wrought in her life. "Would you like to see my equipment in action?" she ended. "If so, the next time you are in Birmingham and have time to come to the hospital, I would be pleased to see you. I'm so thrilled and excited with my Possum I thoroughly enjoy showing off. I hope I can look forward to seeing you."

The "Right Honourable" came, sending advance notice of his arrival and creating a flurry of activity in the hospital almost rivalling the visit of the Queen Mother. He was friendly and informal, a delightful conversationalist, and Hilary enjoyed the encounter to the full.

"Dear Hilary," he wrote on April 23rd, 1969. "I was delighted to meet you on Friday, last week, and to see you work your marvellous equipment. It really is a very notable achievement, and it must make all the difference in the world to you."

Noting the pandemonium occasioned by such visits, Hilary gleefully rattled off some verses.

> If you wish to cause a stir,
> Make the Sister tear her hair,
> All you need do is relate
> That soon a Minister of State
> Is coming here to visit you,

Then quietly watch the great "to do".
Doctor, matron, Governor too
All come up to look at you,
Peruse your Possum, check the code,
As if afraid it might explode.
They vanish as from all about
Cleaners come to sort you out.

On the ward it's chaos too.
And just before the man is due,
Nurses rush from left to right,
Pushing ill folk out of sight,
Hoping, praying, all is well,
But with so many — who can tell?
A cheerful voice, a charming smile
As "The Right Honourable" chats awhile.
His retinue soon fades away
As busy people must not stay.
The visit over, all is still,
Patients can once more be ill.

The move, in January, fulfilled her worst fears. It was a nightmare. Hilary had been unhappy in this ward before. She and the Sister had never seen eye to eye. Now there were further complications. During her months of insecurity she had gradually stepped up her drugs to keep herself communicating as long as possible. Now she agreed with her registrar that she should cut them down, stop her extra half-injections and return to a strict four-hourly routine. But other changes were made without her knowledge and two hours after an injection she could hardly move. The intentions were good but the results disastrous.

Eric and Mona endured agonies. More than once they found her in an uncommunicating condition and knew she had been so for hours. Though Mona had made it plain that she would gladly drive the twelve miles to bring Hilary round after a routine in case the nurse failed, she was seldom called.

"No need to worry," Sister told them one day when Hilary was incommunicado. "She's perfectly safe. The ventilator will be going. It will keep her alive."

"Clinically, yes," replied Mona, almost in despair. "I don't want her just alive. I want her living!"

"She's capable of recovering herself if she wishes," said one consulting physician, when Hilary had been in a non-communicating condition for some seven hours. "Of course she must be psychologically affected after such an ordeal and if she withdraws from choice she can end it when she likes. No human being could go through all this and remain undisturbed."

How foolish, thought Mona. Because they have never seen this before, they assume no one could stand it. They just reached their limit.

5

Possum created a great new roster of friends. Some visited her. Some wrote, and she wrote back, initiating a long and lively correspondence. The vast majority of them she would never meet. And of course all of them she would never really see.

There was Ernie Harman. He saw an article about her in the *Birmingham Post* and knew that he had to see her. "I did," he remembered, " and met the most remarkable person in the world." After he retired, he tried to see her two afternoons a week. Ernie was in a wheelchair. When he visited her on one ward, she was so placed that it was impossible to manoeuvre his chair into a position to do any "toe-talking" — a method still used by many of her relatives and friends. She had to type, then the nurse had to read it, the typewriter being six feet off the floor. It was a friendship which flourished and was mutually stimulating. Hilary's courage and determination were for Ernie both humbling and inspiring.

"I feel that she has been instrumental in checking the progress of my epilepsy," he confessed with gratitude.

There was Victor Bingham. He was attending an annual meeting of the Timperley Tape Talkers, of which he was founder and president, a voluntary club which, using their own tapes, performed readers' service for the blind, disabled, shut-ins. The secretary asked for someone to do a programme tape for Hilary. There were few volunteers. Victor did not have time for the commission, but he had heard of Hilary.

"What kind?" he asked reluctantly. Music, came the answer. Someone had heard she liked arias and organ. He made a tape with about two dozen tunes. It did not come back for three months. Good! He wouldn't have to send very often. But he had retired now, having accumulated forty-four years in the postal service, plus a heart disability. He sent another tape in October with four times as many tunes. It came back nine days later. They started an active correspondence. Hilary told him what sort of music she liked and he began sending her a tape every week, its signature tune, "Danny Boy". They discovered they had much in common — music, a knowledge and love of Liverpool, which was his home, a keen interest in people, a sharp eye and ear for colour, sound, motion. They might well have been called "soul mates".

He began taking infinite pains with the weekly tapes, recording music she said she loved best : symphonies, numbers by Jim Reeves, Glenn Miller, Scottish dances, Viennese waltzes, marches, banjo bands, arias, especially tenors. He caught on tapes the sounds of birds and animals, the cries of gulls, the whistles of tugs on the Mersey. He made recordings of the cattle market in Cardiff, of a blacksmith at his forge, of an English hunt, with the blowing of post horns, the baying of hounds, the pounding of hooves, a man shouting, "Yoiks! Tally ho!"

Once Hilary wrote that she would like to have lived on a farm, so he took her to one farm in fantasy. They stood at a farm gate while trains came past, puffing, clanking, whistling; then walked to the barnyard, where they heard a medley of animal sounds, horses on cobblestones, a cat meowing, cows, sheep, pigs squealing for their mother; then sounds of children's voices happily at play.

Best of all, he visited the I. M. Marsh College and recorded the voices of many of her old friends. Mrs. East : "Surprised to hear from me, aren't you, love? This gentleman friend here is telling me all about you. Cheer up and don't let your spirits go ever away from you, because you'll always have me walkin' beside you. Remember, Hilary, I will always and have always thought of you, and always shall. This is from me, Annie East, as you always knew me. Bye bye, dear one, and God bless you."

Miss Jamieson, who had taken Miss Crabbe's place as principal : "Have been looking at the lovely slides Mr. Bingham has taken. I have written descriptions on them so you will know just what the buildings are and where they stand. Last week when I was interviewing candidates I met one girl who had been inspired to apply to this college because of your marvellous example. I wouldn't dare not to accept her."

He made recordings of the student's carol concert, with comments of some staff members. "Hello, Hilary. I wish you were here. Hope our singing has brought back memories of when you were at college." . . . "Hello, Hilary. I was in college with you. Have been thinking a lot about you, read articles in the papers." . . . "You never met me, but I teach English at I. M. Marsh. We were at Blaenddol this morning and brought back a big bunch of holly to decorate Round Hall. Remember how it used to look at Christmas?"

Victor would send her a four-track, five-inch double tape every week, with a little rose enclosed in it. When she returned it, she would specify what she wanted transferred to another permanent tape. He marvelled at her memory. Once he was unable to find a song from a tape sent five weeks previously. "Don't you remember?" she wrote. "It was just after such and such a song." Always she wanted Annie East's messages kept and the ones from college. "Love to Charlie," she would end her letters, a diminutive for Charlotte, Victor's wife.

Billie James, the British Representative of the Global Tape Recording Exchange, suggested that Hilary be made an honorary member, so she received many of the club tapes, always returning them with a typed note. commenting on her messages in tape. At her request she sent some poems to be read to the British Newstapes that she compiled for international broadcasting. Two of them were read over the Australian radio.

With many of her new friends she had no contact, even by tapes. They never visited her. They may or may not have written her letters. Yet she was bound to them in a fellowship closer than might be engendered by innumerable visits or years of correspondence. It was a fellowship of suffering, of life renewal, of triumphant independence. For they were Possum users, like herself.

The Possum Users Association (P.U.A.) came into being in 1968 at the instigation of Miss Beeston, Head Occupational Therapist at Southport Promenade Hospital and became a registered charity one year later. Its first Newsletter was issued and soon a little magazine was published, called *Possability*. Membership in the Association was open to ALL severely disabled people and those wishing to help them. Its purpose was to contact as many disabled people as possible, to exchange views and criticisms of the electronic equipment different ones had tried, to show what uses the equipment could be put to for the greatest advantage of the user and what opportunities might be available in employment. Also, equally important, it hoped to raise funds to purchase equipment not furnished by the National Health Service for those unable to obtain it. Hilary wrote one of the series of articles called "My Story" for *Possability*.

"I am a myasthenic," it began, "and before you all start buzzing frantically for someone to pass the nearest dictionary, I will try to explain. . . ." and ended, "You all have experienced the thrill and excitement of independence regained, and must be as grateful to P.O.S.M. as I am. I wonder if you also, like me, now find there are not enough hours in the day."

Other Possum users wrote their stories for *Possability*, and she had them read to her. With some she exchanged letters. She felt as if she knew many of them as intimately as the friends who visited her.

She carried on a lively correspondence with Robert Bowell, the editor, a young man with amyotonia congenita (deficient muscle tone from birth) who lived in Bristol. A tiny human dynamo huddled gnomelike on the seat of a wheelchair, through the aid of devoted parents and volunteer teachers he had become a chartered accountant. Now, with the aid of Possum and a set of electronic fingers by which he operated a PSU 1, a telephone, a dictation machine, and an eight-switch input typewriter, he was able to handle accounts for some fifty clients, engage in chess tournaments, attend the Baptist church (whose level entrance permitted use of his Possum-controlled wheelchair) — all in addition to his rapidly growing work as editor of the quarterly magazine *Possability*. In the latter he was assisted by a volunteer, Peter Wilkinson, a solicitor, who came each Monday evening to help read material, play records, and sort out mail.

"I consider myself extremely fortunate," Robert summed up his blessings, "in having so many friends, Possum, and parents who are both willing and able to let me live a normal life."

Hilary had met David Hyde. He visited her on her birthday in May 1969, with his mother and Roger. They were demonstrating Possum at Woodlands Orthopaedic Hospital in Northfield, only about two miles away. David invited her to join the Possum Users' Association Committee as an honorary member, and she accepted. To the treasurer, Christopher Docwra Jones, she sent cheques as often as she was able to accumulate funds for P.U.A., through money she saved herself, contributions of friends, and proceeds from the sales of donated articles managed from her hospital room by friends and family. Christopher, a respiratory polio patient, was a successful solicitor in Kensington with a thriving law practice, which he conducted from his iron lung with the help of Possum by a dictation machine, door lock, intercom, and other aids.

Others of the association Hilary knew less well, but she followed their names and stories gleaned from *Possability* and other sources with avid interest.

Cyril Kohler, paralysed from the neck down after a bombing raid. Because of Possum and his blow-suck pipe he could operate a light, a bell, a tape recorder, and, crowning glory of all, a telephone. He could read all day without help, using a page-turner. He could type with a rubber-tipped stick held in his mouth. His devoted wife could now leave the house on short errands, knowing he could get help if necessary. Oh, his beaming smile spoke louder than words, he was blessed indeed!

Betty Witham, a polio victim, encased in an iron lung for sixteen hours each day for more than fifteen years. "Since I was in Form III at King Edward's," thought Hilary. How life must have changed for her because of Possum! Now she could operate T.V., two radios, control heat, open the front door, call for aid, turn on the phone and talk over it through a microphone! Jean Jefcoate's school had raised money to buy her a typewriter. As she lay in the iron lung, she could look into a mirror above her head while she typed, blowing and sucking through the small tube. What if she did have to see the letters she typed upside down? Lucky to be able to see them at all! Hilary could picture her lying there, hour after hour, pretty, smiling, long red hair streaming out behind her.

Brenda Hansford, who had experienced the first indication of Motor Neurone disease on her wedding day. Strange, it was difficult to handle her suitcase! Her hand kept getting worse, her condition becoming finally so serious that her young husband was permitted to come home from the army. They had better have a child soon, the doctors advised, or it would be too late. They had a son, a beautiful normal boy. Because of Possum Brenda was now able to stay alone while her son was at school, her husband, a draughtsman, at work. She could call for help from nearby if necessary, operating her Possum by the slight movement of her legs which enabled her to sway her knees from side to side. They lived in a small neat house in Rugby, beautifully kept by her handsome, devoted young husband. Friends contributed money and bought her a typewriter, and she was able to earn small amounts by typing manuscripts for an author of children's stories. But the family's chief interest was collecting stamps of every kind for P.U.A. Boxes and boxes of them were stored all over the place. Over 30,000 they had collected in all.

"I'd like to do something like that," thought Hilary.

Winifred Hale, a double amputee because of syringomyelia, which she had had for nearly thirty years, confined constantly to bed, no movement below her neck. Because of Possum, the first one in the West Country, she was able to come home from hospital to her family's quaint old house in the country, at Aust, near Bristol. From her bed she looked out on the garden, a constant delight, and she was able to see the great new Severn bridge being built. Her father, over eighty, had taken care of her, until one morning he failed to come to her room. She rang her bell. No answer. She waited an hour, thinking he might be asleep. Then, thanks to Possum, she was able to phone her sister, who came immediately, and found him dead. Without Possum, who could tell? They might have lain there in the house together, the dead and the living, without anyone coming for days. A family was found to live with her, so she was able to remain at home, frail, motionless, wispy thin, but indomitably cheerful.

"How lonely she must be," thought Hilary, wishing she could share her own visitors and excitement. "But I'm glad she's at home and can look at her garden."

Dick Boydell. Perhaps his story was most dramatic of all. A spastic, a chairbound athetoid. Who could guess that within that grimly contorted body, with its useless hands and arms, its garbled speech that made communication almost impossible, there was hidden away a normal intelligence? Who — but a mother? When he was four and a half, she began teaching him to read. For five years she gave him lessons every day, never knowing how much he was absorbing : reading, history, geography, mental arithmetic, nature study. Then she obtained a teacher's manual and proper textbooks. He was registered with the B.B.C. as a

14—H • •

one-pupil school. In his early teens his father gave him lessons in algebra, chemistry, calculus.

His parents bought a caràvan and took him all over the country, determined to give him every experience he had read about. They visited museums. They sailed on the Norfolk Broads. They flew in a plane at London airport. They even took him on the Underground, one Sunday, when the city was quiet. His father helped him and his mother down the escalator and saw them on a train, then raced back to his car and travelled to a terminus fifteen miles away. When they arrived, he was there waiting. But even they had no idea of the quality of that hidden intelligence until — Possum.

Dick's father saw a demonstration of the Possum equipment at the Royal College of Physicians. He went to see Reg Maling. Most Possum users at that time used mouth control, hopeless for Dick. Foot switches were suggested, and Dick was the first person to have a foot-operated Possum. They got him a typewriter through the Spastic Society. Hour after hour he slogged away at the code, learning the difficult foot movements. After nine days he wrote a letter and called his mother to see it. She could not believe her eyes. It was dated January 13th, 1964 and was written to Mr. Maling. Not only did it contain no mistakes in spelling or punctuation but it included several suggestions for revision of the switches to improve foot control, also some ideas for improvements of the typewriter's letter adaptations to the Possum equipment. After more than thirty years of imprisonment the doors of communication had been flung open. His mother wept. It was a miracle.

Dick Boydell proved to be a mathematical genius. Soon he changed to a four-switch control, later to an eight. He gave demonstrations of Possum in London, Wiesbaden, Rouen, Dublin. He took up amateur radio, passing the requisite examinations for a transmitting licence with a foot-operated Morse key based on his Possum control. He studied electronics and computer programming at the Spastic Society's Further Education Centre at Oakwood and after passing an aptitude test (the first person ever to do so with 100 per cent) started working for the Ford Motor Company as a computer programmer, using a later development of Possum equipment, the word-store typewriter, with 460 stored words, only three small movements required for every word or phrase. He was given a complicated job of programming with a time limit of six weeks. He did it in three. It went through without a mistake.

Mr. Hammersley wrote from the Systems Office of the Ford Motor Company : "All in all I feel that no reference I could give would do full justice for Dick Boydell's grasp of computing but hope that this letter manages to convey some idea of just how high he is in my estimation."

Bravo! thought Hilary. Only someone like herself could comprehend the wonder of such release from prison. But she had previously known the fulfillment of free communication and expression. How much greater the sense of release for a bold spirit which had been locked away in silence for a lifetime!

It was the story of Elizabeth Twistington Higgins which thrilled her most. In some ways Elizabeth might have been Hilary's own fairy-princess-dreams-come-true. She had been a professional dancer and teacher of ballet. Then in 1953 had come realisation. "I've got polio, haven't I?" and "I'll never dance again!" Hilary knew, oh, how well she knew, what that sudden arresting of beloved MOVEMENT must have meant. Disabled from the neck downward, Elizabeth had lived for years in an iron lung. Determined to remain creative, she had learned to become a mouth-painter and had painted striking pictures, of flowers, of dancers, which had sold all over the world. "Another bond in common," thought Hilary, "our love of art and painting." Fascinated, she listened to Elizabeth's story as told through her Possum dictation machine in her little autobiography so aptly named *Still Life*, learned how she had taught herself to breath consciously so that during the day she could leave her iron lung, returning to it each night from her home to the hospital.

Now, thanks to Possum, she was returning to ballet, not to dance, never that again, but to teach it! In addition to her basic unit, which made it possible for her to live in her own home during the day, she now had a battery-operated voice amplifier especially arranged by Roger and an adapted tape recorder. By blowing on the mouthpiece attached to her wheelchair, she could supply her own music, and without undue effort her voice could be heard on stage from the back of the stalls in a quite large theatre. Sitting at her typewriter, she could play the music of a dance theme over and over again, work out the dance sequences in her mind, then teach the choreography to her pupils.

Deciding to create her own version of the *Pas de Quatre* to music by Pugni, a ballet originally presented at Her Majesty's Theatre, London, in 1845, she was training a group to perform the intricate sequences at the Chelmsford Civic Theatre. Once again she was able to create MOVEMENT, beautiful, flowing, rippling mobility full of her own pulsating life.

"Though much has been taken from me," the little book said at its close, "much has been given in return. . . . Determination, will power, and constant effort are needed on my part, but only with the co-operation of others can I achieve results."

"Yes, oh, yes!" thought Hilary. She would never see Elizabeth Twistington Higgins or most of the other Possum users, but they were all akin. Here in this new fellowship was a cause worthy of all her whirlwind energy and tremendous strength of will. Thanks to Possum, she was realising her primary purpose : to live life to the full with all the assets left to her. Now she had an even stronger compulsion : to help others to live.

6

"A thousand and one nights," thought Hilary, her gratitude mingled with awe. No, multiply the line of the old fable by two and you would still have too small a number. Nearly every night for almost ten years Mum and Dad had driven the ten miles from West Riding to the hospital, stayed for hours to perform innumerable duties, driven the ten miles home again, whatever the weather — fog, rain, cold, heat, sleet, snow, wind — night after night after night. Which was the greater miracle — Possum, which had opened up a new world of communication, enjoyment, safety, or this miracle of love which had spent itself in constant self-giving for the life it had created? There was no comparison. Whatever the testing, love would always win.

The burden on Mona and Eric during these years of Hilary's moves was almost intolerable. With the new emphasis on technical nursing the hospital was unable to provide the attendance necessary for her long and complicated night put-back. It was understood that her parents would come every evening and perform the routine which prepared Hilary for the night. In case they were ill, as they were once with the flu, it meant a major rearrangement of the nursing rota. Sometimes Mona and Eric were able to leave by midnight or a little before. Not always. It depended on Hilary's condition. They must be perfectly assured of her safety.

On one ward she was experiencing an especially "low" period, partially because of a change in her drug therapy. One evening they had gone as far as they could with her routine. It was eleven thirty. She could give them no signal. The night sister was alerted, and she gave a reduced dose of prostigmine instead of the pyridostigmine due at this hour, the former being much quicker in effect. Within a few minutes Hilary could signal. They were able to complete her routine and leave by a little after one in the morning.

Three nights later a similar situation arose, but this time Sister would not give the injection. Orders were that Hilary was to be allowed only the pyridostigmine until her two o'clock injection. Mona and Eric must sit by the bed, waiting, until the time came. They had no choice except to stay. Those who had made the rules were off duty. Those on duty did not know the routine. Without communication they could not make her comfortable. At two a.m. the injection was given. In a few minutes Hilary was able to communicate. Mona and Eric left that night at two forty a.m. There were many such episodes.

The excess of responsibility was not all at the hospital. During recent years Nan Nan had come to live with Mona and Eric. She had suffered a stroke and required attention and care. They were of course glad to have her. Betty and Doug were helpful, taking her out at weekends, giving her special treats, but it was on Mona that the burden of daily obligation must fall. Between home and hospital she and Eric were suspended in constant tension. Without extraordinary commitment and co-ordination, plus an ability to laugh at circumstances, both nerves and tempers would surely have snapped under the strain.

Should she give up teaching? Often Mona was tortured by the question. Always the decision was the same. Teaching was her life. Without it she would have been a drying stream, unable to flow outward. Like Wendy — and probably Hilary, if she had had a chance — Mona was a born teacher. Now headmistress of a fine infants' school, she was becoming more and more recognised as an authority capable of instigating new methods of teaching. Regardless of problems at home or at the hospital, no matter how little sleep she was able to get, her school brought release. Here was her self-fulfilment, her *raison d'être*. Each morning the challenge of children's eager faces, of administrative responsibilities demanding all her skills, was like a shot of adrenalin. No, she could not, must not, give up teaching, for others' sakes as well as her own. Without this food for her spirit, she would be unable to give others nourishment. She would be nothing but a weak and lifeless automaton. It was as necessary to her well-being as was Eric's work to his. It was her sole claim to identity as a *person*.

Though the constant attendance at night continued unchanged with each of Hilary's successive moves, and Mona was never free from the expectation of being called at any time of day to restore Hilary to a state of communication, some moves were less traumatic than others. Such was the one to East I A in July 1969. Indeed, as Hilary was wheeled along the corridors to her new port of call, the dread of moving was tempered by a slight sense of anticipation. It was on this ward two years ago that she had first learned about the miracle of Possum. Who could tell? Perhaps it could be the birthplace of another miracle.

Mike Norton, who had taken charge of her Possum equipment when Bob Edge left the hospital, had the trolley chained to the wall of the new room, the buzzer outside Sister's office. Hilary knew some of the nurses. Sister Brown, still in charge, was exceptionally competent. She looked after her patients well and had learned Hilary's routine quickly. She was very much concerned about her spells of noncommunication.

"If we can avoid head jolts, Hilary," she suggested, "when your mother is not here, perhaps the nurses can manage not to 'put you out'."

It was her idea that they try an adapted version of the "Australian lift", a "mini" put-back in which the pillows were not moved out and Hilary's head was not subjected to so much up and down movement — a great improvement because she could be lifted up the bed by two nurses with a third supporting her head, and when she was put down the action was more gentle and controlled. As it was usually on the big lift up the bed to take out all pillows that noncommunication developed, fear of being left uncommunicative for long periods was much lessened.

Another person who made life easier on these rounds of wards was Vic Currie. Understanding her needs, she often became a liaison between Hilary and other members of the staff. Though the majority of the nurses were reasonably patient with her toe-talk and waited to read whole sentences, some were unco-opera-tive. If they were in a hurry or didn't like what they thought Hilary was saying, they would stop reading and guess — not only frustrating and annoying, but dangerous. She couldn't bellow, "STOP! OUCH!!!" if they were pulling a limb out of joint, twisting her neck, getting a kink in the pipe. Then in sheer desperation Hilary would send for Vic, who was a tremendous help when communications went awry, with nurses, doctors, matron. She saved Mum many calls in cases of emergency. Hilary was sometimes a help to Vic too.

"Hill, I've found a patient, a terminal case, on East Lower Ground. She loves reading but is too weak to turn the pages. The only page turner I know of costs a hundred pounds. Can you help?"

"Yes," signalled Hilary, "ring Ernie." Success! Ernie Harman was glad to lend his home-made page turner.

Vic brought her students to talk with Hilary, introduced her to other members of the hospital staff; brought Peter, a psy-chiatric social worker of whom she saw a great deal. Hilary liked him exceedingly, though she knew he teased Vic unmercifully. She was distressed when Vic told her she was not going out with Peter any more, delighted months later when they announced their engagement and were married. (How many Peters did this make in her life?)

Vic was one of the first to know when the momentous change was contemplated.

It all started when Hilary learned that instead of East 2 A, as she had expected, her next port of call was to be the Intensive Care Unit (I.T.U.). Hilary knew why. Professor Robinson had told her at least eighteen months before that he would like her to try his new ventilator when it had been thoroughly tested. Moreover, changes in her position were hoped to make nursing her easier for the nurses. There were not enough nurses on the regular wards to try these experiments. She trusted it would not be for the usual six months period. Six months in a prison re-served for people emerging from unconsciousness, critically ill, or dying? It was like looking into a tunnel with a dead end!

Eric and Mona were appalled. They had long been afraid that the hospital would decide it could not cope with her care. The regular wards with their shortage of nurses were finding it more and more difficult. Suppose this was their solution — keeping her in the Intensive Care Unit permanently! Even the prospect of six months in such an atmosphere was dismaying. It would mean losing most of the benefits of Possum, the stimulating contact with visitors, the impact of a living, thinking other world — stagnation! They made an appointment with Hilary's consultant, and he met them in the day room on August 14th, 1969.

Yes, he told them, it was the decision of the administration because of nursing shortage. He explained the experiments that would be made and judged that Hilary's stay there would not be very long. Meanwhile the pressure on the other wards would be relieved.

"But —" Mona protested — "you know Hilary's mental capacity, her dependence on the outer world for stimulation. How can a physically disabled but otherwise normal person be expected to *live* in such a dreadful situation?"

The doctor sympathised but could give them no immediate encouragement. It was possible, he told them reluctantly, that she might have to be nursed in the I.T.U. permanently.

Mona and Eric dared not look at each other. Each was afraid of the horror in the other's face. This might well be a confirmation of their worst fears — that the hospital would eventually find itself unable to cope with Hilary's case and that she might be sent elsewhere, perhaps far away or, equally frightening — home.

It was as if the doctor read their thoughts. "You could take her home," he said quietly.

They stared at him incredulously. It was Mona who replied. "How could we possibly nurse Hilary at home? She wouldn't be safe!"

The consultant did not dispute the statement. Neither did he retract his suggestion. The interview ended, they left the day room. As soon as they were outside and alone, Mona turned to Eric, eyes ablaze. "Let's take her home!" she blurted.

Eric, always the more practical, regarded her steadily. "You really mean that?"

Mona was again overwhelmed by the enormity of the idea. "I — I don't know." One thing she did know, however. She was tired of being constantly afraid. Now that the vague fear had become tangible, something to be fought, she felt suddenly impelled to action. She knew another thing. She could not let Hilary spend the rest of her life in an Intensive Care Unit. "Yes," she said defiantly, "*home*!"

Eric nodded. Presently they went back into Hilary's room.

"We've talked with 'Uncle Michael'," Eric told her, "and there's nothing we can do about the I.T.U. — at least, not right now."

Hilary was conscious of a coldness in her body. She knew as well as they the danger of getting immured in the Intensive Care Unit, and for a long time she had shared their fears. Then she sensed an excitement in Dad's voice, a significant emphasis on the words, *not right now*.

"How would you like to go home?" he asked.

She felt her whole body shaking. It was akin to that strange half-voluntary movement which the desire to laugh sometimes evoked. Home! Was he joking? No, Dad would never do that to her. As he continued, outlining all the difficulties to be overcome and their possible solutions, her mind leaped out of tension, like a race horse at the starting signal, keeping pace with him, solving the difficulties while he was still presenting them, arriving at the destination far ahead of his cautious presentation of the possibility.

"Think hard about it," he said before they went away. "Then let us know if that is what you want."

HOME! Life had been very frustrating lately, even on this congenial ward. Due to staff shortages injections were not always given on time. She was being left alone in stages of non-communication. In the daytime she had the assurance of Possum, but at night she often moved her foot in sleep and lost control of the bell. Worst of all, many nurses, even some of her consultants seemed to consider and treat her as sub-normal. She knew the constant worry it caused Mum and Dad. Surely they would not be under greater pressure if she were at home! Yet would it be possible? Not without Possum, of course, but she knew of many Possum users who would have been in hospital without it. The problems *could* be insurmountable.

Home! By now Hilary was used to miracles. She could create a dozen by a mere flick of her toe. This time she did more than *hope*. She had *faith*. The same incredible persistence which had wrought the miracle of Possum could surely help to launch this one also, and *love*, the third and greatest of the trilogy, that selfless, unwavering devotion of Mum and Dad, would make it a reality.

Already the last element was at work. The next day Eric rang Mona at her school. "Don't be late home," he warned. "I'm bringing an architect to talk over plans for accommodation for Hilary."

At the hospital he outlined the possibilities. "We'll extend the utility room into the back garden and make a small self-contained flat for you. There will be a little kitchen and 'loo' so that nurses and visitors can have everything they need without coming into the house. There will be a door to the outside and a passage to the house kitchen."

Nursing care would be more of a problem. Injections, tube feeds, suction, tracheotomy care, put-backs, Possum adjustments — all would demand regular and competent attention. Even if the Walsall Health Department agreed to supply district nurses, many additional helpers would be needed. But all the family were of one mind. It was going to be done. Wendy, who would share much of the responsibility, was one of the most determined. They were also agreed on another point : under no circumstances was Mum to give up her job. Somehow every member of the family must maintain his identity and precious independence.

Few people were told at first, Vic Currie, Rachel, Sister Tatlow, and of course Roger. He had thought for a long time that Hilary could be cared for outside the hospital and promised enthusiastic co-operation. Many plans had been made before there was any discussion at the official level. By early September plans for the extension had been sent to the Town Hall to secure planning permission. Mr. Abrams, Professor Robinson, and Hilary's consultant neurologist had been approached. Early in October Eric and Mona had an official meeting with Vic Currie about nursing. She began writing to many organisations for help, the British Red Cross, the St. John Ambulance Brigade, convents, the Salvation Army.

Official moves were slow and cautious. As it seemed advisable for a third party to make the initial approach to the hospital authorities and Roger had successfully dealt with them previously, he was asked to deal with them now about equipment.

"There is some possibility," he wrote, "of Hilary moving home from the Queen Elizabeth Hospital, and Mr. Pole has asked us for advice (as much as we can possibly give him) on the problems that he is liable to encounter and also what prerequisites may be necessary for the essential electrical services and equipment . . ."

The consultant neurologist thought at first that the hospital should contact the Ministry; then he advised Eric and Mona to write to Mr. Ennals. They received assurance that the matter would receive careful attention.

After many weeks the technical teams swung into action. There were innumerable memos, letters, phone calls, visits, between Roger and the hospital, Roger and Eric, the hospital and Eric, re power supplies, ventilators, storage heaters, electrical sockets, generators, air pumps and cylinders, medical equipment. It would take up to a year from the inception of the plan to its fulfilment. A long wait for the excited Hilary!

Meanwhile other less momentous happenings were claiming her attention. The lustre of anticipation was a bit dulled by an event in November. Noonie was with her one evening, laughing, joking, reading to her, when Mum and Dad came. Hilary was quick to sense emotion, tension, in the visitors she knew best. She sensed it now, even before they entered.

"Hello," said Noonie. "You're early."

"Yes," said Dad. He was never one to hedge. "I've some sad news, I'm afraid." Hilary went ice cold. "'It's poor old Chiaro — killed. A car."

She should have felt relief. Nothing had happened to a member of the family; but the coldness remained. Chiaro — that beautiful bit of quicksilver, of sapphire eyes, of light and shadow — her Chiaro! To be at home, yet never to feel the moist loving tongue, the velvet softness snuggled into the curve of her arm! Strange, she had not felt like this at the news of Grom's death — or Nan Nan's! "Oh, you have a letter from Nan Nan," Mum had said. "We had a phone call. She passed away last night." There had been no shock. Nan Nan had been on holiday with two relatives, had died in her sleep. Hilary had felt sadness, of course, loss, but it had all seemed natural. Nan Nan had never been herself since her stroke. Perhaps it would have been different if Hilary had been more involved in both their deaths, sorted through their personal belongings, gone to their funerals. Never in life had she attended a funeral.

She was almost ashamed to feel such grief over Chiaro. It

seemed childish, worse yet, pagan. Just a cat! But it wasn't *just* a cat. It was Chiaro. By the time she wrote her circular Christmas letter in December, however, she could treat the loss with objectivity.

"We no longer have Chiaro (my Siamese cat.) He was killed in November. Shandy, my corgi, was very forlorn indeed, but has now recovered his appetite and high spirits."

The letter related more cheerful news.

I wrote an article for the magazine *Responaut* (for gadget-aided people) and was surprised to get a letter from the editor of *She* asking if she could reproduce the article and photos in the January 1970 edition. Even more surprising, I've been paid for it!!!

Now sit down and prepare for the big news. I AM GOING HOME! After much discussion it's been decided possible for me to be nursed at home. It will take some time, but six months should do it. Dad has permission to build an extension to the house. Nursing could be a problem, but we are exploring every possibility — agencies, friends, married nurses with families, nursing orders, etc.

My niece Joanna Louise, is one year old now, gorgeous blue eyes, a platinum blonde. I love having her come to see me.

Ian, my brother, and Beth went off to Brunei (Borneo) in May. Ian is working for the civil engineering firm, Costain's, building an airport. At the moment they are clearing tropical jungle, draining swamps, etc. Beth is teaching at the Anglican Mission School.

Mum and her school have been on T.V. again.

Her typewriter was clicking and clonking overtime these days. Her toe was in danger of getting writer's cramp. Then suddenly the machine decided not to print capitals, an embarrassment certainly if one wanted to write formal letters, but no deterrent to much of her routine typing. She had discovered some months before that without capitals she could type much faster. Moreover, a letter from a friend had suggested that she try an adapted form of speed writing, using single letters, numbers, and leaving out vowels. Sh tht ths grt idea nd wrt nthus rply mns vwls. Very speedy for her, but hardly so for other people to decipher! She had been far too wholesale. However, she now found a modified code very useful for notes, conversation via typewriter, informal letters. Briefly, it was as follows: "u" for "you", "r" for "are", "b" for "be", "2" for "to" or "too", "4" for "for"; leave out single vowels, as in cmmnt, pssm; with short words the context would show whether "f" stood for "if" or "of", "t" for "it" or "at", etc.; where two vowels came together, it was easier to omit one, as in "esy" for "easy"; when words started with a vowel it was best to include it, as "alod" for "aloud", "alwys" for "always".

She had explained it in an article for *Possability*, hoping that it might give suggestions to other Possum users. "I hpe m xplntin s cler enogh 4 u & tht sme f u wll fnd ths frm f shrthnd usfl."

"I notice Hilary has gone in for a special shorthand code," wrote Roger to Mr. Milnes, the hospital administrator. "Hers is probably the most heavily used machine ever issued."

Too heavily! "dear roger," she wrote in January, "my typewriter over-indulged at christmas and is still tipsy on capitals, so in due respect to its hangover i'm only using small type!"

Eric and Mona took the typewriter down to Aylesbury that weekend, and Reg Maling worked on it all one day and night. On Sunday they had lunch with Roger and Jean in their home on World's End Lane at Weston-Turville.

"It's the first Sunday lunch I have had in a real *home* for many years," confessed Mona a little wistfully. "For the last nine years we have had Sunday lunch in a little restaurant near the hospital."

Roger took the typewriter back to Hilary the next day. To his intense amazement he was able to step up the speed switch within half an hour of his getting the control to speed Number 4, which meant that she was typing at twice her original speed.

She continued to use both small type and shorthand for much of her informal writing, and her visitors became adept at reading it. Even a stranger was expected to decipher something like the following:

"who is it
o k ta who — yes — do you know mr and mrs atkinson
my parents liv near atkinsons
ive been here 9 year
very well
very lit yes ive got fan
i can swi foo yes

tape
yes write-lot
will
yes
shw resl
know atkinson co
ta very much
nos da."

Letters kept pouring in to be answered. The article in
Responaut and in *She* produced a spate of new friends and
admirers.

"Hi, Hilary!" wrote one fan. "Looking at your photos accompanying the *She* article I have quite fallen in love with your
feet. Did anyone ever tell you you have such pretty toes — quite
sexy, in fact!"

"You don't know me," came a note from Agnes A. Higham in
Winnipeg, "and I am old enough to be your grandmother, but
I would like to be your friend as I know you are the bravest
girl I know."

The most thrilling letter came from the Edward Shelley High
School, Walsall.

"During recent school assemblies your article which appeared
in the magazine *She* was read. A great interest arose from both
staff and pupils, and we are now in the process of making various
efforts towards a machine similar to yours. We thought you
would like to hear about this because of your association with
this school."

Smashing! Now perhaps someone who couldn't afford it would
be able to click-clonk.

Another exciting letter had come some months before from
far off Oklahoma in America, from a polio quadriplegic, Mary
Jane Comstock, who had seen an article by Ernie Harman in a
magazine called *Wide Horizon*.

"Even your name sounds happy," wrote Mary Jane, impressed
with Hilary's contagious cheerfulness.

"That's what it means," went the reply. When Mary Jane
wrote that she collected names as a hobby, Hilary sent her a
long list, ascribing a personality to each one : fair or dark, good
disposition or ugly, virtuous or a bit wicked.

"You should try your toe at fiction," suggested Mary Jane, who wrote short stories for religious magazines.

Hilary had no time for fiction, but later that year she did set her toe to some serious religious writing. Her friend Janet Smith had become a lay preacher and was now head of a Methodist Boarding School. She asked Hilary to write her a service, something that might affect the activity of her young pupils, make them *do* something, shake them out of their complacency. Hilary complied, drawing on her vast memory store for hymns, prayers, scripture, and sermon material. Janet read it, had it taped, and it was a great success, much appreciated by her girls and their parents. They were especially impressed because in it Hilary had made no mention of her own situation at all! There was also the inspiration of very useful reading and marvellous illustration.

The sermon was terse and practical, based on the text, "Love One Another". After relating a short story by Ivan Turgeniev about a Russian beggar who had considered a warm friendly hand clasping his own swollen filthy fingers a more welcome gift than money, Hilary ended her sermon with some advice gleaned from her own experience.

"It wasn't food or money that made the beggar smile with joy, but the fact that a man spoke to him and shook hands with him. It is this personal contact these lonely people need — companionship — to feel wanted. They need someone to talk to, with whom to share a cup of tea. Every one of us can help in this way. Just a little time and thought can make some lonely person very happy. When you go shopping, call in to see if you can save someone a journey. Make it an excuse to call in for a chat. Send a postcard when you are on holiday. Please help." She closed with a quotation from Kahlil Gibran. " 'You give but little when you give of your possessions. It is when you give of yourself that you truly give.' "

7

The dreaded exodus to the Intensive Care Unit came inexorably closer. In December Hilary's consultant neurologist, Professor Robinson, and Mr. Abrams had come to explain to her

what they would like to accomplish for her while she was in the
I.T.U. Instead of a dead end the projected stay there was now
being considered a preparation period for her safe-treatment.
They wanted to try a new ventilator, change her position, give her
a thorough series of medical tests and reorganise her routine to
make it easier for home nursing.

On Monday, February 9th, 1970 she found herself whizzing
through corridors. East to West at a speed even Jackie Stewart
would have admired. Arriving, she found to her surprise that
she was sharing her new abode with a gentleman. However,
Possum and J.W. were too much for him. He retreated to his
own ward, leaving her in sole possession of the "dirty" end of the
unit. (There was no lack of soap and water. "Dirty" was just
nursing slang for non-sterile.)

The first three days were almost intolerable. Mum was dreadfully upset. The quarters were barely big enough for nurses and
patient. Most of Hilary's personal belongings had been sent
home. Visitors were afraid to come and stay. The I.T.U. was
certainly different from any other ward — like a row of well-
equipped glass houses linked by intercom. There was every con-
ceivable mechanical and electrical gadget. Hilary felt like an
intruder — also like a specimen in a goldfish bowl. After the
usual pestiferous X-rays, blood tests, and other preliminaries, she
was moved to a corner of the sterile unit. Luckily her nine years
of hospital had ousted any blushing violet scruples! Curtains and
screens were nonexistent, and ablutions, as well as other intimate
ministrations, were performed for all the world to see. Peace was
nil as well as privacy, for there was action twenty-four hours a
day, torture for her ultra-acute sense of hearing. For almost the
first time in her hospital career she felt lost and sorry for herself.

Not for long, however. This was not a dead end. It was — it
must be — a corridor leading home. Sister James, Professor
Robinson, Dr. S. — all became firm allies in this battle for
independence. All soon became her friends. Dr. S. became
adept at "toe-talk". An expert with ventilators, constantly
helpful and understanding, he was absolutely certain that she not
only could but should be nursed at home.

"We will never start anything," he promised her, "without
consulting you first and telling you exactly what we are trying
to do."

Knowing about the innovations helped, but they were still

ordeals. One was the introduction to two new ventilators, a Cape and a Harlow, one power operated, the other driven by gas, in her case compressed air. The Harlow was no bigger than a shoe box, with very light pipes, plus an air cylinder which could fit on her bed, the Cape much bigger but independent of air supply. Not that she divorced J.W. completely. She was merely two-timing! Always apprehensive when trying a new ventilator, she kept him by her bed "just in case". But, though the sound and feeling of the new Cape were unfamiliar, she suffered no dis-comfort or distress.

"If you're offered a more up-to-date ventilator," was her advice to other responauts, "at least try it before saying no!"

There were other bonuses. One was a bright pink sheepskin, not to cover her but to lie on. Talk about the lap of luxury! A real boon for a bed or wheelchair patient, the ultimate in com-fort and a dream to launder.

There were thrilling ideas in the melting pot. One was a sheepskin-lined "shell" which would support her in a sitting position, fitting her body like a glove. All essential equipment (ventilator, air cylinder, sucker, etc.) would be attached to the frame in some way, making her a self-contained unit. If successful, it would diminish the complicated and painful business of tortu-ous put-backs. Lucky molluscs, born complete with shells! It was no easy task making hers. Because her body resembled that of a badly stuffed rag doll. She usually lay on her right side, sup-ported by mounds of pillows in odd places. Before any moulding could be done, she had to be turned on to her back in a sitting position, a gruelling process for all concerned.

The "plastics" team from Stanmore moved in, complete with sheets of Plasterzote and a special oven. Operations started at the top, the major problem being her neck, which was about as use-ful in supporting her head as a blob of jelly. After having her head lifted and swathed in hot plastic innumerable times, she was given a much needed rest. The team went nurse hunting, returning with a subject of Hilary's height and build to act as a model. But the mould did not work well, so it was decided to make a plaster cast of Hilary's neck from which the Plasterzote could later be moulded. Her neck and the back of her head were liberally coated with a substance resembling cold porridge, followed by the application of soggy strips of impregnated bandage. After drying, this was carefully prised away, easily from the skin but not so from the hair. Now Hilary knew what it felt like to be scalped — slowly!

There were ideas also to let her see. There was still normal vision in one eye, less in the other. Only immobility of the lids prevented sight. At the moment the opththalmic team were working on two ideas : magnetic spectacles, or special contact lenses, with ridges at the top to prop the lids open. The contact lenses would keep her eyes moist and avoid damage resulting from the inability to blink.

A good thing, perhaps, she could not know that neither of these experiments — the plastic mould or the eye gadgets — would prove feasible in the near future. Yet these were secondary compared with the great expectation : GOING HOME.

News of the possibility had finally swept round the hospital. Some were sceptical. "She'll be back in a month!" "If you go home —" nurses frequently said. *When*, corrected Hilary firmly to herself. But most of her nurses shared her excitement. Jennie, the lovely Jamaican who had been on East 2 A during Hilary's second time round was here on the I.T.U. also. She and Esther, an Irish auxiliary, could handle Hilary's routine very capably. From one of his trips to Ireland Esther's son brought Hilary a shillelagh. Janet Thacker, whom Hilary had also met before, on East 2 B as a "green" junior nurse, was as capable with her routine as with the complicated care of the seriously ill patients in the I.T.U. There was great excitement in the unit when Janet became engaged. Hilary's interest in the romantic life of all her nurses never flagged. She was thrilled when Sister Tatlow (Tatty) came and whispered in her ear, "Hil, I've met a super person!"

The weeks and months would have seemed endless to one less used to waiting. But what were six months beside ten years? Preparation for an African safari would have seemed like that for a picnic by comparison. A polar expedition could hardly have taken more planning. "Operation Homeward!" There were innumerable people, hospital departments, organisations involved : the Possum team, Mr. Milnes the hospital administrator, Miss Currie, Professor Robinson, Sister James, Dr. S. who masterminded the whole project, Hilary's consultant neurologist, the Walsall health service which agreed to supply the extra nurses, the M.E.B. (Midland Electricity Board), the B.O.C. (British Oxygen Company), and of course Eric and Mona with the major responsibility of building the extension, equipping it, finding voluntary helpers — in fact readjusting their whole lives to fit the new situation.

"We can only send her home," stressed Mr. Milnes, "once we are assured that a stage has been reached in her medical programme where we feel nothing can be done for her in the hospital and there is no advantage in her staying." So thorough was the hospital in its reappraisal that Hilary's sojourn in the I.T.U., scheduled for a few weeks, was extended for several months. In fact, it was not until April 1970 that both the hospital and the National Health Service were satisfied that the move was advisable and that Mr. David Ennals sent a letter of approval to Eric and Mona.

The hospital was more than co-operative in planning for the necessary medical provisions. In addition to supplying much of the equipment for Hilary's home care — ventilators, sucker, Air Viva resuscitator, tracheostomy tubes, Ryles tubes, spare pipes — they agreed to keep sufficient equipment at the hospital so that she could be re-admitted at short notice should the need arise, also to arrange for twenty-four-hour access to the spare equipment to be kept at the hospital. Hilary's consultant neurologist arranged for a briefing conference with Dr. Milne, who would be Hilary's general practitioner.

The local authority would provide syringes, needles, swabs. The Ministry through prescriptions, would supply catheters, drugs and other medical needs. The B.O.C. would fit out the garage and keep a good check of cylinders at hospital expense. The M.E.B. would be responsible for power. Eric and Mona would provide Complan and other personal needs.

Roger, acting for the Possum team, made numerous recommendations both to the hospital and to Eric concerning electrical circuits, an emergency self-starting generator, spare ventilators and suction units, a reciprocating type of pump (with spare), a variable transformer, two cylinders of air with interlinking tubing, taps, and a pressure gauge. Every precaution must be taken to provide alternative means in case of mechanical or electrical breakdowns.

Weather delayed the start of building until the end of March. Then carpenters, builders, engineers, electricians moved into the rear of the house at 3 Fallowfield Road and turned the quiet garden into a madhouse of activity. Shandy, whose favourite pursuit was standing inside the glassed-in porch and barking at every sign of approaching life, human or otherwise, almost developed canine bronchitis. As for the extension, he seemed to regarded it as a sophisticated kennel and staked his claim by christening the wall! Joanne treated it as a playroom.

"The roof's on . . . The window's in . . . There's concrete on the floor . . ." Each evening Eric and Mona gave detailed reports.

Hilary followed each step with intense interest. Her room was to be twelve by fifteen feet, with a ceiling of knotty pine and a tiled floor. The door into the rest of the flat would be by her bed head; opposite it a high but very wide window facing east and filled with a view of flowering cherry and almond in the spring. To her right would be a double-glazed, double sliding french window, opening on to the terrace and forming her own front doors. On her left the wall would be full of "Spur" shelving with birch shelves for all her Possum equipment and enough room for her books and wooden animal collection. Next door would be a tiny kitchen, with an automatic washer, a dryer, and a tea-making kit, a "loo" beyond.

"We'd better stick to something neutral in walls and curtains," said Mona, "until you get home. Then you can furnish it more to your own taste."

"Then I can —" Hilary started to spell excitedly.

"I know!" Mona jumped to forestall the conclusion. "You can have the monk's bench in your room!"

For once Hilary did not mind the jumping ahead. "Sm!" she swiftly spelled. Smashing!

Except for the shelves, the monk's bench would be the first thing to go into the new room. In Hilary's vision it already sat under the high window in all its intricately carved glory, heavy oak lid bearing a visitor's book and a bouquet of flowers.

May 27th was a red letter day. She was given the most precious birthday present she had ever had, the key to her own flat. It was hung on the head of her bed, where it would still be found for years to come. The big double-glazed sliding door was in, so were the decorators. Fortunately there was only one other patient in the unit, so they were able to celebrate her birthday in style. The hospital kitchen staff had made her a birthday cake, and there was a bottle of sherry, soon diminished by the many visitors. It was like a second coming of age, as exciting as the first, for it also symbolised independence.

Activities at the Queen Elizabeth now accelerated to a hectic speed. Dr. Milne, who would be her general practitioner at home, and the Chief Nursing Officer for Walsall came to see her to get some idea of her requirements and to view her equipment. There were lengthy conferences in the board room between hospital and local authority staff to discuss equipment, nursing, safety precautions, and of course finance. Thankfully she was spared these meetings. Vic or her anaesthetist kept her up to date with the results.

June . . . Towards the end of the month the Walsall Health Department were able to tell her that Hilary could have two district nurses for her ten a.m. and two p.m. routines from Monday to Friday and one at weekends. There would also be a night help during the week who would come at nine p.m., assist with the ten p.m. routine and stay with her until seven a.m. This was a great relief, since night time had been one of her major concerns. Private nurses would be prohibitively expensive, and she could not expect Mum or Dad or Wendy to attend her at night. The helpers would not be qualified nurses, permitted to give injections. This posed some problems. She talked the matter over with the medical staff, and it was decided to try an oral dose of pyridostigmine, a drug similar to prostigmine but acting more slowly, instead of her two a.m. injection. It was successful. The family should learn to give the injections. Wendy had already learned, so Mum was victim number one. Armed with a syringe and several needles, she was sent off to practise on an orange. Then it was Dad's turn. Both were good pupils. Walsall started to send district nurses each week to the hospital to help with Hilary's routines. She soon made friends with all of them.

About this time there came another bonus. When the local health authority were looking into aspects of Hilary's nursing care, they sent an official to see the new building accommodations. As a result a grant was obtained from the local authority to help with the building expense, and they were able to obtain an exemption from rates. Through Ann Dobson, editor of *Wide Horizons*, a magazine for the disabled, Hilary obtained information from the ministry about rate relief on buildings used expressly for invalids and disabled people, and she was later able to share the details with other Possum users through *Possability*.

July . . . There was a press conference at the hospital, resulting in some newspaper publicity.

"Going home . . . Most Remarkable Patient," headlined the

Birmingham Mail on July 6th, and continued, "A Walsall woman described by a consultant neurologist as possibly 'the most seriously handicapped person alive', is to go home after ten years in hospital. . . . Due to her dependence on others, Miss Pole, now 31, needs a nurse constantly in attendance. Walsall's Deputy Medical Officer, Dr. John Burrows, said, 'We will have district nurses with her for many hours of the day, but we cannot give 24-hour coverage. We are hoping to find volunteer nurses or other suitably qualified people who are prepared to look after her."

She was divorced from John Willy (final decree) on July 1st, and attached to her new Cape ventilator. "Cod", as she called it (after Cape Cod) was fairly large but so streamlined it would not spoil the new decor. Power driven, it entrained its own air and had a handle just like a car-starting handle, which could be turned by hand in case of power failure. She would also have the Harlow, the tiny light machine working on compressed air. Clamped to the head of her bed, it would render her completely mobile. Then, if all else failed, she would have an Air-Viva resuscitator, a hand-operated bag resembling a small rugby ball.

Slowly the roster of helpers — nurses, readers, just plain sitters — grew. Though pay was offered, most were volunteers. Pat Wyles agreed to come on the first Saturday night of each month. Anne Smith would continue to come each Monday night to wash Hilary's hair and stay until eleven. Peter, the husband of Mona's deputy, a Methodist minister doing social work, would come on Sunday nights to help. Margaret Brookes agreed to come and read on Sunday evenings, bringing a new friend, Amy. Norah Deakins, wife of Les, secretary of the Warwickshire County Cricket Club, would come and read, type, help the nurses, do odd jobs. Offers came in response to advertisements, to newspaper appeals, to local church publicity, to personal solicitations.

August . . . Hilary was running a race with Wendy, who was expecting another baby towards the middle of the month. She vowed she would be home before it arrived.

8

The day of the great migration was set, Tuesday, August 11th. The decorating was finished. Mona and Eric were working furiously in every spare minute, re-laying the terrace, making a pond, clearing away the building rubbish, putting up the "Spur" shelving, transferring some of Hilary's belongings from the loft. And at the hospital the pace accelerated. The ambulance men came to measure Hilary's bed, then went to the house to measure the doors. A press conference was arranged at the hospital with an embargo on release until mid-day on August 11th.

The night of the tenth Roger and his young wife Jean worked until the early hours of the morning transferring Hilary's Possum equipment from the hospital to the new flat. They were just as excited as Eric and Mona and equally involved in the flurry of preparations. Their interest was as much personal as technical, though, if successful, "operation homeward" would be by far the greatest triumph Possum had yet achieved. If Hilary could do it, who couldn't? They assumed duties well beyond the scope of Roger's technical obligations. Early on the morning of the eleventh they were laying the last of the square concrete slabs on the terrace over which the ambulance team must pass on its trip round the house to the entrance of the new flat.

Hilary woke up feeling as excited as the most daring adventurer. Safari? North Pole expedition? This was even more momentous — a journey to a new life! She had an earlier routine than usual, at eight a.m. The nurses were as excited as she was. Many came from other wards to indulge in last minute toe-talk.

"Ta . . . Ta . . . Ta . . . Ta . . ." She kept spelling out thank yous.

At nine thirty Roger arrived to finish dismantling Possum and to take photographs of her departure and journey. Then came furious activity. Dr. S. attached two air cylinders to the end of her bed, put her on the tiny Harlow ventilator. At a little after ten they were ready to move. Still on her bed, she was wheeled along the maze of corridors, lifted into the ambulance. For the first time in months she felt the warmth of sunlight, fresh air on her cheeks. For the first time in five years she was for a few brief moments out of doors. But it would not be the last!

Anne Bradford, a nurse from the I.T.U., Margaret Payne, one of the Walsall district nurses, and Dr. S. travelled in the ambulance with her. The convoy consisted of two police outriders, the ambulance with flashing blue lights, then Roger and Jean in their van, followed by the Chief of the Ambulance Brigade. The police escort was because of the very slow rate of travel, to give Hilary as smooth a ride as possible. Exciting, V.I.P. treatment! The ten-mile, police escorted journey along the M5 took about an hour.

Hilary loved the trip. Lack of sight was no deterrent to enjoyment. She revelled in the smoothness of the M5. She had never been on a motorway before. John Styles described every detail of the course — fly-overs, tunnels, expressways, how high or how low the road was, names of factories, canals, railways, even the crops in the fields. Great fun!

She knew by the turning when they reached Fallowfield Road, followed by the motion of the ambulance as it was backed into the drive. Then the ambulance men, with the aid of the police, lifted her bed and carried it round the house to her room. She felt like a bride being lifted in strong arms over the threshold of her new home.

There were Mum and Dad. She could see even without vision their unshed tears. There was Wendy. Aha! Hilary had won the race. The birth of Baby Emma was still at least two weeks away. There was eighteen-months-old Joanne, so surprised to see Aunty here that she just stood staring and mouthing, "Ooooh, look!" There were Margaret Hoare, Anne Smith, Wendy and Peter, and several other friends. And of course there was Shandy, most vociferous of all. Somebody lifted him on to the bed, a squirming soft red bundle, and she felt his slobbering welcome.

The hospital had asked the press and television to stay away from the house to avoid adding to Hilary's "considerable emotional and psychological upheaval" on experiencing the great transition. When she heard of this statement, Hilary was "hopping mad". Ridiculous! After moving her from ward to ward every six months for the last five years, did they still not know what to expect? However, she was glad that they had kept the press away, because it was a private affair. Much better to have friends round her instead of strangers!

While Mum and some of the others in the party served coffee to the bevy of attendants, Wendy read Hilary the post. There was a great pile of cards, letters, tapes, telegrams, records of phone calls, even a message from Ian and Beth in Brunei.

"Welcome home will phone eight a.m. Saturday fifteenth. Stop. Dad have office telephone amplifier if possible. Bethian." There was a wire from Aunty Betty and Noonie, on holiday in Austria : "See you soon."

"Welcome home. So glad. Lots of love. John Bunty and Tim. Just adopted baby."

The one from Ernie was lyrical :

> Yippee you've ridden out to west,
> We know you love West Riding best,
> The trail you took leads many ways
> To comfort, home, and happy days.

After photographs had been taken and coffee served, Hilary was left in possession of her new domain with only family and a few helpers in attendance. Now she could really bask in the joy of ownership. She did not need to see it with her eyes, though obliging fingers were always ready to lift the lid of her good eye for a brief view of some detail. She knew how it all looked : the walls and tiled floor almost the same colour of palest sage green; on her left the entire wall of shelving for her Possum equipment; the beloved monk's bench under the high window, already decked with flowers; the long sliding french doors to her right, with a minute wisteria on one side of the outside terrace, a camellia on the other. Already she was planning additions to the decor. In the wall space to the right of the high window would hang the beautiful big brass rubbing which three of the King Edward's High School girls and their boy friends had done for her; perhaps close to it the still life flowers which she herself had painted. Oh, she had a host of plans for this domain of hers!

The Possum team was busy. Roger and Bob Blackburn, another technician, had brought Hans Persson, a young Swede who was working with them for a time preparatory to going back to Sweden to help install Possum equipment for the Swedish government. All three spent the whole afternoon drilling holes and climbing, hiding wires, clambering on the roof, trying to find the best place for aerials, future garden alarms, and other equipment.

A "mini-party" had been planned, mostly family and a few others who would understand if in the rush of activity the affair did not run smoothly. In addition to the complications of Hilary's homecoming, Wendy might be rushed any minute to the hospital! However, the party mushroomed. All and sundry began issuing invitations, and friends popped in by the dozen to celebrate. It was a gorgeous evening. Small tables, chairs, and cushions were scattered all over the garden and terrace. The table indoors was laden with fifteen or twenty different cheeses, plus biscuits and bread. Wine was there for the pouring. It was only the hospital which had underestimated Hilary's resilience. Still "fighting fit", she revelled in every minute of the celebration. It was super! Now she could actually entertain in her own flat. She felt like a queen newly come into her kingdom.

When Nell Jones, the first night help, arrived at nine p.m., she must have been somewhat overwhelmed to find a party in full swing. If so, she gave no sign. All the workers soon learned that events at the Pole's were unpredictable. Nell, who had had little or no briefing and only three days' notice of this duty as one of the health department's night service personnel, was much more overwhelmed by her responsibility. However, Dr. S. stayed for the night, sleeping on a settee in the lounge so that Nell could tap for him if his help and advice were needed. She was given a demonstration of the equipment and shown how to communicate with Hilary. (After three weeks she was teaching another night helper, Joy Holland.)

Though the press was not present at the actual homecoming, they swiftly sprang into action. In the evening editions throughout Britain the event was headlined.

Manchester Evening News, Tuesday, August 11th, 1970. "BRITAIN'S BRAVEST PATIENT GOES HOME. The girl doctors and nurses call Britain's bravest patient went home to a tearful family welcome today — after nearly ten years in hospital. It is the first time since December 1960 that Hilary Pole has been outside of the Queen Elizabeth Hospital . . ."

(Tearful! They had to laugh at that. It was certainly one of the happiest days the family had known. No one had shed a single tear, not even of joy. They finally concluded that the report must have been made over the telephone and that what actually was said must have been "cheerful"!)

Blackpool Evening Gazette: "BRAVE HILARY LEAVES HOSPITAL. After nearly ten years . . ."

Daily Telegraph: "Bravest Patient Goes Home after Ten Years . . ."

The Times: "A PARALYTIC TRIUMPHS . . ."

Liverpool Echo: "A BRAVE GIRL GOES HOME AFTER TEN YEARS . . ."

Birmingham Mail: "Back home after ten years in hospital . . ."

Walsall Observer: "TRIUMPH OVER GRAVE ILLNESS. With new ventilator, operated from compressed air cylinders, she is able to move about . . ."

"Rot," was Hilary's reaction to such excess of palaver and occasional misstatement.

Similar articles appeared *ad infinitum* for the next month, the news spreading far beyond the bounds of Britain through the Associated Press.

The Oakland Tribune, California: "SHE SPEAKS WITH HER TOES . . ."

New Jersey Herald: "ALMOST TOTAL PARALYSIS BEATEN AFTER TEN YEARS . . ."

The Globe and Mail, Toronto: "Life still a challenge. FORMER GYM TEACHER CAN MOVE ONLY TOES . . ."

Australia: "TOES SPELL HER LESSON IN COURAGE . . ."

As the days passed interviews with the chief actors in the drama were publicised, quotes given, details of Hilary's new life chronicled.

The hospital was reported in the *Express and Star* as saying, "The transfer has been successfully completed, but it is likely to take her two or three weeks to recover from the journey and adjust to her new environment." (Ha! They should have seen her party the first night!)

The same article quoted Mona: "I never believed that it would be medically possible to have my daughter home again. We are overjoyed." and Eric, "Hilary has been wonderful throughout the long years. At no stage has she ever shown any embitterment. She has a positive attitude towards life."

"She will be under the constant care of her local doctor," the article continued. "The nursing service of Walsall Health

Authority has appointed additional nurses for twice a day visiting. In addition a night helper will be provided by the local authority from Monday to Friday to ensure that there is someone at Hilary's bedside 24 hours a day. An appeal for volunteers has brought 20 replies. In all, 17 volunteers will be involved every week."

A quotation from one of the hospital doctors was a marvel of succinctness. "She has a tremendous personality, and, though she cannot move, manages to impose her will on people."

There were many feature articles which made discerning comments. Wrote Emma Butler in *Pulse*, "I would describe her as the most mentally active disabled person I have ever been privileged to meet."

"Is there any way *Pulse* readers could help you?" she asked at the close of her interview.

"Stamps, please," click-clonked Hilary instantly, then elaborated in her short hand (or should it be short*foot*?) "To raise funds 4 p u a mmbrs collct so i'm alwys vry grtful 4 any help."

In an article titled "Hilary's World", Rosalind Chalmers commented, "It might even seem to some that this is the sort of case advocates of euthanasia envisage, for one could hardly have a greater number of disabilities and still be living. If you could call it living? But to anyone who knows Hilary, even indirectly through her letters or articles, such thoughts are ludicrously irrelevant."

Perhaps Laura Gillan, writing about "The Brave Cheerful World of Hilary Pole" in September 1970 in the *Express and Star*, came closest to shrewd and sympathetic discernment.

"The first thing a stranger has to realise is that there are two Hilary Poles.

"There's the body on the bed, inert, unresponsive, unable to speak, open its eyes, move a hand, smile, or otherwise reply to the visitor's greeting. There's the bizarre effect of tubes, one to the throat and one to the nose, the sagging jaw line, the protruding tongue.

"It seems pointless to say anything, to do more than whisper across the bed to a third person, 'How is she?'

"But you say hello, aloud, just to seem polite, and suddenly the typewriter on the shelf beside the wall begins to chatter. And as the message comes across you realise that now, for the first time, you are meeting the real Hilary Pole, that inside that immo-

bilised body is a vital, sensitive, fully conscious woman with a
lightning brain, a sharp turn of phrase, and a vital thought that
she wants to get across . . ."

Miss Gillan was as curious about Hilary's parents as about
Hilary.

"I could be quite submerged by all this," Mona told her. "But
I'm keeping on with my job as head mistress. It's much better
that Hilary and I retain our independence."

Eric also made his contribution. "There's no room for senti-
mentality or pity. We hate all that sugary stuff. Hilary retains her
independence and individuality, and we respect her privacy as
much as we can."

They indulged in some toe-talk. "Beginning, a, b, c, d, etc." or,
if there was no initial flick of the muscle, "Beginning, l, m, n, o,
etc."

"Hi," greeted Hilary. Then, instead of telling about herself,
she "talked" about Possum and the need to publicise it.

"I-t m-a-d-e s-u-c-h a d-i-f-f-e-r-e-n-c-e t-o m-e," she spelled.

Hilary click-clonked the concluding words of the interview on
her typewriter. "I have no fears, and I am very happy. It has
been a very successful move."

She could have said it in two words : "I'M HOME."

9

Now Hilary could get down to the real business of living!

Worries were at an end. She felt completely secure. No more
waking to find herself alone, wondering if her bell would be
answered, getting late injections, struggling with the inept and
painful experiments of new nurses. No matter how good a
hospital was, it could never be a substitute for home. The first
five years had been tolerable; she had felt an integral part of a
community. But once she had started moving she had no longer
belonged anywhere — drifting. Now, to be home, to have a
flat of her own, personal belongings around her, to be able to
say, "This is mine", was a tremendous joy. She was once more
a part of FAMILY, could participate in its trivialities as well as
its major issues. Shandy could wander in and out at will. She

could see the garden, even be wheeled out into it, hear the birds, have Joanne play in her room or sit on her bed to "read" her a story. It was living again!

Shortly after her installation all the helpers came for an evening and Dr. S. explained in simple terms her medical equipment so that all would understand her alarm system and know what to do in an emergency. Mrs. Payne, the senior home nursing sister, Edna Doggett, and some of the other district nurses had already been to the hospital to learn something of the routine. Fortunately it was Mona's holiday from school, and she spent time every day doing the routines with successive nurses. Mrs. Payne stayed on duty for many weeks as the "constant", so that there would be only one new nurse at a time. Anne Smith helped Mona with the ten p.m. routine and assisted in instructing the new night help. Before the summer holiday was over the whole staff of district nurses, about thirty, had been met and briefed. They were quick to learn, and with Mona always available the period of adjustment was less difficult than many of Hilary's experiences on new wards in the hospital.

Eric also gathered together his band of volunteer mechanics, and a representative from the Cape Engineering Company came with a spare machine, which he dismantled to demonstrate day to day maintenance. In case of serious trouble a Cape engineer was on call twenty-four hours a day — and that really meant twenty-four!

Not only did the company give regular servicing, but if there was the slightest difficulty their representative arrived in record time. Soon after Hilary came home she found the motor noisy. Probably she had not noticed it in the confusion of the I.T.U. A Cape service man came with a new motor and stayed until nearly midnight getting every part insulated against the smallest vibration. Later one night the pressures on the Cape seemed to aggravate a chest congestion. Dad rang Hank Shumacher, a company engineer, around midnight. When his advice failed to settle the problem, Hank drove from Warwick, about thirty miles at one in the morning, staying until three; then came on each of the next few days to make sure the equipment was in order. During a power crisis some months later a representative was constantly checking. Service was equally prompt and efficient at two in the afternoon or two in the morning.

Thanks to expert management (largely Mona's) a daily routine was developed which would continue almost unchanged

10.00 a.m. Two district nurses arrive, give injection, feed, bedpan (nurse one on Hilary's left lifts her head, while nurse two on the right turns her on to her back, then nurse one lowers her head and both lift her to the pan), suck, face wash, off pan, blanket bath (feet and hands dabbling in the water, gorgeous feeling!)

11.15 a.m. Buzz for Nancy, the family treasure, to bring coffee, which Hilary the good hostess, always shares, having her cupful poured down her tube. Teeth cleaned, turned again on to her side, put back comfortably on her mountain of pillows, hair combed, Possum connected, another feed, and the nurses leave soon after twelve.

12.15 p.m. Clearing up of post with volunteer, tapes on, typing.

1.00 p.m. News on the radio. If Dad is at home, he and volunteer and Nancy have dinner.

2.00 p.m. Afternoon routine with two nurses and volunteer, injection, feed, pan, another put-back, a cup of tea for the nurses.

3.15 p.m. Departure of nurses. More typing, listening to "Waggoners Walk" and Sports Desk on the radio, feed.

4.30 p.m. Mum home, departure of volunteer, more typing.

6.00 p.m. Injection and feed by Mum or Dad, suck, type, radio.

8.00 p.m. Evening volunteer to work or read.

9.00-9.45 p.m. Night help, injection, feed, nursing routine by Mum and Dad, with night help or volunteer, "milking" of ventilator pipes, top up humidifier, checking second ventilator, change of nightie, put-back for the night, shawl over shoulders.

11.00-11.30 p.m. Dad making coffee, Shandy on the bed for a biscuit, departure of volunteer; Dad sets up the talking book, ear piece, or personal tape; Mum checks the drug for the night help to give at 1.00 a.m. and gets provisions for night.

11.30-11.45 p.m. Mum and Dad to bed, night help in charge puts pads of witch hazel on left eye, glycerine on tongue and cuticle cream on nails; talking book on.

1.00 a.m. Feed and drug (orally), off to sleep. During the night, half-hourly hip and reverse hip twist alternately, even when asleep.

6.00. Dad gives injection, helps to lift up the bed, goes back to bed, night help feeds.

7.00. Dad comes down; night help goes.

8.00. Feed. Listen to book or tape or just cogitate.

8.30-9.00. Dad to work, volunteer comes, Mum to school, Nancy comes.

10.00 a.m. The round starts again.

The weekly routine was almost as predictable, reminding one of the old silly song, "Monday, roast beef, Tuesday, string beans, Wednesday, sooo-up . . ." All the volunteers came every week on a certain day. Wendy's responsibility was chiefly on Monday and Tuesday.

For the first few months after Hilary came home Wendy and her family were living at West Riding, waiting for their new house in Chasetown to be built. After they moved into it in March, every Monday morning Peter would bring Wendy, Joanne, and baby Emma before going to the comprehensive school where he was a mathematics teacher. Joanne would then go to nursery with Mum while Nancy looked after Emma (and loved it!). The family would stay at West Riding Monday night, for Wendy was on duty again Tuesday until two p.m., when she would collect Joanne and Peter at their schools and head for home.

For Hilary Wendy was almost an extension of self — hands, voice, movement. She sorted post, read it, filed it, helped to answer it. She varnished nails, sorted out tapes. She was expert at the routine and popular with the new nurses. She was able to take over from Mum on an occasional weekend, later for a week's holiday. At Christmastime she shopped, wrapped, addressed cards, even brought Hilary the Christmas pudding mixture to "stir", so she wouldn't miss her Christmas wish! She acted as interpreter for visitors and helpers. And if any time was ever left over during her visits, she read aloud. Without Wendy, and the sacrifices she made willingly for Hilary's sake, the routine of days and weeks would never have rolled so smoothly.

On Monday evening, from seven thirty to ten came Brenda, mother of three children, to type and read, while Anne Smith washed Hilary's hair. Ward sister? Not any longer. On several occasions when Anne tried to exert professional authority, she was squashed in no uncertain terms! Hilary was the sole arbiter of action in this, her own domain.

"She remains indomitable," Anne marvelled. "She exhausts me at the end of the day with her energy. She continues to irritate me at times, to make me furious when she seems to use her mother's last ounce of energy, but she still holds my unquestioned loyalty."

There *had* been a few tears at the homecoming, after all, unknown to Hilary. "For me," confessed Anne, "seeing her carried out of the ambulance at 'West Riding' was a miracle. She had defied all medical predictions and survived in spite of everything. I'm ashamed to say I had a little weep, but don't tell Hil, she'd be disgusted.")

On Tuesday afternoon came Rikki, an old pupil of King Edward's High School, about Mum's age, to help the nurses, do Hilary's nails, read; and from eight to ten Jessica, who had heard of Hilary at church; from nine forty-five to eleven thirty, after putting her two young children to bed, Maureen, who had learned to help Mum with the late routine.

There was Joyce, always available and willing to help. Mum was on holiday when Hilary came home, so apart from the nurses and the occasional social visitors, she was in attendance all the time the first week; but Joyce came for her volunteered time on Saturday afternoon at two. She helped fetch and carry and watch, then sat and read to Hilary for a few minutes, but there was cricket on the radio, so she just sat with her book and knitting. But Joyce would never be content with merely "sitting". She quickly learned to stay alone with Hilary for short periods while Mum went into the garden, then to the local shops; later to the golf course with Dad for an hour after finishing with Hilary's routine. Finally Joyce learned to help with the whole routine, injections and all — a godsend to Mona, relieving her occasionally from the constant pressure of home duty. Harry, Joyce's husband, also became involved in all sorts of odd jobs for Hilary and for P.U.A.

The rest of the week was equally filled with volunteers; Doreen and her thirteen-year-old daughter Heather, who assumed the task of typing the card index for Hilary's more than two hundred records; Nell, a widow; Sylvia, who had heard of Hilary through the Young Wives' Group at church; Margaret, a member of the Walsall Ladies' Circle, and Jean, who came on Thursday morning, helped the nurses until noon, went home to get her husband's

lunch, came back from two until four. Ernie Harman came in
his wheelchair whenever he was able.

There was Pauline Morley, who had met Hilary at the consecration service of St. Martin's and who felt inadequate at first
but learned so much through Hilary that she became an auxiliary
nurse on Walsall District. There were the two Anns, Ann Snell
and Ann Boyd, who came one after the other on Thursday
nights, Ann Snell to type some of Hilary's fast accumulating
material; Ann Boyd to do the right routine with Mona and
the helper, also substituting for any volunteer unable to come.
Learning of Eric's fondness of pastry and realising that Mona
had little time for baking, Ann Boyd baked a tart or a pie for
him whenever she made one for her husband and two small
boys. Eric loved them!

On Fridays came the always faithful Norah Deakins, followed
by Joyce and Trixie. Trixie also learned the routine and stayed
to help Mona at night. She came also every other Saturday
(when either Mona or Eric had to be on all-night duty), becoming
the third person of the team to help put Hilary to bed.

All day, from Monday to Friday, there was Mrs. Platt, the
cheerful, efficient Nancy, far more family godmother than daily
household help, ready at the whirr of the buzzer to bring coffee,
run errands, prepare lunch for visitors, attend to the needs of
Shandy, watch Wendy's children, eager at all times to assist.

"Yes, Hilary, love, what can I do for you?"

At the weekends there was no Nancy, and the helpers were
fewer. There was only one district nurse, so she and Mona performed the routines with Eric as the third pair of hands and
coffee maker. Joyce came again on Saturday afternoons, and at
night three volunteers shared the rota, Pat Wyles the first Saturday in the month; Ann Webb, qualified as a Health Visitor;
and Betty, a trained midwife. When the latter had to give up on
account of ill health, Mona and Eric took over this duty.

Sunday afternoons were high points for Hilary. During the
cricket season, if there were no home match for Warwickshire
at Edgbaston, John Allison came and gave her a ball by ball
commentary of the John Player Sunday League Match, staying
until the matches ended at six forty-five p.m. It was a fabulous
treat. If Warwickshire were playing at Edgbaston, John had to
stay at the ground, broadcasting his commentary on the Birmingham Hospital Network, but he always taped it and brought it to

her when the match was over. Hilary's passion for cricket never cooled. The month she returned home she wrote a long hilarious description of a match called "Commentator's Nightmare". It made John howl with laughter.

"Bowlers like Procter," it began, "who hike a good two-thirds of the way to the boundary between each delivery, must be the Commentator's nightmare. . . . England are 47 for 1. Procter is still walking back. The batsman out today — Edrich, caught Engineer, a fine catch diving to his right, bowled Procter 7 . . . Procter starts his long trek back . . . He's walking back, walking, walking . . . let's count his steps, 2, 3, 4 . . . 23, 24, 25 . . . 44, 45, 46 . . . What can I talk about! Score has not changed, nor the field. Try the weather? The crowd? Cold sweat trickles down my back. I just hope Procter is sweating too!" . . . and so on to the hilarious end. "It is me for the Tavern, running all the way! I'm not coming back, coming back — coming back — coming — com —"

Out of the cricket season John often brought his stereo tape recorder and speakers, and they would listen to a variety of music tapes, taking turns to choose. Fortunately they had the same tastes, classical and jazz, both loud. If either of them had written any new poems, they exchanged them.

Hilary remained interested in all the surrounding cricket clubs. The Warwickshire County Club sent her a membership card so that she could visit its grounds if possible.

"Dear Hilary," a message accompanied one small package. "Whilst not wishing to incur the wrath of your Yorkist father, and by so doing restart the Battle of the Roses, we would be pleased if you would kindly accept this small token from two members of the greatest county in these Isles. With our very best regards, Gerry Ennis and Harry Arnold." The package contained a blue tie with red roses and the inscription LCCC "Lancashire County Cricket Club".

Margaret Brookes and her friend Amy Cooper, a widowed nurse, came together on Sunday evenings, and they all did crossword puzzles and anagrams, usually to the frustration of the visitors. Poor Margaret could hardly get the anagram written down before Hilary's bell would ring furiously with the answer. Amy developed the habit of doing the *Daily Mirror* puzzles in her lunch hour and saving them for Hilary, enjoying to the full the advantage it gave her over the other two. "Please look it up,"

Hilary would insist if there was the slightest doubt about a clue and they were soon surrounded by dictionaries, atlases, Shakespeare, language books, histories, quotation collections. Margaret, only five feet tall, had to climb on a chair to reach them. Meanwhile Amy was kept busy continuing the crosswords, as Hilary could not brook wasting time. Starting with the puzzles from the *Sunday Express*, they went on to the ones from the *Birmingham Evening Mail* and the *Daily Mirror*, usually doing three in the evening. It was work, work, work, but hilarious fun.

In fact, fun usually became mixed with work, whatever the team and whatever the hour. Dad, Noonie, Hilary — all were proficient contributors.

"Look at those words on Jane's uniform," Dad chaffed. " 'District Nurse?' I'm threatening to take the 'N' off and put 'C' on."

The atmosphere was contagious. "Now look, Hil," said one of the night helpers, dressing her in a glamorous nightdress, "I'm not going to get up to let your men friends in."

"Don't worry," tapped Hilary promptly. "They've all got keys."

When she first came home, there were only two people sharing her night duty, but the number soon increased to five. All were employed by the council — Nell Jones, Joy Holland, who had had some nursing experience during the war, Irene Taylor, Lily Dean. Only young Eleanor Evans, mother of a roguish baby boy, was qualified to give injections, so when she was on duty Dad could sleep until seven. Sometimes Eleanor brought the baby during the day, and Hilary always asked to have her eye opened so that she could see him.

Children were her delight, especially Wendy's. When Emma Jane was born, two weeks after her return home, she again experienced the thrill of vicarious motherhood. It was not long before she and Possum became baby-sitters-in-chief. Emma, placed on the bed, settled quite happily to sleep on her tummy, close enough so Hilary could sense her slightest movement. If she cried, the buzzer was always at toe-touch.

But Joanne was her special joy. The blonde two-year-old soon assumed the prerogatives of a self-delegated nurse. She would sit on Hilary's bed and "read" to her. She revelled in standing on a stool and pouring the two-hourly dose of Complan down the tube. "Me, mummy, me mummy, my feed Hayay!"

When given an old syringe, without a needle, and a swab, she would apply it with great gravity to the proper area, waiting obediently, like other injectors, for Hilary to indicate the point of least sensitivity. "Me give Hayay 'jection!"

There were contacts with other children. Pictures drawn especially for Hilary came from nursery and church school classes. Many of the letters she received came from children. There was one big batch from a Comprehensive School near Sheffield, full of laudatory descriptions of their school and eulogies on the school pig, which had just produced twelve piglets.

But there was one especially sobering letter.

"Dear Hilary, My name is ————. I am a skin head. I wear bovver boots and braces and jeans and Levi staypress trousers turned up to show big size nine boots off. I have been involved in many fights with greasers who are long-haired leather jacketed youths. I have been placed on probation and have a criminal record. Yours truthfully."

The close of the letter was amusing, its substance tragic. That any boy of fifteen should be proud of a police record!

It was heaven to be again with the family. Ian and Beth came home on a six-week holiday in October and November, and Ian spent much time with Hilary. Instantly they were on the old affectionate but no-holds-barred brother-sister footing — no sympathy, no pity, only a complete give-and-take understanding.

"Hi, Hil. Getting pretty cocky, what, living in your own flat and bossing a whole regiment of servants."

She listened with intense interest to his problems of converting millions of square miles of jungle and swampland into an international airport; to his adventures in learning to fly; to his colourful descriptions of life in a strange country. They exchanged reminiscences, jokes, private confidences. But under the surface of light *camaraderie* Ian felt sometimes depressed and a little guilty. Hilary was his sister, and they shared a unique relationship. Was he shirking responsibility in letting his parents and sister carry the full load of her disability, sacrificing their welfare to his own inveterate ambition? It was sensible and practical, he tried to tell himself, to put his career first, and yet — the sight of Mum and Dad and Wendy expending themselves seemingly beyond the limits of endurance was sobering. He took the gnawing sense of guilt back with him to Brunei.

Hilary's determination to survive was as much altruistic as

selfish. She wanted to prove to other disabled people that return home from hospital, comparative independence, living life to one's full capacity, were all possible. If she could do it, surely any disabled person could. She wrote articles for *Possability*, telling about her Possum equipment and the recent attempts to improve it Though the mouldings for her "shell" had been made to fit, unfortunately the material had not proved strong enough for a permanent support, so the project had been temporarily shelved, awaiting an expert in industrial plastics who would be interested enough to help. Since her return home, Mr. Sabell of the Department of Ophthalmic Optics at Aston University had made her a special contact lens for her left eye. (She lay on her right one.) It was a large lens covering the whole eye with a ridge on the outside to prop up her lazy eyelid. She could manage its use two hours at a time without discomfort, not for reading, but for seeing her room, visitors, photographs, objects. It was like magic.

Before leaving hospital, she had been asked to edit one of the editions of *Responaut*. What an opportunity! She could give a blueprint of her experience in coming home, explain the co-operation of the National Health Service and the local authority in providing equipment and financial help, detail the successful hunt for helpers, describe the mechanics of her electrical arrangements, ventilators, and, of course, fundamental to all else, the benefits of her Possum. She could give information on the new government allowances and pensions for disabled people.

"I have had financial help from various organisations : Sutton Coldfield Round Table, Invalids at Home, the Margaret de Sousa Deiro Fund, and the Florence Juckes Award of Birmingham Soroptomists."

She could enthuse on the broadened horizons which life at home had brought.

"Now I can hear the sounds of living, of birds in the garden, 'baby-sit' with seven-months-old Emma. Joanne, two-and-a-half, plays in my room, chatters to me, 'helps' look after me. Last thing at night my corgi comes on my bed and takes his biscuits from my hand. If I want to listen to an opera or concert I can have the doors and windows closed, turn up the volume, and 'let it rip'. Friends can bring their children to see me, and if I want to type, listen to records or gossip half the night, I am free to do so. This personal freedom and privacy is very important."

The editorial was the least of her problems. It was the time of the great postal strike. When the strike was just a rumour, she was still plodding through her Christmas thank-you letters, trying to finish an article for *Possability*, as well as collecting articles for *Responaut*. When the strike became certain, she spent every available moment "toe-bashing" — even after being settled for the night, when she usually listened to her talking book. Poor Possum must have thought she had gone mad! Material for *Responaut* had to be at the printer's by mid-April. Luckily some of her friends and acquaintances were travelling round the country and became a fleet of private postmen, delivering mail and collecting articles — but it was worth it. The magazine came out on time, a picture of herself with Joanne feeding her on the cover, and she was invited to edit another issue for 1973.

The power strike of 1970 could have been far more awkward, even dangerous, without the co-operation of the Midlands Electricity Board, who warned the Poles of the exact time of probable power cuts, but fortunately managed without cutting Hilary's supply. Possum and electricity — without the two homecoming would not have been possible, and since that time Possum's miracles had multiplied. Besides the house buzzer and bell, there was a garden alarm to summon help if Mum and Dad were outside. Even the garden fountain was wired to Possum! Children of all ages were fascinated watching it come on and go off as if by magic.

Also there was a new loudspeaker telephone. Olwen Strange, who had been a patient in the hospital and had often visited her, had a senior position in the Post Office. Mona told her one day that they had been unable to get a loudspeaker telephone because Hilary could not speak over it. Olwen made an investigation, some one came to look over the situation, and soon Hilary had her telephone.

The most important addition, however, was a second typewriter, the result of private donations and of a gift from the Sutton Coldfield Round Table, a cheque from the latter arriving in December 1970. Now Hilary could use the first machine for gossip and chatter with visitors, the second for private letters, poems, and articles. She kept both typewriters busy, especially the "literary" one; but information, advice, inspiration — they were only the bones of the new life she wanted to create. The flesh must also be provided, the material substance essential to enable disabled people less fortunate than herself to purchase equipment. Raising money for the Possum Users' Association was now a major interest and *raison d'être*. She became a general in command of her vast regiment of friends, an organiser *par excellence*.

Many gifts for the cause came as the result of her articles, her return home and its attendant publicity. They ranged from two pounds to a thousand. Pupils of Edward Shelley made toffee apples, lemonade and biscuits to sell at school breaks, arranged discotheques, and raised two hundred pounds which Hilary sent to Roger. One of her helpers had had an invalid daughter, Marian. A tree falling on the coach in which she was travelling had caused severe head injuries. For two years she had been unconscious and had only recently died. Marian's parents insisted on donating a thousand pounds, a small portion of it to complete the payment for Hilary's second typewriter, the rest to be used in P.O.S.M. research.

The Possum Users' Association printed a Christmas card for sale, featuring a beautiful still life of flowers by Elizabeth Twistington Higgins. Hilary wrote a poem for it. Perhaps it had been conceived in those moments towards the end of the year when baby Joanne had been placed beside her on the bed.

> On such a bitter, frosty night
> The stable hay was sheer delight
> To Mary, knowing that, by early morn,
> The child she carried would be born.
> That, where the humble beasts had trod
> Would lie the infant, Son of God,
> To whom, with joy and love, we pray
> To grant us peace this Christmas day.

In 1970 the Association had been in existence only two years, and it had few members. Not wishing to run a risk of loss, the committee had printed only 3,000 cards. They did not know Hilary! Hopefully, realising her enthusiasm, they gave her five hundred cards to sell.

Robert Bowell, the editor of *Possability*, was in charge of sales. "She had hardly had them for three weeks," he related afterwards, "when one lunch time I received a telephone call from Walsall. It was Hilary's father. Hilary had a message. She wanted another 3,000 cards! I was almost struck dumb. Thinking I was dreaming, I said 'Yes', then added confusedly that I would let her know later after speaking to the printer. Not only did she manage to sell these extra 3,000. She sold by Christmas 5,000 cards for the P.U.A.! . . . We always say now that if we receive any large donations from people we don't know, they must be friends of Hilary's."

She collected used postage stamps. After friends and family had soaked, sorted and counted them, Joyce, one of the helpers, and her husband Harry would pack them in thousands and take them to Brenda Hansford. Hilary collected Green Shield Stamps, milk bottle tops, tinfoil, articles of every sort for jumble sales. One side of her room was turned into "Ye Olde Possum Shoppe" bulged with donated contributions of cards, wrapping paper, home-made crab-apple jelly, aprons, fancy goods, peg holders, tea cosies. It was often Wendy who took the responsibility for managing the shop.

The merchandise was as systematically arranged (by Wendy and other helpers) as the contents of the array of wall pockets over the monk's bench, bearing the conspicuous markings: Personal Replies, Personal, To Be Sorted (two of these), Listening Library, Address Book, Sorted (two of these), Jotter Paper — Help Yourself, Tape Circulars, Information. Bold notices might announce: PLEASE GIVE SOME GREEN SHIELD STAMPS FOR P.U.A. . . . YOUR HELP WOULD BE MUCH APPRE-CIATED ON MARKET STALL DAY . . . OPEN AIR MARKET. PLEASE SIGN. On one of the shelves were tins marked: POSSUM CASH, SALE MONEY, CHRISTMAS CLUB, STUDIO MONEY, STAMPS. Order was meticulous. Hilary knew the location of every item, and woe to that helper by whom an article was misplaced.

The work burgeoned. A jumble sale at St. Martin's Church in Walsall, even on a day of pouring rain, yielded sixty-four pounds, later increased to over a hundred. Friends from all over the country sent donations for a stall at Walsall Market on Saturday, November 13th. On Friday evening the family and friends were up until all hours, packing and pricing. When the first van load arrived about seven thirty in the morning, calamity — no trestles! But the problem was solved. The sale yielded a total of three hundred and twenty pounds, almost enough to buy some Possum user a typewriter!

Someone like Pamela la Fane. It was Joyce who read Pamela's story to Hilary, a story Pamela had written herself which was published in the magazine *Woman*, called "Warrior in a Wheelchair". A victim of rheumatoid arthritis, Pamela was put in a hospital for incurables at the age of twelve and remained there for twenty-eight years — all that time in a geriatric ward, submerged in an atmosphere of sickness, of old age, of mental stagnation. For eight years she never saw a tree or felt the warmth of the sun. All that made her life bearable was her love of reading. She wrote a book, taught herself shorthand. Then a visitor from the National Health Service came, was shocked at her condition. She was thoroughly examined. If she could find a companion helper, she was told, she could be freed. The Wandsworth Council found a flat for her and paid for it. She found someone to stay with her. The National Health Service supplied her with a basic Possum. Now she was living a life of independence, attending evening classes in writing, spending holidays in Jersey at a hotel for disabled people, going to concerts at the Royal Albert Hall!

Yes, it was for people like Pamela la Fane, thought Hilary, that she must use all the strength of her remaining faculties to make life more worth living.

10

"Dear friend," tapped Hilary in December 1971. "I have been home for over a year now and am looking forward to my second Christmas in the flat." It was the introduction to over three hundred circular letters that she sent out at holiday time.

A year! She had proved beyond a doubt that it could be done. It was possible for even a most severely disabled person to be nursed at home instead of being shunted off into an institution. If a small county borough like Walsall could effect such a miracle, surely there was no excuse for other areas. Hats off to all concerned — Possum, the volunteers who had exhibited such staying power, the co-operation of all the different services involved, and especially the FAMILY.

For it was the family, of course, who had made it possible. It is doubtful if even Hilary understood fully the price each one gladly paid for her well-being and independence . . .

Wendy, with a husband and family of her own, yet travelling many miles day after day, week after week, to sit, to read, to become willing confidante, to act as hands, as feet, as voice, as intermediary in a hundred capacities; expertly organising collections and sales and other projects for Possum; subordinating her own special talents and personality to become, in effect, an extension of Hilary . . .

Eric, spending his days in the competitive, worrying world of the business executive, then going home post haste to Hilary with gay, "Hello, darling" and a joke for the departing volunteer; making a lark of the long and tedious routine which consumed the late evening almost to midnight; serving gallons of coffee; rising at six to give the injection before snatching a few moments more of sleep; taking his turn at sitting up all night every third Saturday; always cheerful, always, or nearly always, even tempered; always resourceful and ready to cope . . .

Mona, especially Mona. She knew what it must feel like to be the keystone of an arch. Suppose someday she cracked? Thank God for the hours of release in creative activity, when she could be *herself*. Without them she would have, not cracked, worse, exploded from the dynamite of inner frustration. She filled the necessary roles — teacher, nurse, housewife, hostess, wife, mother, grandmother — with efficiency, imagination and, usually, incredible patience. A half hour on the nearby golf course was a precious luxury, a week's holiday a sojourn in paradise.

It was inevitable that there occasionally should be moments of tension between herself and Hilary. There always had been. As a child Hilary had deeply resented the adult authority which, by divine right it seemed to her, had taken precedence over her precious common sense. Now she was reduced to even greater dependence than when a child. But she was an adult, and she insisted on being treated as one. She *must* exert her will, dominate her environment, in order to survive. Mona's energy and patience were frequently taxed to the limit, yet, unlike Eric, who had a temper like Hilary's and could occasionally release his tensions by stumping round and slamming doors, she remained taut and calm under the most agonising pressures. Even Hilary, who could "bash" angrily with her toe, was more capable of expressing her frustrations.

No one knew better than Hilary the depth of Mona's selfless devotion. It was always Mum who bore the brunt of the burden, no thanks were wanted or expected. Dad could slip out from under, both by circumstance and temperament. He was often not needed at the ten p.m. routine. He could often manage a game of golf on a Sunday morning, "cat nap" at odd hours, even go to sleep while making "toe talk". Not Mum. She was the "constant", never free of nagging responsibility. A perfectionist, excellent at any job she undertook, incapable of "switching off", she would gladly expend her energy two hundred per cent if necessary, wholeheartedly, cheerfully. If a job needed doing — dishes unwashed, the house untidy — conscience pricked her. The only reward she asked was to see a task well done. Hilary could understand how Mum felt. She felt the same way herself. Perhaps the occasional tension between them made for harmony, like a violin string tuned to a pitch. Both respected the other's prerogative to show herself a person in her own right. Hilary understood Dad, too, for she was like him. It was well that he could relax and laugh under pressure, for in addition to home responsibilities he was under tremendous anxiety and strain in his work as a business executive. The relationship of all three was one which only a deep mutual love could have made harmonious. Its successful endurance was a testimony to that love.

It had been an eventful year. Hilary reported :

The most exciting family news, was the arrival of Christopher Mark, born to Beth and Ian on July 1st. They leave Borneo in June, spending their end of contract leave in South Africa with Beth's family, where Christopher will be christened, then come home before Christmas '72.

Wendy, Peter and family moved into their new house in March. Joanne is now three and a great help. Emma is sixteen months and a real tyke. She is walking, or rather running. She has no physical fears, so has many nasty tumbles and just gets up and does exactly the same thing again. She calls me 'goo-girl'. Anyone looking after her needs a thousand eyes.

"Another Hilary," said Aunty Betty, regarding the plump ash-blonde imp of a cherub with wondering tenderness.

"Mum and Dad spent a few days with Aunty Betty and Uncle Doug at Droitwich," the letter noted, "then in August they spent a week at a hotel in Shropshire, with a heated outdoor swimming pool, golf course, etc. Yes, Mum has taken up golf! She and Dad are now members of Walsall Golf Club."

The year brought new adventures in friendship. Victor Bingham, long a disembodied voice on his faithful weekly tapes, had at last come with his wife from Liverpool to visit. Sylvia Malcolm, a myasthenic with whom Hilary had corresponded for years, came from Devon to spend a week in August. They discovered that they shared not only an unusual disease but a similar approach to life.

"Cut your coat according to the cloth," Sylvia described Hilary's philosophy, "or let's get on with what we've got and not concern ourselves too much with what we haven't got."

The year brought another development. An American woman asked permission to write a book about Hilary. With some reluctance Hilary consented. If your experience could perhaps help other disabled people, it might be worth baring your soul in public. The woman came from America to visit her. Then started months of furious delving into the past, of click-clonking every spare moment of the day and often into the night, for they were working against time. There was to be a concert at the Royal Albert Hall in November 1972 for the benefit of the Possum Users' Association, and it seemed desirable that the book should come out on that day (Could Hilary possibly manage to go? Gina Bachauer was playing her favourite of all favourites, Beethoven's Emperor Concerto!) Reams of onion skin paper flew back and forth across the ocean. Always the perfectionist, Hilary applied her critical ear to every sentence, every phrase, every comma. As usual, it was Mona who shared the brunt of labour and tension, communicating for hours by toe-talk, typing until midnight and after, reading, re-reading, and re-reading.

But at last it was over. Hilary was glad to leave the past behind and return to the living present. Not that you want to forget the past, she would have expressed her feeling, you just don't want to dwell on it. Now is so much more important, and there is so much to do, so many things to enjoy!

You can't breathe? What of it? You have two efficient machines ready to pump air into your lungs.

You can't see — at least not much and not long at a time? But you have a razor-sharp mind which remembers where everything is in your room, the books you have read, the pictures you have seen, the knowledge you have acquired, the experiences you have enjoyed — yes, even the joyousness of dance. You have ears that can hear music and reading and bird-song and can tell whose steps are approaching long before they reach your door.

You can't eat? Ah, how people pity you for that! At first they were even reluctant to talk about food in front of you. They needn't worry. Complan is quite adequate for nourishment, and it's astonishing how often coffee, sherry, even champagne, find their way down your tube — yes, and you send a hint of their flavour back up to your tongue! True, you can't stand people's sucking and chewing over you, but you quite enjoy talking about meals. Once, when you could eat, you loved making up exotic dishes. Now when you think about food, you enjoy remembering the simple things — a lavishly buttered crust, a lump of cheese with an English tomato, fish and chips with lots of salt and vinegar, potatoes in their jackets running with butter. Mmmm!

You can't dress up and go out? No, but you have pride in your appearance. There are the twenty-seven nightdresses hanging in your wardrobe, minis, maxis, midis, lawn for summer, nylon for winter, even a sheer black one that Peter Dunn, who bought it for you, calls "Sin and Degradation"! You can pick nightdresses and jewellery to fit your mood — the pink lacy one with a jade ring and bracelet, the lavender one with amethysts, the silver grey over pink with moonstones, the black with a red velvet ribbon; and a bedspread in either matching or contrasting colours. You can have perfectly manicured nails, thanks to Wendy or one of the helpers, with a choice of two dozen varnishes — wild red, cotton candy, passionata, pistachio, swamp fire, platinum, to name only a few. You can enjoy the fragrance of your favourite "Blue Grass" perfume and lotions. Yes, you have by no means said goodbye to feminine vanity.

"I'm vain," you confess, insisting that when Roger takes your picture you be shifted to a more becoming position. "I don't want pictures with my head tied and my face shining."

"What do you do with your time?" wonders a reporter who is interviewing you for a bit on a television programme. Do with it! Once your typewriter starts click-clonking about that, it can go on for hours. You soon have the reporter madly scribbling and almost tearing his hair.

And what about the future? Ah, this is the question people

are afraid to ask you. They think you must have secret and
terrible fears. Suppose the time should come when that flicker
of movement in your toe grew less and less, when it ceased
entirely — what then? Suppose the experiments the scientific
people are working on, to provide contact with your Possum
through some sort of electronic impulse instead of movement,
prove a pipe dream? Suppose you no longer have communication with the outside world?

It's hard to make them understand that you have no fear. As
long as people will still communicate with you as though you were
able to answer, it will be all right. It will be difficult for them,
of course, but you will not be any different mentally. As long as
they understand that you are still *you*, continue to give you
information, as long as there is still a relationship, some means
of communication can be found. Look at Joanne. She can't read
the typewriter, can't make toe-talk, yet there is wonderful communication between you. No, you are not afraid of the future.

Meanwhile there is the present. *Life*. All yours. To enjoy. To
use. Perhaps you are luckier than most people, because you can
savour its very essence, undiluted by complexity and activity.
Life! Remember that prayer you chose for Janet's service from
Prayers of Life, by Michel Quoist? That expresses it all in a
nutshell.

I went out, Lord.
Men were coming and going,
Walking and running.

Everything was rushing : cars, lorries, the street, the whole town
Men were rushing not to waste time.
They were rushing after time,
To catch up with time,
To gain time.

Good-bye, Sir, excuse me, I haven't time.
I'll come back, I can't wait, I haven't time.
I'd love to help you, but I haven't time . . .
I can't think, I can't read, I'm swamped, I haven't time.
I'd like to pray, but I haven't time.

*   *   *

Lord, I have time,
I have plenty of time,
All the time that you give me,
The years of my life,
The days of my years,
The hours of my days,
They are all mine.
Mine to fill, quietly, calmly,
But to fill completely, up to the brim.

AFTERWORD

Since this book went to press in England, some exciting things have happened to Hilary.

Just before Easter, 1972, Hank, the young man who serviced her ventilator, brought a colleague with him an electronics expert. This friend, Bernard, thought he could improve Hilary's means of communication. He designed a gadget resembling a wrist watch which she could wear around her right ankle. In its padding is a very sensitive crystal which picks up the slightest tremor from the Achilles tendon, and sends an impulse along a fine flex to an electronic device which she calls a "bleeper", fastened to the head of her bed. Now it is no longer necessary to place one's hand on her ankle in order to "talk". She is able to "bleep" when the correct letter in the alphabet is reached.

This proved so successful that Bernard made a pad for her other ankle, in which there is even less range of movement but sufficient for this extremely sensitive mechanism. This operates her Possum equipment — bell, buzzer, typewriters, radio channels, tape recorder, talking book. The new arrangement is a wonderful improvement over the cumbersome device fastened to the side of her bed and activated by contact with her toe.

One day Bernard heard Joyce and Eric discussing the possibility of a more mobile bed, and he and Hank undertook to build one. It is a masterpiece, a complete life-supporting unit. Ventilator, batteries, and sucking machine are built in under the bed. There are side flaps that let down to permit passage through an ordinary door. It even contains a cupboard for drugs, linen, and other supplies!

With the progress of the disease her tongue had become unnaturally and painfully swollen. In May an army of doctors, nurses, and technicians moved into the house with their elaborate equipment and amputated the front part of the tongue, reshaping it to normal size, a vast improvement in both looks and comfort.

In November I went again to England for the activities attending the book's publication.

The concert for the benefit of the Possum Users Association was held in the Royal Albert Hall, as planned, with Mr. A.G. Jefcoat, Roger's father, the impresario, and — another miracle, it seemed to all of us — though the doctors refused to approve the trip, Hilary the indomitable came! An ambulance went from London, organised and driven by Eddie King who donates this splended voluntary service for the disabled in his spare time, and brought Hilary the 120 miles from Walsall, with Mona, Eric, and Wendy substituting for doctors and nurses. There were some anxious moment when we wondered if the bed was too long to fit in the hall, but finally the doors closed — just.

In one of the luxurious red-velvet-curtained boxes Hilary lay and listened to Gina Bachauer's matchless rendition of her favorite Emperor Concerto and Sir Adrian Boult's masterful conducting of the London Philharmonic in Schubert's great C Major Symphony — the first time she had actually attended a concert in over twelve years. Afterward the beautiful and gracious Duchess of Kent came from the royal box to talk with Hilary and other Possum users. It was a highly successful event, with 5,000 in attendance. 180 of them in wheelchairs, and it yielded over £6,000 for the Possum Users Association. What a lot of typewriters and other equipment that will buy.

"Fabulous!" was Hilary's summing up when she arrived home at four-thirty the next morning.

Four days later she came to London again for a reception at the Oriental Club where the book was officially launched. Royalty graced this event also in the person of Prince Philip, whose interest in people and intense concern for problems of the disabled were evidenced as he made himself late for another appointment to spend time with Hilary and other members of the Association committee.

Fully as thrilling for Hilary as the presence of royalty at both these events was that of her brother Ian and his wife Beth, on leave between assignments in Brunei and Nigeria. Later that same week she herself entertained at an autographing party in her home, with more than a hundred relatives and guests attending. Her autograph, carefully typed on slips of paper, was pasted beneath mine in all the books.

Excitement over? Not a bit of it! When I left she was immersed, with all her family and nurses and thirty-odd volunteer helpers, in activities for her "Fayre", soon to be held for the benefit of the Possum Users Association.

In June, 1973, my heroine was awarded the M.B.E. in the Queen's Birthday Honours, for her service to the disabled. "I was stunned," confessed Hilary, " had it been possible I would have gasped." She celebrated the awarding of the M.B.E. at home with a family party. Her medal and a letter from the Queen came just in time. "I wore the medal that evening," write Hilary, "though by rights my ventilator should have been sporting bow tie and tails. There were more than a hundred guests, there was hardly room for me."

She continued her activities, selling nearly a thousand books in all and raising many thousands of pounds for other disabled people. Then one day in June, 1975, I received a cable. HILARY DIED WEDNESDAY MORNING. SHE WAS VERY HAPPY. MONA AND ERIC. Hilary — happinesss. Her name described her life from beginning to end.

How? It was sometime before Mona's letters gave the whole answer. . .

" . . for some months Hilary had suffered occasional periods of deep distress with her breathing due to a blocking of the trachea. In her last month this happened two or three times. It was thought necessary to investigate under anaesthetic, probably stretching the tissues and removing loose fragments to clear the passage. We did not know, nor Hilary, the gravity of her condition. She was dying. She was calm and happy and had planning the whole day ahead. It was to be very busy . . . She never awoke. . ."

" . . .You ask, 'How did we cope?' " Hilary had lived on borrowed time for fifteen full, happy, worthwhile years. We were happy in her feeling of purpose and fulfilment but could not ask that she endure one more day than she was given. Her work was done.

The last event she organised was a concert in the Walsall Town Hall. The Canoldir Male Voice Choir sang. It was a wonderful concert. Hilary enjoyed every minute of it. Yes — she was there, in spite of breathing problems. She was trying to raise £500, the balance for a Possum controlled typewriter for a disabled woman whose speech was failing. She raised the money and ordered the typewriter on Saturday, June 14th. She died on June 18th.

She has left a lot of happy memories. She was FUN. You know how much she inspired us all. In her memory we have decided to work as a group for the Possum User's Association under the name of the Hilary Pole Memorial Committee." How true, that pungent line in her poem, "It is my body, not my mind in bed!" She was far more alive than many of us who can breathe and swallow and see and move. Certainly if immortality is the triumph of spirit over body, something we all hope in the fullness of time to achieve, then Hilary attained it long ago.

The Author